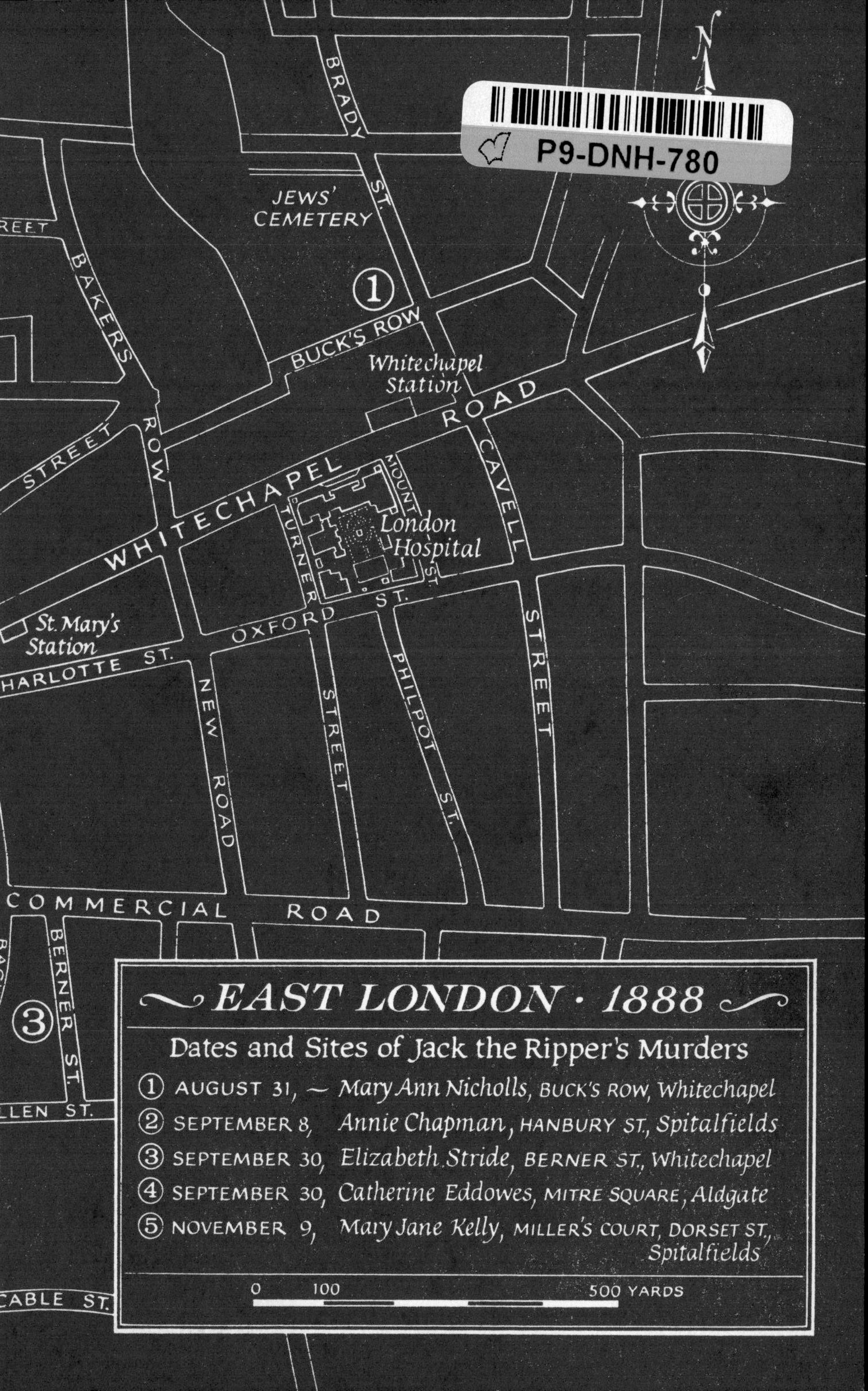
P9-DNH-780
N
BRADY ST.
JEWS' CEMETERY
REET
BAKERS ROW
BUCK'S ROW
Whitechapel Station
STREET
WHITECHAPEL ROAD
MOUNT ST.
CAVELL STREET
TURNER STREET
London Hospital
OXFORD ST.
St. Mary's Station
HARLOTTE ST.
NEW ROAD
PHILPOT ST.
COMMERCIAL ROAD
BERNER ST.
LLEN ST.
CABLE ST.
EAST LONDON · 1888
Dates and Sites of Jack the Ripper's Murders
① AUGUST 31, — Mary Ann Nicholls, BUCK'S ROW, Whitechapel
② SEPTEMBER 8, Annie Chapman, HANBURY ST., Spitalfields
③ SEPTEMBER 30, Elizabeth Stride, BERNER ST., Whitechapel
④ SEPTEMBER 30, Catherine Eddowes, MITRE SQUARE, Aldgate
⑤ NOVEMBER 9, Mary Jane Kelly, MILLER'S COURT, DORSET ST., Spitalfields
0 100 500 YARDS

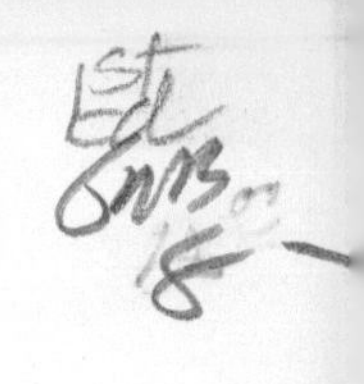

WHEN LONDON WALKED IN TERROR

To Mae —
Read this some night when the wind howls outside your windows —
[illegible]

WHEN LONDON WALKED IN TERROR

BY

TOM A. CULLEN

ILLUSTRATED

The Riverside Press Cambridge

HOUGHTON MIFFLIN COMPANY BOSTON

1965

First Printing R

Library of Congress Catalog Card Number: 65-14078
Printed in the United States of America

To

Tom and Elizabeth Van Dycke

"Whilst we conventional Social Democrats were wasting our time on education, agitation and organization, some independent genius has taken the matter in hand, and by simply murdering and disembowelling four women, converted the proprietary press to an inept sort of communism".

George Bernard Shaw in a letter to
The Star *dated September 24, 1888*

CONTENTS

ILLUSTRATIONS

A map showing the sites of the Ripper's murders appears on the endpapers.

The author wishes to thank the British Museum, Cassell and Company Ltd., and the publishers of Punch *for permission to reproduce some of the illustrations listed above.*

WHEN LONDON
WALKED IN TERROR

INTRODUCTION

THE SMELL OF BLOOD

HORROR ran through the land," reads a contemporary account. "Men spoke of it with bated breath, and pale-lipped women shuddered as they read the dreadful details. People afar off smelled blood, and the superstitious said that the skies were of a deeper red that autumn . . ." It was the autumn of 1888, and England, still slightly hung over from the previous year's celebration of Queen Victoria's Golden Jubilee, watched with apprehension as her grandson, Wilhelm II, ascended the throne of Germany.

But it was not the advent of Kaiser Wilhelm that caused men to speak with bated breath or drained the color from the lips of their womenfolk. It was not the prospect of war, distant in 1888, that caused some to imagine that they could smell blood from afar. The horror which ran through the land and caused cranks to speak of a revisitation of Cain was inspired by a series of murders quite without parallel in the annals of crime. The autumn of 1888 was the period when a mysterious killer was abroad in the streets of London's East End, striking down his women victims without warning, slitting their throats, mutilating their bodies in hideous fashion, and escaping through police cordons to murder again. "Jack the Ripper" was the name which he gave to himself, and by which he was to be known to posterity. It is a name which still strikes chill to the heart.

All too soon that autumn the bloodshot sunsets which some

interpreted as portents were blotted out by thick, sulphurous fogs of the variety that are known as "London particulars," and thus a new dimension was added to terror. At the height of the Ripper scare, Russian, Polish and German immigrants arriving in Whitechapel refused to stay there even temporarily, so great was their fear of the unknown killer. And even the local Cockneys would not budge from their hearths after sundown. The landlord of The Star and Garter, near Commercial Road, going broke, put the blame for his troubles squarely on Jack the Ripper. "People aren't going out at night any more," he complained to the bankruptcy receiver. "Since the killings, I hardly get a soul in here of a night." Even in the quiet, tree-lined squares of Belgravia and South Kensington the curtains were drawn a little tighter than usual, and their masters had difficulty in persuading the servant girls to post a letter after dark.

South of the Thames, in Blackfriars Road, a Mrs. Mary Burridge, a floor-cloth dealer, was so overcome in reading the *Star's* lurid account of one of the Ripper murders that she fell dead, a copy of the Late Final clutched in her hand. Perhaps it was this paragraph that had caught her eye: "A nameless reprobate — half beast, half man — is at large . . . Hideous malice, deadly cunning, insatiable thirst for blood — all these are the marks of the mad homicide. The ghoul-like creature, stalking down his victim like a Pawnee Indian, is simply drunk with blood, and he will have more."

Not all of London stayed at home. Richard Mansfield, the American actor, opened at the Lyceum in August in *Dr. Jekyll and Mr. Hyde* and was an instant success, his interpretation of the monster Hyde in particular giving satisfaction. Playgoers who were disgorged into the gaslit Strand while still under the spell of the Lyceum shocker found new thrills in store for them when their ears were assailed by newsboys shouting, "Murder! Murder! Another Whitechapel Murder! Read all about it!"

This was a case where it could truly be said that reality counterfeited art. And not only in the Strand was the silence shattered by the news vendors' cries. From sedate Pembroke Square arose this anguished *cri de coeur* addressed to the *Daily Telegraph:*

> Sir — Can nothing be done to prevent a set of hoarse ruffians coming nightly about our suburban squares and streets yelling at the tops of their voices, and nearly frightening the life out of the sensitive women and children of this neighborhood? Last evening, for instance, their cry was "Special" — "Murder" — "Paper" — "Jack" — "The" — "Ripper" — "Caught" — "Paper" — "Whitechapel" — "Paper" — "Got him at last" — "Paper" — "Murder" — "Ripper" — "Paper" — "Murder" — "Got the Ripper" — "Paper" — "at last." These awful words were bawled out about nine o'clock in a quiet part of Kensington; a lady who was supping with us was so greatly distressed by these hideous bellowings that she was absolutely too unnerved to return home save in a cab because she would have to walk a hundred yards or so down a quiet street at the end of her journey by omnibus. Now, I venture to ask, sir, is it not monstrous that the police do not protect us from such flagrant and ghastly nuisances?

2

How many murders did Jack the Ripper commit? There is no agreement on this subject among either the amateur criminologists or the police experts who have studied the case. Some say eight, others say eleven, but as many as fourteen murders have been attributed to the Ripper, including slayings which occurred long after 1888. In fact, the Ripper became a sort of collective for murder, a convenient repository into which all the unsolved crimes against women of a violent or sadistic nature were dumped. According to Sir Melville Macnaghten, onetime head of the Criminal Investigation Division at Scotland Yard, "The Whitechapel murderer committed five murders and no more." After studying the evidence closely I am inclined to agree with Sir Melville.

The five murders were committed in the ten-week period from August 31 to November 9, 1888, and they occurred within an area of about one-quarter mile square. They had certain characteristics in common. All of the victims were seized apparently from behind and had their throats slit. In all but one case there was some attempt made to mutilate the bodies, though there was no evidence of sexual assault. In two of the murders organs were removed from the victims' bodies. The murders were marked by increasing savagery, leading to the double murder of September 30, and to the blood saturnalia of Mary Jane Kelly's murder on November 9, after which the carnage ceased as suddenly as it had begun. With the exception of the last-named homicide, the murders all occurred out-of-doors in the dark alleys and byways of London's East End.

Finally, the killings all occurred either on the first weekend of the month, or the last weekend, and between the hours of midnight and 5 A.M., causing one Dr. L. Forbes Winslow, M.B., LL.D. Cantab., D.C.L. Oxon, to work out an elaborate "lunar theory." The murders were committed, according to Dr. Winslow, either when the new moon arose, or when the old moon had entered its last quarter. "Lunatics are strongly influenced by the various periods when the moon changes," he adds, almost as though it were a matter of common knowledge.[1]

[1] The possibility that Jack the Ripper and the unknown killer responsible for a series of bizarre stranglings in Boston in 1962–63 were both victims of "moon madness" was advanced by Dr. E. A. Jannino, of Lynn, Mass., at an international conference on forensic medicine held in London in April 1, 1963. "Modern scientific investigation with electrical waves emanating from humans indicates a change in electrical potential twice a month coincident with the full and new moons," Dr. Jannino declared. "A maladjusted group studied had the highest voltage readings," he added.

3

Who were the Ripper's victims? "Wherever there was laughter and the gaiety of the can-can . . . Wherever there was beauty, HE was lurking in the shadows," reads a 20th Century-Fox handout for *The Man in the Attic*. Indeed, in the many film versions of the Ripper story, his victims have usually been pictured as music-hall actresses or barmaids.[2]

Nothing could be further from the truth. In reality, all five of the Ripper's victims were prostitutes, or "sisters of the abyss," as the Victorians preferred to call them — in fact, they had reached the last rungs of the ladder descending into the abyss. They were, with one exception, middle-aged drabs, the very dregs of wretched humanity. All five had strikingly similar case histories, a fact which seems to have been overlooked by most writers who have dealt with the subject. All had been married at one time or another, and were either widowed or living separated from their husbands, with children farmed out to relatives or in orphanages. One was in the early stages of pregnancy at the time of her murder.

All were chronic alcoholics, the factor which seems to have contributed most to the breakup of their marriages and of their homes; and at least one was so far gone with Bright's disease that she had only a few more years to live at best. They lived in the fourpenny lodging houses of Spitalfields, East London — that is, when they had the price of a doss. Otherwise, they slept with the other down-and-outers in parks, or along the railings of Christ Church, Spitalfields.

Their complete and utter destitution is the most shocking denominator that they had in common. Twenty-four hours before she was found murdered, Mary Ann "Polly" Nicholls was turned away from a bug-ridden doss house in Thrawl Street be-

[2] See Appendix A.

cause she lacked fourpence for a bed. Her body, which had been disemboweled, was identified by the "Lambeth Workhouse" markings on her flannel petticoats. A comb and a broken piece of mirror found in her pockets were her only possessions. Thomas Hood might well have had Polly in mind when he penned these lugubrious lines:

One more Unfortunate,
Weary of breath,
Rashly importunate,
Gone to her death!

4

The Ripper's experiments in anatomy were discussed from the pulpit, and *The Times* devoted four and five columns to them daily in reports which are still regarded as gems of their kind.[3] Among those who brought their intellect to bear on the problem of the Ripper's identity were George Bernard Shaw, then a young music critic, and Arthur Conan Doyle, whose first Sherlock Holmes story, "A Study in Scarlet," had been published only the year before in Beeton's Christmas Annual.

Nor was interest in Jack the Ripper confined to London. In a letter to *The Times,* "Elderly Gentlemen," who had been traveling extensively about England, told of the widespread excitement which the Whitechapel murders had occasioned, particularly among the humbler classes. "Last week in an agricultural county," he wrote, "I shared my umbrella during heavy rain with a maid servant, who was going home. 'Is it true, Sir,' said she, 'that they're a-cutting down the feminine seck in London?' And she explained herself to mean that 'they was a-murdering of 'em by ones and twos.' "My own main interest in the

[3] *The Times* reports are reprinted in the anthology, *A Treasury of Great Reporting,* edited by Louis L. Snyder and Richard B. Morris, as models of crime reporting.

matter," the writer added, "is that I, myself, have been taken for the murderer. And if I, why not any elderly gentleman of quiet habits?" Why not, indeed?

The Ripper's fame quickly crossed the Channel to inspire murder by emulation in the Montmartre district of Paris and to culminate in the grisly deeds of Joseph Vacher, the peasant who is said to have murdered eleven people in the 1890's. His celebrity also spread to America, where it crowded out other news from the papers. In particular, the *Police Gazette* devoted columns of print to Jack the Ripper, while the *New York Graphic* dug up Dr. J. G. Kiernan, a noted medical authority, who swore that the Whitechapel killer was a cannibal pure and simple, "a type fortunately rare in Anglo-Saxon lands, but not infrequently met with in Russia, Germany, Bohemia and France," according to the learned doctor.[4]

Finally, Queen Victoria, from her widowed seclusion at Windsor, took as lively an interest in the murders as did her humblest subject, and she peppered her Home Secretary with suggestions as to how the Ripper could be captured. ("Have the cattle boats and passenger boats been examined? Has an investigation been made as to the number of single men occupying rooms to themselves? The murderer's clothes must be saturated with blood and kept somewhere . . .") When her suggestions appeared to have been ignored, she fired a telegram at her Prime Minister, Lord Salisbury. "This new most ghastly murder shows the absolute necessity for some decided action," she complained, referring to the Mary Kelly murder of November 9, 1888. "All these courts must be lit, and our detectives

[4] The Ripper apparently was well known in southern Italy, too. In his memoirs, Cambridge Professor Thomas Okey, who was born in Spitalfields, tells of being asked to act as cicerone to two young Neapolitan lawyers who were visiting London in 1881. "When I asked how I could serve them, with one voice came the request, Could I lead them to the scene of one of the Giacomo-lo-Squarciatore murders?" the professor relates.

improved." "You promised me when the first murder took place," she reminded the Prime Minister, "to consult with your colleagues about it."

5

The years have brought no abatement in interest in Jack the Ripper, as far as Londoners are concerned. In fact, he has become a figure of folklore, as I discovered when I wrote to three East London newspapers in the hopes that some of their readers might be able to shed light on the Ripper mystery. The response to this appeal was surprising in view of the fact that the murders occurred seventy-six years ago. Most of those who replied were old-age pensioners in their late seventies and eighties (the oldest person I interviewed was ninety), but they remembered the events vividly either through witnessing them as children, or through listening to their parents talk.

Some of my informants were genuinely mistaken as to their facts. One old man, for example, got the Ripper murders mixed up with the Sidney Street Siege, which occurred in the same area at a much later date, and which was made memorable by the presence of young Winston Churchill, then Home Secretary, who risked his neck to watch police shoot it out with two Lithuanian anarchists. But thanks to them, I found that the Ripper is still very much alive, at least, east of Aldgate. East End mothers still frighten their offspring with the bogey, "The Ripper will get you if you don't watch out." And these same offspring skip rope chanting, "Jack the Ripper/Stole a kipper/ Hid it in his father's slipper." (In Argyll, Scotland, the rhyme has to do with the Ripper "cutting his throat with Sunlight soap.")

The image of Jack the Ripper which East London retains, as I discovered from these interviews, is straight out of Victorian melodrama. He is the waxen-mustached villain of *Maria Marten, or Murder in the Red Barn,* who was hissed by the parents of present-day East Enders when he played the Paragon or the old Pavilion music hall in Whitechapel Road. "I can see Jack the Ripper just as plain as I see you sitting there," exclaimed Mrs. Annie Tapper, a short, stout Polish woman in her early eighties, whose iron-gray hair was cut short, and who wore glasses of the unbecoming National Health variety. We were seated in the kitchen of the Council flat near the Cable Street docks, which Mrs. Tapper shares with her third husband. Mrs. Tapper was a girl of nine when, she claims, she not only saw Jack the Ripper, but waited upon him in a shop, selling him the bunch of grapes ("Almiras, I think they was called — those pale green ones") which were reported (erroneously) to have been found still grasped in the hand of one of the murder victims. "I'll tell you what he looked like as sure as this is Friday." She paused while the Blackwall elevated train roared past, rattling the kitchen windows. "He was tall and dark — foreign-looking, I would say — with a black, pointed beard. I couldn't tell you the color of his eyes for he kept looking down. But he wore a bobtail coat with striped trousers and he carried a Gladstone bag." She paused, searched her memory for some overall impression. "He looked like he was dressed up for a wedding, only he didn't have a top hat," she concluded.

Hand luggage, such as Mrs. Tapper described, is to be encountered everywhere along the trail of the Ripper. Sometimes it was a Gladstone bag, but most usually the bag described was made in shiny black oilcloth, or "American cloth," as the Victorians called it. Such bags had been popular novelties in the 1880's, but after the Ripper made his debut anyone spotted in the East End with this black badge of murder in his hand was not only in peril of arrest, but in positive danger of his life. One who narrowly escaped arrest as Jack the Ripper was the late Bransby Williams, the music hall star, then a lad of eighteen and just starting out on the boards.[5] Williams, who died in 1961 at the age of ninety-one, was noted for his Dickensian impersonations and was a great favorite of Edward VII. But at the time of the Ripper murders he was a wallpaper designer from Hackney doing an occasional turn in the East End working men's clubs, where the actors onstage competed with the costers who hawked their whelks and mussels in the hall. "I was on my way to such a club in Poplar one night," he related, "when I was stopped by the police, who were looking for Jack the Ripper. They questioned me, then asked me to open the black bag in which I carried my make-up and props. Imagine their surprise when a bloodstained knife was found in the bag — my surprise, too, I might add, for I forgot that I was carrying this damning bit of evidence. The blood, of course, was paint," he added, "and the police, seeing that I was just a crazy young actor, sent me on my way."

The image of Jack the Ripper which East London retains on its retina is as remote from reality as the red paint on Williams's knife. At the same time, it is essentially a class image. In East London eyes the Ripper was a "guv'nor," a "toff," or "one of Them," and he was "dressed up for a wedding," to borrow Mrs. Tapper's conceit. Interestingly, none of the East Enders I talked to who, like Mrs. Tapper, claimed that they had information concerning the Ripper had ever volunteered this information to the police.

6

"If nonsense were solid," wrote Sir Robert Anderson, who headed Scotland Yard's CID at the time of the Ripper murders,

[5] Another was John Burns, "The Man with the Red Flag," who led the Great Dock Strike of 1889, and who became a Cabinet Minister later. Burns was on his way home from a dock workers' meeting late at night when he was stopped by the police and questioned.

"the nonsense that was talked and written about these murders would sink a dreadnought." Indeed, the Grand Fleet. No other multiple crime in British history has excited so much speculation or seen such a proliferation of theories, to the point where guessing the Ripper's identity is still a popular parlor game.

Some have laid the Ripper murders at the doorsills of homicides convicted and executed for other crimes, notably Dr. Thomas Neill Cream, the poisoner, who on the gallows is said to have cried out, "I am Jack the ———" just as the trapdoor was sprung. (The flaw in this theory is that Cream was serving a sentence in a United States penitentiary at the time of the Whitechapel murders.)

Still others have advanced the theory of the "invisible killer," an assassin so cloaked in anonymity as to be invisible to the ordinary public and to expert trackers alike. A policeman would be such an invisible person, his presence at or near the scene of the crime being so plausible as to eliminate him entirely as a possible suspect. Thus "Jack the Copper" was born, a theory shrewdly exploited by Thomas Burke in his short story, "The Hands of Mr. Ottermole," the Ottermole of the story being a police sergeant who strangles with his "great, white-gloved hands."

A priest or clergyman would likewise be invisible. Maurice Heine introduced "The Reverend Ripper," complete with frock coat and dog collar, in an essay which he wrote for *Minotaure*. In an imaginary dialogue in hell, the reverend boasts to the Marquis de Sade how he has outwitted the London police, who are too dull to conceive that "the mask of charity could cover the face of crime." "Jill the Ripper" falls into this same category. Conan Doyle was among those who believed that the Ripper, if not actually a woman, disguised himself as such in order to escape notice.

I am indebted to Colin Wilson, himself the author of a novel based on Jack the Ripper, for the information that General

Booth, of Salvation Army fame, suspected his own secretary of being the killer. Why? Because the unfortunate secretary dreamed of the crimes before they were committed.[6] Finally, when a member of the illustrious Russell family was mentioned as a suspect in a television program devoted to Jack the Ripper, Bertrand Russell came back with a sharp rejoinder. "I am astonished by your suggestion," Earl Russell declared. "I have never heard of it before, and I most emphatically deny it."

The British press has done its share to keep the Ripper alive. Hardly a year passes but the Ripper story is rehashed under the rubric of "Great Murder Mysteries," and "new evidence" is brought forward — evidence, be it added, that would be of interest to no one but a clinical psychiatrist. For example, *Reynolds News,* in February 1959, published an interview with a retired blacksmith of Worthing, aged eighty-two, who claimed, "The Ripper was my Cousin Frank." His proof? Cousin Frank was caught redhanded, so to speak, way back in 1888 with a razor and a bloodstained collar in his briefcase; the blacksmith, who was then a sharp nipper of eleven, remembered it distinctly. In November 1958, a man wrote to *Empire News* denouncing his own father, who, it appeared, committed the Ripper murders as a boy of fifteen. The writer obligingly enclosed a copy of the father's death certificate. For the benefit of those who are contemplating future "confessions" of this nature, Scotland Yard informs me, "As far as the criminal investigation of the crime is concerned, the case is closed."

7

Five murders occurring within a period of ten weeks, all the victims from the same class, living in the same doss houses in the same streets — how is it that the Ripper was never caught,

[6] Colin Wilson says that he gleaned this bit of information from the magazine *Tit Bits* when he was a boy of eight.

or at least, that his identity was never established? Why has this remained the greatest murder mystery of all time?

In the following pages I hope to indicate how their prejudices so blinded the Victorians that they were unable to discern the figure in the carpet. The Ripper murders outraged all the Victorian virtues and sensibilities. To the Victorian mind, they could only be the work of a killer who came from the "lower orders." Obviously, no man of education and family background would consort with such low creatures as prostitutes, let alone to slay them and cut up their bodies. And, by the same reasoning, the assassin must be of foreign origin; no Briton could be guilty of such heinous crimes.

"The celerity with which the crimes were committed is inconsistent with the ordinary English phlegmatic nature," points out a reader of *The Times,* who goes on to say that the anatomical skill displayed by the murderer "is possessed, to a not inconsiderable degree, by foreigners engaged in the *charcuterie* and other kindred trades abroad." Another *Times* reader, who signs himself "Nemo," starts his letter with, "Having been long in India and, therefore, acquainted with the methods of Eastern criminals," and goes on to conclude that the murders were committed by "a Malay, or other low-class Asiatic coming under the general term Lascar. When the villain is primed with his opium, or bang, or gin," writes Nemo, "and inspired with his lust for slaughter and blood, he would destroy his defenseless victim with the ferocity and cunning of a tiger; and past impunity and success would only have rendered him the more daring and reckless." The Victorians quite obviously preferred to believe that the Ripper murders were the result of a demoniacal impulse, or a brainless *Lustmord,* or killing for killing's sake. Therefore, it somehow followed that their perpetrator must be a foreigner.

That Jack the Ripper was a homicidal maniac of the most dangerous variety is undeniable; and yet a pattern existed. I have already indicated the peculiar unity of these murders in the matter of timing, locale and choice of victims with similar backgrounds. Why these particular whores? And why this particular quarter mile, the "evil quarter mile," as Reverend Samuel Barnett, of Toynbee Hall, called it? And why, having chosen his victims, did the Ripper proceed to carve up their bodies in such a hideous fashion, and to leave them exposed on the public highway?

Had he weighted the bodies with stones, and lowered them into the Thames, they might never have been recovered; or if they had surfaced in due course it might have been difficult, if not impossible, to determine the cause of death as being due to accident or to murderous design. The walls outside the Thames Police Station at Wapping were plastered with notices headed "Dead Body Found." Many of those fished from the Thames were female tramps of the sort the Ripper specialized in, whose relatives had not even bothered to report them missing. Unidentified, they were soon hustled into a pauper's grave.

The inescapable conclusion is that the Ripper deliberately sought to make these murders as public as possible. Far from trying to cover up his deeds he signposted them, hung red flags around them, so to speak. Here, if ever, was murder that advertised, that shouted from the rooftops. But what was the Ripper trying to say? Perhaps he was trying to say something quite simple, and perhaps it was only the obtuseness of his Victorian audience which jammed the message, insane though it may have been.

In the course of these pages I shall trace the criminal history of Jack the Ripper step by step. With rare exceptions, I shall adhere closely to the evidence as it was developed at the various inquest hearings, or in statements to the police or to the press. (London newspapers reported the Whitechapel murders in amazing detail, including the verbatim testimony of inquest witnesses.) In the few instances where I have reconstructed conversations, I have again based myself closely on the written or spoken testimony of the persons involved. Secondly, I shall examine the various theories concerning the Ripper's identity that have been put forward by previous investigators before advancing a theory which, in my view, is more consonant with the facts in the case. Finally, in the interests of dispelling the fog which has surrounded this murder mystery for the past seventy-six years, I shall reveal for the first time the names of three men against whom Scotland Yard held "very strong suspicion." In particular, I shall identify the individual to whom police suspicion finally narrowed. "I am inclined to exonerate the last two, but I have always held strong opinions regarding No. 1," declared Sir Melville Macnaghten, who became CID head six months after the Ripper murders. "The more I think the matter over, the stronger do these opinions become." This man's name has never before been made public. He was not a foreigner nor did he come from the so-called "lower orders." He came from a good family in Dorset, he was educated at Oxford, and he was called to practice at the Inner Temple bar in 1885, just three years before the reign of terror began.

CHAPTER I

MURDER IN BUCK'S ROW

As he turned into Buck's Row on his way to work at Spitalfields market, George Cross broke into a tuneless whistle. Not that the market porter had anything to whistle about as he hurried along the empty street at 3:20 A.M., Friday, August 31. To the contrary, the day, although it had not yet dawned, stretched ahead of him dreary and endless in terms of fruit crates to be unloaded and stacked in the market sheds. The whistle was the forlorn response of every man faced with such a prospect. But Cross had additional reason to keep his courage up, for Buck's Row was one of the meaner back streets of Whitechapel, and located midway along its length was Barber's horse slaughterhouse, which had given the neighborhood an evil reputation.

All day and sometimes late into the night butchers in bloody aprons could be seen coming and going at the slaughterhouse, and the air was filled with the stench and sounds of dying animals. The presence of so much death in the midst of so much tightly packed humanity was thought to be an unlucky omen foreboding human sacrifice; and although no crimes against the person had actually occurred in Buck's Row passersby were inclined to give the slaughterhouse a wide berth at night. It was with these thoughts in mind that Cross quickened his pace and began to whistle like a demented songbird.

He was nearly opposite the slaughterhouse when he saw lying on the opposite side of the road a tarpaulin; at least he concluded that it was a tarpaulin, probably fallen from a knacker's wagon where it had been used to cover the horse carcasses. Had his trade been other than that of a porter, he would have passed by without troubling to examine the object. But, sensing that he had discovered something of value, he crossed the road to claim it as salvage. Coming closer, he saw that what he had mistaken for a canvas shroud was, in fact, a human form.

At this moment Cross heard a man's footsteps coming toward him on the same side of Buck's Row and, almost instinctively, he stepped back into the shadows to await the newcomer's approach. But the newcomer had perceived *him* at a distance and, perhaps fearing an ambush of some sort, likewise took evasive action. The two might thus have circled each other stiff-legged like two hostile dogs had not Cross recognized in the stranger a fellow porter named John Paul. "Oi, mate," he called out, "give us a hand. There's a woman lying here, but I can't make out whether she's drunk or fainted."

The two men bent down and examined the woman's body as best they could. Cross touched her face, which was warm. He then lifted her hands, but they were curiously limp. The porter straightened up. "She's copped it," he said, his voice suddenly strangled by fear. "She's deader'n a haddock." It was less from any evidence afforded to him by the senses than from instinct that Cross knew the woman was dead. But the other man, Paul, was not so easily convinced. "I think I can hear her breathing," he announced, "only it's ever so faint." He then suggested that they shift the body. "Come on, mate, let's get her on her feet. She's probably just dead drunk." But Cross backed away. "Not me," he said, "I ain't touching her." The market porter shivered as he stood there scanning the silent street fitfully lit by its gas flares. There was no one in sight, to be sure, but suppose that someone were lurking in the shadows and watching these proceedings. Suppose that that someone had lately been with the woman lying there, was, in some way, connected with her death.

"Come on, let's get out of here," Cross cried to his companion. And so the two of them set off at a brisk pace not stopping until they reached Baker's Row, where they encountered Police Constable Misen of H-Division, Whitechapel, and reported their find. The curious part is that although both men had examined the woman's body, neither of them had discovered that her throat had been cut almost from ear to ear.

2

Buck's Row was part of the regular beat of another policeman, Constable John Neil, Badge 97-J, who passed along this wretched street at half-hourly intervals. At 3:45 A.M., or just about the time when the two porters were reporting their gruesome find, P.C. Neil's bull's-eye lantern shone on a dark heap in the road that had not been there when he made the rounds of Buck's Row thirty minutes earlier. Holding the lantern high, he made out that it was the body of a woman. She was lying on her back with her eyes open and staring. Her bonnet had been knocked off and was lying in the gutter, and her clothing was disarranged. Stooping down, the policeman felt her arm, which was quite warm from the elbow joint upward — "warm as a toasted crumpet," he was to testify later. He also noticed the sour reek of gin. But it was only when he sought to raise the woman in the belief that she was drunk that he discovered her throat had been cut, and that blood was still oozing blackly from it.

Quite illogically, his first reaction was, Here's a woman who has committed suicide, and his eyes almost mechanically sought for a weapon near her body. Finding none, he was puzzled. It was then that the crimson word "murder" blotted itself on his consciousness, and the constable started up as though half expecting to find a homicide hovering nearby with knife poised in hand. Certainly every instinct told him that the killer could not be far away. His beat took only twelve minutes to walk, and, allowing for stops en route, he must have passed the very spot where the body now lay at 3:15 A.M., and on that occasion he had neither seen nor heard anything out of the usual. P.C. Neil was undecided whether to remain with the body or to report his findings at headquarters when, hearing Constable Haine pass on the neighboring beat in Brady Street, Neil called to him, "Run for Dr. Llewellyn — a woman's been murdered."

Twenty-four hours before she was found with her throat slit, Mary Ann Nicholls, for that was the name of the murdered woman, had been evicted from a doss house at No. 18 Thrawl Street, Spitalfields, because she lacked fourpence for a bed. "Never mind, I'll soon get my doss money," she boasted. "Look what a jolly bonnet I've got now." And she pointed to the piece of straw finery trimmed with black velvet which was later found in the gutter beside her body, but which was then perched at a jaunty angle on her head. Begging the lodging-house deputy to keep her bed for her until she had raised her miserable coppers, she set forth into the night. What she did in the next twenty-four hours will never be known.

The last person to see Mary Ann Nicholls alive was Emily Holland, her roommate at the Thrawl Street flophouse, who encountered Nicholls at the corner of Osborn Street and White-chapel Road at 2:30 A.M. Friday, August 31, or less than an hour before she was found murdered. "Polly" Nicholls, as she was known, was very drunk and staggered against the wall, according to her friend. She said that she was kipping in a doss house in "Flowery Dean Street," where "they sleeps men as well as women." She also said that she had made her doss money three times that day, but had spent it on drink. Her friend tried to persuade Polly to come home with her, but Polly mumbled something about having another try at raising the price of a bed. She was last seen staggering eastward along Whitechapel Road.

3

The Spitalfields area made notorious by Jack the Ripper was no more than a quarter-mile square. It lay between Commercial Street and Brick lane with Whitechapel Road as its southern boundary, and it contained the worst of London's doss houses and slums. Ironically, its epicenter was Christ Church, Spitalfields, built in 1729 by Sir Nicholas Hawksmoor, a pupil of Wren's, when the parish was still inhabited by prosperous Huguenot silk weavers.

But long before the events of this story Spitalfields had fallen upon evil days. When Henry Mayhew visited it in 1861 he found "800 thieves, vagabonds, beggars and prostitutes" living within an area of 400 square yards. It was, in Mayhew's words, "one of the most notorious rookeries for infamous characters in the metropolis." Charles Booth, the pioneer sociologist, ringed the area with black when he drew up his famous Poverty Maps of London in 1889 to denote it as "very poor, lowest class . . . vicious, semi-criminal." It was no accident that Dickens made Fagin traverse Spitalfields in order to reach Bill Sikes in nearby Bethnal Green. It was not accident, either, that Jack the Ripper chose it as his theater of operations.

The area can even be narrowed down to four or five streets, streets "where murder was considered as a dramatic incident, and drunkenness as the buffoonery of the stage," in the words of Charles Booth. Thrawl Street, Fashion Street, Dorset Street, Flower-and-Dean — we shall encounter these names over and over again in the course of this narrative, for it was here that the victims of Jack the Ripper lived, and it was here that they met their horrible deaths. We shall see how the Ripper penetrated ever deeper into this area until at last he seems to have come to the very heart of the evil which he sought there.

By some miracle Spitalfields has been preserved almost intact. The doss houses are gone, but the gloomy, brick Victorian tenements which replaced them are still there. The Irish laborers who gather in front of the now derelict hulk of Christ Church on Friday nights to hire on as market porters are the spiritual descendants of the starving silk weavers who sold their labor at the same spot in the 1760's. Today the sinisterly narrow tombstones which marked the graves of the poor have been swept back against the walls of the churchyard to make room for a children's playground. But if you visit this same churchyard on any afternoon you will find the "meths" or the "Jack drinkers," as the derelicts who drink methylated spirits are called, sleeping it off on the park benches.

Their ancestors slept on these same benches all during the reign of George III, and during that of George VI, for that matter. Then, as now, the churchyard was known as "Itchy Park," a nickname which was richly merited. "They are covered with vermin," a police superintendent explained to one of Charles Booth's social surveyors, referring to the destitute who slept rough in the 1880's. "The police don't like touching them," he added.

Jack London found the antecedents of today's meth drinkers asleep in Itchy Park when he visited there in 1902, the year of Edward VII's coronation, and the sight sickened him. "It was a welter of rags and filth, of all manner of loathsome skin diseases, open sores, bruises, grossness, indecency, leering monstrosities and bestial faces," he wrote. Of the dozen or so women who huddled on the benches, London's guide told him, "They will sell themselves for thru'pence or tu'pence or a stale loaf of bread." This was the evil quarter-mile in which Jack the Ripper was to operate, and it was from the ranks of just such female tramps as the American writer found huddled together that the Ripper chose his victims, of whom Mary Ann Nicholls, also known as "Polly," was the first.

4

It was 4 A.M. when Dr. Rees Ralph Llewellyn, police surgeon, arrived in Buck's Row to examine Polly Nicholls's remains. Dr. Llewellyn was thoroughly annoyed at having been aroused from his slumbers. Again, he viewed with distaste the curiosity seekers who had begun to gather. He could, of course, have ordered the police to erect screens around the body and could then have proceeded with his examination in semi-privacy. Instead, he chose to make only the most cursory of examinations before ordering the body removed to the mortuary.

He noted that the woman was lying on her back with her legs straight out, as though she had been formally laid out. The throat had been cut from ear to ear, completely severing the carotid arteries, but only a small pool of blood had collected in the gutter from the throat wound — "not more than would fill two wineglasses, or half a pint at the outside," according to the good doctor. (This absence of blood led to the belief, later abandoned, that the woman might have been murdered elsewhere, and her body carted to Buck's Row.) The surgeon was surprised to find that her arms and legs were still warm, indicating that she had not been long dead. She wore a rusty-colored ulster with seven large brass buttons, and underneath that a brown linsey dress, two flannel petticoats, each stenciled with the words "Lambeth Workhouse," and a pair of close-ribbed brown stays. Black woolen stockings and elastic-sided boots completed her attire. The only personal articles found on her were a comb and a piece of looking glass.

Had Dr. Llewellyn lifted the flannel petticoats he would have made a startling discovery. The woman had been disemboweled, a condition which the tightly laced stays served partly to conceal. Starting in the lower left part of the abdomen, the gash ran in a jagged manner almost as far as the diaphragm. It was a deep gash, completely cutting through the tissue. There were several incisions running across the abdomen; also three or four cuts running downward on the right side. All had apparently been caused by a long-bladed knife, moderately sharp and used with great violence.

Dr. Llewellyn did not stay to make these discoveries, however. Clearly, this homicide did not impress him. He was, in fact, so eager to get back to his bed that he left the scene before the body had been taken away, telling the police to send for him "if anything important transpires." It was only later, when pressed by reporters, that he amended his impressions. "I have seen many terrible cases," he told the pressmen solemnly, "but none so brutal as this."

Meanwhile, the riddle of the dead woman's identity did not go long unsolved. The "Lambeth Workhouse" stencilings on the petticoats swiftly led to the body being identified by the workhouse superintendent as that of Polly Nicholls, aged forty-two, an "unfortunate" of no fixed abode. Another item found on her person, a bit of broken mirror, led police to pick up her traces in the Spitalfields lodging houses, for this concession to vanity indelibly stamped Polly as a doss-house inmate, just as the markings on the petticoats betrayed their origin. Such an amenity as a mirror was not to be found in the Spitalfields stews, therefore their inmates carried bits of broken looking glass around with them.

5

Polly Nicholls was a Whitechapel whore, which tells us much, for they were a species apart. These were no lasses with fresh blooming cheeks, newly arrived from the provinces and fallen upon evil ways. Nor were they the pale, rather elegant young milliners' assistants whom one could pick up at night in the Haymarket, or in Lower Regent Street, and who offered at least an allusion of gaiety and charm. No, these were female tramps whom poverty and gin had robbed of whatever allure they might once have had, and, in this respect, Polly Nicholls was typical. Only five feet two in height, she gave an overall impression of drabness, with mouse-colored hair, a sallow complexion, and five front teeth missing from her lower jaw, souvenir of a brawl.

Brawls were not infrequent among them. In his memoirs Cambridge Professor Thomas Okey, who was born in Spitalfields, pictures the women of this district as "swearing, fighting, clawing, *ritu forarum,* with lacerated, bloody faces and breasts." This occurred, of course, when they were drunk, which was often. Alcohol was their means of rebelling against a society which condemned them to making matchboxes at tuppence farthing a gross. It was their means of hitting back at husbands who begat children in too quick succession.

Yet, for the collectors of human eccentricity, these women had a certain appeal. They were sharply limned — it was as though the constant battling with life had flayed away all externals. And they were fiercely independent. Not for them the workhouse — they preferred to vagabond, sleeping rough in Itchy Park, when they lacked the price of a kip. The knowledge that they had no farther to fall seems to have given these trollops a certain courage, even humor.

Polly Nicholls's story reads like the dreadful example in one of those temperance tracts beloved of the Victorians. She had been married to William Nicholls, a printer's machinist in the Old Kent Road, and had borne him five children, but she appears to have spent her afternoons in saloon back parlors instead of looking after her brood, and in 1881 the marriage broke up. Nicholls accused his wife of desertion, while the latter accused him of running off, during her last confinement, with the midwife. In the police courts during the course of the next few years Polly with unremitting fury was to hound the printer for maintenance for herself and the children. For a while Polly went to live with her father, Edward Walker, a blacksmith in Camberwell, but it was the same old story of drunken quarrels, and although her father did not turn her out, he undoubtedly was glad to see her go.

Her next stop in the Hogarthian cycle was at the Lambeth Workhouse in Prince's Road, where, as we have seen, she was an inmate for a while. Then in April, 1888, she went to work as a domestic servant at Ingleside, Wandsworth Common, which she described in a letter to her father as "a grand place with trees and gardens back and front." Her father must have relished the irony of the next sentence. "My employers are teetotallers and religious," she wrote, "so I ought to get on." But Polly did not get on. One can picture her in that rather rarefied atmosphere, her head with its frilly maid's cap bowed as the master of the house read the lesson each morning before breakfast, and all the while Polly wrestling with the terrible temptation. In the end the craving for drink proved too strong: Polly stole £3 from her employers ("betrayed her trust," in the Victorian phrase), crossed the river and lost herself in the purlieus of London's East End.

For the past four months she had flitted from one Spitalfields doss house to another, finally ending up at No. 18 Thrawl Street from which she was evicted on August 30, 1888, because she lacked fourpence for a bed.

6

The London press gave the murder in Buck's Row prominent display, which is rather extraordinary considering the number of violent crimes reported at this time. In scanning the press for this period one is astounded by the number of reports of women who had been beaten or kicked to death, jumped on until they were crushed, chopped, stabbed, seamed with vitriol, eviscerated, or deliberately set afire. In the preceding year thirty-five murders were recorded in the Home Counties alone (seventy-six murders if one includes infanticides) and of this number only eight convictions were secured, the majority of these crimes remaining forever unsolved.

What was there about the murder of an obscure prostitute in Buck's Row that sent editors scurrying to the newspaper morgues to dig out clippings filed under the heading "Unsolved Murders"? The answer was to be found in the clippings themselves. A number of "unfortunates" had been slain under mysterious circumstances in London's East End in recent months, but until Polly Nicholls' body was found in Buck's Row this fact, or rather this coincidence, did not register with the public. It was as though the mind, like some electronic computer, had quietly been storing the information all along, but now, with this latest coincidence, bells began to ring, lights to flash, and the answer which tumbled out looked suspiciously like serial murder.

First of all, there was "Fairy Fay," which was the rather whimsical name the press gave to the unidentified woman whose mutilated body was discovered near Commercial Road on the night of Boxing Day, December 26, 1887. "Fairy Fay" lost her life as a result of a wrong decision: she decided to take a shortcut home when the pub in Mitre Square where she had been drinking all evening closed after midnight, and in the dim warrens behind Commercial Road she was struck down and carved up by an unknown assassin.

Even more brutal was the murder of Emma Smith, a forty-five-year-old prostitute, which occurred on Easter Monday, April 13, 1888. Returning home at about 1:30 A.M. after a night's pub crawl, Emma was accosted by three men who assaulted her, robbed her and left her for dead in Osborn Street,

Spitalfields. Rushed to the London Hospital in Whitechapel Road, she was found to be suffering from a rupture of the peritoneum, which had been perforated by some blunt instrument used with great force, according to the house surgeon. She lingered a few hours in agony before succumbing to her injuries, but she was unable to describe her assailants other than to say that one looked to be no more than nineteen years old. Robbery appeared to have been the motive for the Emma Smith murder, leading police to believe that it was the work of one of the organized gangs, such as the Hoxton Market or the Old Nichol Street gangs, which preyed on prostitutes. These gangs offered "protection" in return for a cut of the prostitute's earnings, and the theory advanced was that Emma Smith had failed to pay up.

But if "Fairy Fay" and Emma Smith were killed for their pitiful earnings, as seems just barely possible, there was no ready explanation for the murder of Martha Tabram, which occurred four months later in almost exactly the same spot where Emma Smith had been assaulted with a blunt instrument. Because the Tabram murder was as senseless as it was frenzied, many crime experts have attributed it to Jack the Ripper.

7

Martha Tabram differed from the prostitutes whom the Ripper claimed as victims in one important respect: she was a "soldier's woman." If the Whitechapel whores constituted a distinct species, as seems to have been the case, then the soldiers' women were a subspecies, characterized by unflagging loyalty to Her Majesty's services. Tabram walked a regular beat, and that was down by the docks where she picked up soldiers who were stationed at the Tower of London.

Henry Mayhew, that tireless chronicler of the London underworld, speaks of soldiers' women as being low, cheap and often diseased. He describes one of these infected creatures whom he spotted in a music hall as "contaminating the very air, like a deadly upas tree." Of another of these camp followers he says that her arm was scarred where it had been run through with a bayonet. "The sodgers is such bleedin' cowards," she confided to Mayhew, "they thinks nothing of sticking a woman when they'se riled, and drunk, or they wop us with their belts." It was to this class that Martha Tabram belonged.

Early on the morning of August 7, 1888, a single, piercing cry of "Help!" "Murder!" shattered the silence of the George Yard buildings in what is now Gunthorpe Street, Spitalfields. It awakened Mrs. Francis Hewitt, manageress of this block of flats, but she was not unduly alarmed. Cries of murder were fairly common in this neighborhood, where husbands beat up wives with monotonous regularity. Besides, it was the morning after the August bank holiday, and drunken couples were still straggling home from the pubs, or from outings farther afield to Epping Forest or Clacton-on-Sea. Paying no heed to the cry, Mrs. Hewitt turned over and was soon fast asleep again.

Cabdriver Albert Crow, who lived in the George Yard buildings, returned home from work at about 3:30 A.M. after an exhausting day carting holidaymakers around in his hack. As he climbed the stairs of the block of flats, he noticed someone lying on the first floor[1] landing. "But I am so used to finding people sleeping there," he told the inquest jury later, "that I took no notice of it — not even to find out whether it was a man or a woman." Crow fell into bed exhausted and did not awaken until late that morning.

John Reeves, another tenant, slipped in what proved to be coagulated blood as he descended the stairs on his way to work an hour and a half later. By this time it was beginning to get light, and Reeves could make out, lying in the pool of congealed blood, the body of a woman. Martha Tabram, for it was her

[1] In England, the floor above the ground floor.

body that the stevedore had discovered on the stairs, had been stabbed thirty-nine times. Most of her vital organs had been punctured, and the wounds had been inflicted apparently by some sort of dagger.

Missing details of the last hours Martha had spent alive were supplied at the coroner's inquest by Mary Ann Connolly, alias "Pearly Poll," a tall, masculine-looking woman with a face sodden and reddened by drink. Pearly Poll was an inhabitant of one of the most notorious thieves' dens and brothels in Spitalfields, Crossingham's lodging house in Dorset Street, which may have accounted for her reluctance to testify. During her interrogation by the police she had threatened to throw herself into the river if the lawmen did not leave her alone; and now, in the witness stand, she complained that her chest was "queer," that she could not speak above a whisper, and in the end a policeman had to act as interpreter for her.

She said that she had been with Martha Tabram on the night of the murder, and that they had been picked up in Whitechapel Road by two soldiers, one of them being a corporal, who stood them to drinks at The Blue Anchor. They had been among the last customers to leave this pub, and afterwards the two soldiers had stood haggling with their drab companions over the price of their favors. The price settled, the couples parted, Martha going with her soldier in the direction of the George Yard buildings while Pearly Poll led the corporal up a dark close known appropriately enough as Angel Alley. It was then 1:45 A.M., and that was the last Pearly Poll saw of the ill-fated Martha Tabram.

The Pearly Poll saga had an epilogue. Convinced that she was not telling the whole truth, but was in fact shielding someone, Inspector Reid of Scotland Yard escorted her to the Tower of London, where a parade that must surely have been unique in military annals was held for her benefit. Drawn up in formation in the square facing Pearly Poll were all the noncommissioned officers and privates who had been absent on leave August 6–7 when the outrage was committed. Poll, for her part, was dressed up in all of her cockney finery for the occasion, with a great plumed hat and a dress trimmed with pearl buttons.

Asked if she could identify either of the two men who had been with the murdered woman, she scrutinized each of the soldiers in turn with her head cocked to one side, for all the world like an inspecting general. Then slowly she shook her head. "'E ain't 'ere," she announced.

The same farce was enacted at Wellington Barracks in Birdcage Walk where Polly was taken for an identity parade of the Coldstream Guards. But this time Polly changed her tactics. Without hesitation she picked out two men, one of them a corporal, as having been her companions on the night of the murder. That the purpose of this stratagem was to shake off the police was evident, for both of the guardsmen had unimpeachable alibis; the corporal had spent the evening at home with his wife, while the other guardsman had returned to his barracks at 10:05 P.M.[2]

Sir Melville Macnaghten, who became head of the CID at Scotland Yard after the Ripper murders, was sure that Pearly Poll had recognized, at the Tower of London identity parade, the two soldiers she had been with and that she had refused to identify them. He was also convinced that the Tabram murder was not the handiwork of Jack the Ripper, and on this latter point I am inclined to agree. Tabram's throat had not been cut, as was the case in all of the Ripper murders; nor did the wounds inflicted upon her body show any anatomical skill.

[2] An unexpected result of the Tabram inquest was that soldiers stationed in the Tower of London were forbidden to carry bayonets or any sidearms while on leave. This information was given to me by James W. Bousfield, whose mother ran a boardinghouse at No. 4 Star Court (now Planet Street) where Martha Tabram lodged. Bousfield, aged eighty-three, showed me one of the key chains which Tabram had hawked for a living, and which he had retained as a souvenir after the murder.

Seemingly, they were the work of a man in a blind frenzy, rather than that of the cool but misplaced gynecologist that was Jack the Ripper.

Three East London prostitutes murdered in less than eight months, and all in the same wretched locale: this fact was bound to register with the public. It is not surprising then that when a fourth murder, the one in Buck's Row, was reported the public should jump to the conclusion that all were the work of the same hand.

CHAPTER II

A GRISLY COMIC INTERLUDE

EAST LONDON, whose 2,000,000 population was then greater than that of either St. Petersburg, Philadelphia or Berlin, had not a single mortuary worthy of the name in 1888. When East London prostitutes such as Mary Ann Nicholls were found murdered, their bodies were placed in a shed behind the workhouse in Old Montague Street — "a disgraceful hole-and-corner hovel," the *Daily Telegraph* called it, adding that the surgeons who were constrained to perform their postmortem examinations in this shed did so "with the most incomplete appliances for carrying out their delicate and difficult duty."

Equally disgraceful, there was not a single coroner's court where inquests could be held in the whole of East London, although some five hundred inquests into unexplained deaths occurred in the Wihtechapel district alone in 1887. These were usually convened in the smoke-filled saloon bars of public houses, where the jurors were within easy reach of a pint of ale. If the coroner was lucky, he might get the use of the Working Lads' Institute in Whitechapel Road.

It was outside this institute that a small, but excited crowd gathered Saturday morning, September 1, the opening day of the Mary Ann Nicholls inquest; and when the doors opened there was a general rush for the few seats available to the public. The remaining space in this improvised coroner's courtroom was quickly filled by those who had official business —

witnesses looking stiff and self-conscious in their best regalia, detectives conspicuous for their bowler hats and flash clothes, penny-a-line journalists, messenger boys poised to rush the news copy to Fleet Street, and, of course, a thin blue line of the law in the background, the constables of H-Division, Whitechapel, many of them with fierce mustaches, who would be called upon to give evidence.

A hush fell over the courtroom when Wynne E. Baxter, coroner for the northeastern division of Middlesex County, entered, followed by his clerk. Coroner Baxter was wearing "white and checked trousers, a dazzling white waistcoat, a crimson scarf and a dark coat," according to the *East London Observer*, which added by way of explanation for this flamboyant plumage the fact that this Crown officer had just returned from a Scandinavian tour. Because he was to preside at the inquests of three of Jack the Ripper's victims, Coroner Baxter will repay a closer look. In addition to being something of a dandy, he was also a legal expert, having written a treatise on *The Law and Practice of the Supreme Court of Judicature*, which became known thereafter as "Baxter's Judicature." Under the pseudonym of Llewellyn Acton, he also wrote religious tracts of a high moral tone. But it is as self-appointed gadfly to Police Commissioner Sir Charles Warren and his Metropolitan minions that Baxter is of chief interest to us. For the dapper coroner seemed to have conceived it as his mission in life to expose the stupidities of the law guardians. Indeed, the police became so incensed at his carping criticisms and insinuations that the inquest into one of the Ripper murders was wrested from Baxter's hands, even though the murder had occurred inside his bailiwick as coroner.

Gaveling for order, the coroner's officer addressed himself to the jury in a formula that went back a thousand years: "Oyez, Oyez, You good men of this district summoned to appear here this day to inquire for our sovereign Lady the Queen when, how, and by what means Mary Ann Nicholls came to her death, answer to your names." The formalities of the roll call and the swearing-in over, the jurors then adjourned to the workhouse in Old Montague Street to view the remains of Polly Nicholls, and as they viewed the cadaver their faces were a study in conflicting emotions. Some peered intently at the contents of the tin shell as though to memorize every detail; others, after a swift glance, turned their heads away and, indeed, seemed to hold their breath until they had reached the door.

2

George Cross, the market porter, took the witness stand at the inquest wearing the rough sack apron of his trade, and told of discovering Polly Nicholls's body in Buck's Row. Cross had not been certain whether the woman was alive or dead, but had thought that she might have fainted after having been raped. He had not noticed that her throat was cut, or that she had other injuries. Police Constable Neil, who discovered the murder independently, had, on the other hand, jumped to the conclusion that the woman had committed suicide by cutting her own throat. No one saw or heard Nicholls's killer, a fact all the more remarkable when one considers the number of people — Police Constable Neil and the two porters — in the vicinity of Buck's Row shortly after the murder. Either the murderer hid in the shadows when these men approached or he knew the district so well that he was able to slip through them undetected and to escape by some side alley. Three night watchmen were on duty close to Buck's Row, but none of them heard cries or sounds of a scuffle. Three men employed at Barber's slaughterhouse in Buck's Row testified similarly. Mrs. Emma Green, who lived a few yards from the spot where the body was found, said she had heard no one cry out. "I was awake at the time. I couldn't sleep. If the woman had screamed, I must have heard her."

Emily Holland, who gave her evidence in such a frightened manner that the coroner had to urge her to speak up, told of encountering Polly little more than one hour before she was found murdered and of later identifying her body at the morgue. "Were you crying when you identified her?" the jury foreman asked. "It was enough to make anybody shed a tear, sir," she replied. The father of the deceased — a gray-haired and gray-bearded man, came slowly up to the coroner's table, his head lowered, his hands behind his back, and gave his name as Edward Walker, a blacksmith of Maidswood Road, Camberwell. He said that Polly had lived with him for a while after separating from her husband, but that he had not seen her since June, 1886. He had, however, recognized her body at the mortuary by its general appearance, the loss of some front teeth and a small mark on her forehead. Polly was not a particularly sober woman, he testified, but he did not think her "fast" with men. He had not turned her out of the house, he said further, in reply to questions. They simply had had words, and she had left the following morning.

A ripple of interest ran through the improvised courtroom when William Nicholls, printer's machinist and estranged husband of the deceased, took the witness stand. Nicholls was very pale with a full light brown beard and mustache, and he was wearing mourning clothes — a tall silk hat, black frock coat, black tie and trousers of dark material — which he had hired especially for the occasion. He carried an umbrella to complete this ensemble. In this same rented attire he had gone in the company of Inspector Abberline of Scotland Yard to the Old Montague Street mortuary, where he identified the Buck's Row victim as his wife. Nicholls seems to have had a keen sense of drama, for gazing down upon the remains of the poor woman in the open coffin he is alleged to have delivered this curtain line, "I forgive you, as you are, for what you have done to me." On the witness stand, however, he appeared less forgiving. Polly Nicholls was much given to drink, he said. "She deserted me four or five times, if not six," he pursued, "and the last time she left me with five children, the youngest of whom was only sixteen months old."

There now occurred one of those grisly comic interludes which, like the drunken Porter's scene in *Macbeth,* served to separate the horrors that have gone before from those that are to come, and thus enable the mind to support both. Coroner Baxter, by a series of skillful questions, had been endeavoring to show the slipshod way in which postmortem examinations were carried out. For example, the fact that Polly Nicholls had been disemboweled was not discovered until 7 A.M., when Police Inspector John Spratling arrived at the mortuary to make an inventory of her clothing and, lifting up her petticoats, discovered the evisceration. Inspector Spratling, himself, did not remove the clothing, but stood by while two workhouse inmates stripped the body and washed it. Inspector Joseph Helston, of J-Division, was also present.

It was the testimony of these two workhouse inmates, at times wholly at variance with what the police had testified, which provided the macabre comic relief.

Robert Mann, a pauper who was also subject to fits, testified that he was in charge of the workhouse mortuary, and that on the morning of the murder he had opened the mortuary at about 5 A.M. to receive the body of Mary Ann Nicholls. He then went off to breakfast, returning later with his mate, James Hatfield, to undress and wash the body.

Q (Coroner): The police were not present?

A: No, there was no one present. Inspector Helston had not arrived.

Q: Had you been told not to touch the body?

A: No.

James Hatfield next took the stand and said that he had assisted Mann in undressing the body. He likewise maintained that Inspector Helston was not present.

Q: What did you take off first?

A: I took off her ulster and put it on the ground. Then I took off her jacket and put it on the ground.

Q (interrupting): Did you have to cut any of her clothing?

A: Her dress was loose so I didn't have to cut it, but I cut the bands on her petticoats and peeled 'em down with my hands, the petticoats, that is. She was wearing a shirtwaist, and I cut that down the front.

Q: Was she wearing stays?

A: Not that I can recall.

Q: Who gave you instructions to do all this?

A: No one gave us any. We did it so as to have the body ready for the doctor.

Q: Who told you the doctor was coming?

A: I heard someone talking about it.

All this time Coroner Baxter had been patient in questioning the witness, but now a note of sarcasm crept into his voice, sarcasm which was directed more to the red-faced police sitting in the makeshift courtroom than to the poor workhouse attendant.

Q: Having finished, did you make the postmortem examination?

A: No, the police came.

Q: Oh, the police came, did they? And so it was no longer necessary for you to go on with the postmortem?

A: Yes. They looked at the petticoats and found the words "Lambeth Workhouse" on the bands.

Q: It was cut out?

A: Yes, I cut it out.

Q: Who told you to do so?

A: Inspector Helston.

This unhappy police official slumped down in his seat as the coroner fixed him with his most piercing look.

Q: Would it surprise you to learn that the deceased was wearing stays?

A: Yes.

Q (by jury foreman): Why, you tried the stays on the body of the deceased in my presence to show me how short they were.

A: I forgot about that.

Hatfield's answer was all but drowned by the laughter which swept the courtroom.

Q (Coroner, gaveling for silence): He admits that his memory is bad.

3

Dr. Llewellyn, called as a witness, gave the postmortem results. The doctor did not believe that Nicholls had been seized from behind and her throat then cut, as had been widely reported in the press. In his opinion a hand was held across her mouth and the knife then used, possibly by a left-handed person, as the bruising on the decedent's face was such as would result from the mouth being covered by the right hand. Also, the knife wounds had been made from left to right, indicating that they might have been inflicted by a left-handed person. As for the murder weapon itself, it could scarcely have been a sailor's jackknife, in the doctor's view, *but was more likely a pointed weapon with a stout back, such as a cork cutter's or a shoemaker's knife.* This last opinion — almost a chance observation — was to have an important bearing on the whole conduct of the Ripper investigation. The reference to the cork cutter and/or shoemaker was to be remembered long after the inquest had closed, and it was to be combined with one other piece of information, namely that the murder site in Buck's Row was near a slaughterhouse, in order to conjure up a mythical character known as "Leather Apron" as the assassin of the women.

Meanwhile, the inquest into the Nicholls murder ended with the coroner and the coroner's jury in a distinctly rebellious mood. With elaborate sarcasm, Coroner Baxter thanked the committee of the Working Lads' Institute for the use of their room. "Otherwise," he continued, "we would have been forced to hold this inquest in the parlor of a public house, hardly a suitable place." Next he turned to the lack of mortuary facilities in London's East End. "Jury after jury has requested the coroner to draw the attention of the sanitary authorities to this deficiency — without success, I might add," he observed dryly. He then pleaded for adequate public mortuary facilities on health grounds. "Surely if mortuaries are found necessary in the West End, there must be stronger reasons for them here in the midst of so much squalid crowding." Alluding to the slipshod methods of handling corpses, the coroner went on, "Had there been a public mortuary there would also have been a keeper whose experience would have shown the advisability of the body being attended to only in the presence of the medical witness."

The coroner's remarks were an incitement to rebellion, therefore no one appeared too surprised when the jury foreman got up and criticized the Home Secretary, Henry Matthews, for not offering a reward for the capture of the killer. The foreman linked the murder of Martha Tabram with that of Polly Nicholls as the handiwork of one and the same person, and said that had a reward been offered in the former case, the latter murder would never have occurred. "You can bet that a substantial reward would have been offered if it had been a rich person murdered, and that is why, to start the ball rolling, I am prepared to give twenty-five pounds out of my own pocket for the capture of the murderer." "After all," he added, a bit illogically, "these poor people have souls like anybody else."

The funeral of Mary Ann Nicholls took place on September 6. A polished elm coffin containing her remains was driven to Ilford cemetery in the company of a mourning coach containing her father and three of her children. The husband, William Nicholls, rode in another coach. "There was a very large number of spectators present who evinced the greatest sympathy," reported the *East London Observer.* A few weeks later the residents of Buck's Row petitioned to have the street's name changed, and thus it became Durward Street, the name it now bears.

4

Queen Victoria could hardly have been less fortunate in her choice of Metropolitan Police Commissioner than Sir Charles Warren, a major general of the Royal Engineers, whose chief qualification for the commissioner's post seems to have been his ability to handle the Bantu in Grinqualand West. He was a strikingly handsome man, with fierce mustaches and a monocle screwed into his right eye, and he sat a horse well, sometimes wearing the old-fashioned policeman's "chimney pot" hat with his full dress uniform. But his appointment as police chief in 1886 was little short of a national disaster.

The year 1886 was one of great social unrest which started in February when the unemployed tossed paving stones through the windows of the Carlton Club. It was to quell these demonstrations that General Sir Charles Warren was summoned home from Egypt, where he had been posted as Governor of the Red Sea Littoral and in command of the Royal Engineers at Suakin. "The selection of a distinguished general would, it was thought, restore confidence," writes Sir John Moylan, in his history of Scotland Yard, overlooking the fact that Warren was third choice for the job (it had been turned down by Sir Redvers Buller and Lord Charles Beresford).

Warren's method of restoring public confidence was to reorganize Scotland Yard along military lines, and to staff it with Army officers in executive posts. Thus, in 1887, he created two new superintendents, 168 inspectors, 196 sergeants, while the number of constables actually dwindled by 89. He had nothing but contempt for the CID detective branch, which he omitted to mention in the 1887 Annual Police Report. He found room in his report, however, to mention such trivia as the fact that 131 constables had been placed on the sick list because of sore feet ("Boots are a matter of great concern," commented Warren); and that the new-style truncheons, which were made of cocus wood, were to be carried in a side pocket, the truncheon case having been abolished.

All during the terrible winter of 1887, Warren deployed his police against the hollow-cheeked men who demonstrated in Trafalgar Square as though these latter were Kaffirs and his mission was to "civilize" them. This was the winter when the unemployed, to call attention to their plight, picketed the fashionable churches on Sundays carrying banners inscribed with Scriptural texts. It was the winter when Henry Champion, the Socialist, told a meeting in London Fields that if the whole propertied class had but one throat he would cut it without a second thought.

The real trial of strength came on November 3, 1887, thereafter to be enshrined in the Socialist calendar as "Bloody Sunday," when a crowd of unemployed estimated at twenty thousand converged on Trafalgar Square from all parts of London. To oppose this ragged army, Sir Charles took the field with four thousand constables, plus detachments of Life Guards and Grenadier Guards. Lining the parapet of the National Gallery which faces the square were three hundred Grenadier Guards with fixed bayonets and twenty ball cartridges each in their pouches.

"It was all over in a few minutes," William Morris wrote. "Our comrades fought valiantly, but . . . the police struck left and right like what they were, soldiers attacking an enemy." Two hundred of the demonstrators were injured badly enough to require hospital treatment, two of them later succumbing to their injuries. The marchers got "the broken heads they richly deserved," according to *The Times,* which devoted eight and a half columns to a news report of the incident. The paper regretted that "a great many more escaped well-merited punishment."

Bloody Sunday earned Sir Charles a knighthood and the undying hatred of London's working class population.[1] Later he was to boast that the military strategy he employed in Trafalgar Square on Bloody Sunday "was admired not only by experts at the clubs, but by the Social Democrats themselves."

But not all rank and file policemen shared this admiration. A police constable, in an anonymous pamphlet published shortly after the riot, commented: "The majority of police feel that it was a thing to be sorry for. People who previously treated constables with respect and had generally a kind word for them, treated them afterwards with a scowl of contempt."

5

I have dealt at some length upon the personality of Sir Charles Warren and upon its unfortunate effect on the police force under this command, because both, in my opinion, go far toward explaining why Jack the Ripper was never captured. The clashes with the unemployed in 1887 had "exhausted the police and terrified the public," in the words of Home Secretary

[1] Warren's grandson, Mr. Watkin W. Williams, was kind enough to lend me a scrapbook kept by his grandmother, Lady Warren, in which she had pasted newspaper articles and cartoons lampooning her husband. Also pasted in are several threatening letters, one of which is headed by a Jolly Roger in red ink and reads: "To the bloody curs in blue, you bloody liars and cowards, say your prayers . . . Revenge — Deeds Not Words." Another warns, "Beware of your life, you dog. Don't venture out too far. Look out — this is yours." There follows the sketch of a coffin.

Henry Matthews, and this despite Warren's boast in the Annual Police Report that the police had "successfully coped with attempts by unruly mobs to riot in the streets." Not only were the police exhausted, but they had been thoroughly demoralized by Warren's attempts to enforce a military regime. In other words, the Ripper could hardly have picked a better time to begin his anatomical experiments if he were to escape detection. The police were in no state to match wits with one as diabolically clever as he.

Possibly the only man at Scotland Yard who was capable of tracking down the killer was James Monro, the Assistant Police Commissioner and head of CID, and Monro resigned on the last day of August, 1888, after a series of quarrels with Warren. Monro, like many of England's ablest police officers, had learned his trade in India, where he served as Inspector General of the Bengal police. Ironically enough, he was to be recalled to Scotland Yard as Warren's successor and, as police commissioner, to push through many needed reforms, including police pensions. ("The men were his devoted slaves," writes George Dilnot "and he did much to increase their pride in their calling and to ensure their personal well-being.") Meanwhile, Monro's resignation left a huge gap at Scotland Yard: it meant that the detective branch was without an effective head. Robert (later Sir Robert) Anderson, who was chosen to succeed Monro, was a socialite and a barrister whose police experience had until then been limited to ferreting out the secrets of the Irish Home Rule Dynamitards. Anderson's idea of meeting the challenge of his new job was to leave immediately for a one-month holiday in Switzerland.

But Jack the Ripper could not wait for the Assistant Police Commissioner to have done climbing Alpine slopes in search of edelweiss, and of the even more elusive chamois. On the very day Anderson left for Switzerland the Ripper prepared to spring his next surprise. As the CID head sped toward Paris en route to Montreux, the corpse of the Ripper's latest victim lay exposed to the night in the backyard of No. 29 Hanbury Street.

CHAPTER III

THE BACKYARD OF NO. 29

THE BACKS of the tenements which overlooked the yard at No. 29 Hanbury Street rose sheer in the gray light of the September morning like a vast brick cliff pocked with windows. Had one glanced upward from the yard on that Saturday morning, September 8, 1888, one would have made out heads at every window. It gave rather a comic effect, for some heads still had their frilly nightcaps on, while with others the hair was tousled or stood straight up in a fringe, but there was nothing comic about the faces. They were white, strained, as they gazed downward, registering fright or a frozen fascination as though their owners had been mesmerised. And there were children, too, whose faces shone white against the smoke-begrimed brick, like gulls nesting in the side of the cliff, and their cries were shrill with excitement like those of seabirds. What were they gazing at so intently at this early morning hour, this host high in the brick wall? What was there so special about the backyard of No. 29? And why was it swarming with police?

Certainly, there was little about its façade to distinguish it from its neighbors. Like all the other houses in Hanbury Street, No. 29 was built originally for Huguenot silk weavers at a time when their trade flourished. But the Tuscan pilasters which decorated its doorway on either side had long since disappeared. For Hanbury Street had become a slum, "the very heart of the sweating district," in the words of *The Lancet*, the medical journal, which sent a team of medical inspectors to report on conditions there.

The yard of No. 29 was more cluttered with debris than its neighbors, for it was used by its owner, Mrs. Amelia Richardson, in running a packing-case business. There was a passage leading directly from the front door to the yard, which was reached by two stone steps. Between the steps and the fence of the house next door there was a recess about three feet wide. It was around this recess that the police clustered like bluebottles around a festering sore. It was only by dint of straining that the eyes of those who gazed down on this scene could make out in this recess what appeared to be a bundle of dirty rags against a dark patch, but what was, in fact, the body of Annie Chapman, better known to Whitechapel as "Dark Annie."

2

"Dark Annie," said Timothy Donovan, landlord of the rookery at No. 35 Dorset Street where she lived, "was a decent woman in her way. Whenever she had the money she would pay eightpence for a double bed, instead of a fourpenny single, just so she could have the bed all to herself." Such were the standards by which Whitechapel judged its own. But Annie Chapman, aged forty-seven and a widow, had other claims to superiority. She had been married to an Army pensioner named Fred Chapman, who was also a veterinary surgeon, and they had lived for a while in Windsor. Annie was inclined to embroider upon this golden age: thus in the telling, her husband was likely to be transformed from a veterinarian to a doctor and she also spoke of "my home in Windsor," all of which did not endear her to her less fortunate sisters.

Annie never explained why she had left her good provider,

though her husband must have been many years older than she in order to have reached pensionable age. Nor did she ever discuss the two children who were issue of that marriage—there was a boy, who was deformed and in a cripples' home, and a girl who was in an institution in France. But she must have parted from her husband on good terms, for he continued to make her an allowance of ten shillings a week until his death in 1886.

The death of Fred the pensioner seems to have marked a turning point in Dark Annie's life, for thereafter her luck changed. Not only was she deprived of an income which was more than the average factory girl earned in a sixty-hour work week, but her health began to fail. Unaccountably, she began to suffer from dizziness and fainting spells.

Certain writers, in discussing the Ripper murders, have obviously been misled by Annie's pretensions to respectability. They may even have been dazzled by that mythical Windsor home. At any rate they have denied that she was a prostitute. She was, they maintain, a "one-man woman" who attached herself to a man of her choice and lived with him for a long period. Certainly, Annie did live with a sieve maker in Spitalfields long enough to earn herself the nickname of "Annie Sievey," but to insist that she was not a whore is to take the romantic view. No respectable woman even in straitened circumstances would have been found in an establishment such as that in Dorset Street run by Tim Donovan.

Dorset Street in 1888 had the distinction of being the first street to which the police directed their searches in the event of an untraced London crime. Although it was only a short thoroughfare, it was one vast brothel, with no fewer than twelve hundred people crammed from cellar to roof in its common lodging houses, and these included beggars, petty thieves, confidence tricksters and the dregs of whoredom. Should there be further doubt concerning Annie's profession, we have the word of her friend Amelia Farmer. "Annie," said this latter, "was not particular what she did to earn a living, and she stayed out at all hours of the night looking for men who would pay her the price of a bed."

Annie, like her sister unfortunates, worked when she could at those staple slaveries which were reserved for the women and children of the poor — matchbox making and tieing artificial flowers. And like them she sprinkled worthless seeds with a pennyworth of scent and sold these sachets as "sweet lavender," or she hawked such gimcrack notionery as miraculous corn cures and walnut thimble cases. But lately she had been too sick to work at all, as she told the medical orderly at the infirmary. There was nothing that any infirmary could do for Annie. She was tubercular, and she was slowly starving to death, or, as Dr. George Bagster Phillips expressed it in his autopsy report, her body showed "signs of great deprivation."

Her friend Amelia Farmer was genuinely shocked by Annie's appearance when the two chanced to meet Friday, September 7, for she looked even thinner and more haggard than usual, with an unhealthy, bluish tinge to the flesh beneath her eyes. "You look God-awful," her friend informed her frankly. "I've been taken queer," Annie said, by way of reply. "Besides," she added, "I ain't had anything to eat all day — not even a cup of tea." She spoke vaguely about going into a casual ward for a day or two, but she seemed too listless even to take the necessary steps toward this end. Taking pity on her, Farmer slipped a couple of coppers into her hand. "This is for a cup of tea, luv," she said. "But don't have rum," she cautioned. "You know your weakness." Annie knew it all right. She muttered something about pulling herself together, then the two friends parted.

Later that same night, Timothy Donovan found Annie sitting by the fire in the kitchen at No. 35 Dorset Street. The kitchens of most lodging houses were enormous, and Donovan's was no exception, it being intended to serve as a communal center. It was lit by one flaring gas jet, and although it would have been difficult to discern what color they were originally, the walls were now a gravy-brown. Dominating the room was a coke fire which glowed and crackled in a grate large enough to roast a sheep. Above, in a serried line, were tin teapots battered and stained with long use, while higher still on the wall hung the "Rules of the House," one of which stood out in aggressive capitals: NO WASHING ON SUNDAY. Pervading all was that smell which is indissolubly linked with poverty, the smell of toasted bloaters.

Donovan glanced at his watch, noted with surprise that it was 1:45 A.M., then turned to Annie. "You're sitting up late," he remarked, but Annie only gazed disconsolately into the fire. In a somewhat kindlier tone the Irishman asked, "Aren't you going up to bed?" "No," she replied wearily, "I have no money." "Well, you know the rules," Donovan said, becoming noncommittal again. Annie knew the rules, but as she moved toward the door she told Donovan to hold her bed for her. She would find the money somehow, she said.

At some time between 2 A.M. and 5 A.M. Annie encountered Jack the Ripper.

3

It was nearly daybreak when John Davies, a market porter who lived at No. 29 Hanbury Street, discovered Annie's body lying in the backyard of the building — not far, be it noted, from the spot where Polly Nicholls had been murdered eight days earlier. But in savagery this latest murder far surpassed its predecessor. This time the head had been so nearly severed from the body that the killer had knotted a handkerchief around the neck as though to hold the head to the torso.

The body lay in the recess between the backyard steps and

the fence of the neighboring house. The left arm had been placed across the left breast, and the legs were drawn up, with the feet resting on the ground and the knees turned outward. The face, which was turned on its right side, was bruised, and the tongue was swollen and protruded between the front teeth but not beyond the lips; all of which suggested that the murderer had clapped his hand over the victim's mouth, or that she had been gagged to stop her from calling out. The body had been disemboweled and, with some show of surgical deftness, the uterus and its appendages had been removed. As a further bizarre note, two brass rings, evidently wrenched from the middle finger of her left hand, and a few pennies and farthings were laid out neatly at the victim's feet.

Davies, the market porter, ran to notify the police at the nearby Commercial Street station, and they in turn summoned Dr. George Bagster Phillips, the divisional surgeon. In no time at all the backyard of No. 29 was alive with police and men in brown suits and bowler hats, who were obviously detectives. After completing his preliminary examination, Dr. Phillips ordered the body removed to the makeshift mortuary in Old Montague Street.

Among those who followed Annie's body as it was wheeled on a stretcher down Hanbury Street on that gray September morning was a grotesque figure draped with a blanket who might have been a mourner, but who was in fact an excited boy of eleven. "Yes, I was one of those who saw her body being taken away," Alfred Henry Lane told me when I interviewed him at Hathaway House in Hoxton.

Lane, who was in his mid-eighties when we met, was one of those who answered my appeal for information concerning Jack the Ripper which the *East London Advertiser* was kind enough to print. He turned out to be a small, spry man who wore a peaked cap indoors, and who had an air of quiet amusement about him, as though he was enjoying a private joke. He seemed to be secretly amused not only at Jack the Ripper, but at the American writer who had journeyed all the way to Hoxton to interview him, and at himself and his own longevity — that was part of the joke. He showed me a photograph of himself taken when he was a young man with a great wedge of mustache ("the best mustache in Bethnal Green until I joined the Royal Engineers and they made me shave it off"), then he told me his story.

"My uncle had a coffee stall in Hanbury Street, and my mother used to go there very early in the morning to help out. When the Ripper murders started, she took me along for her protection, wrapping me in a blanket against the cold. Not that I would have been much protection" — and here he paused to chuckle — "for I was only a lad of eleven. Anyway, on this particular morning as we neared Hanbury Street we saw a stretcher being wheeled out of No. 29 by two policemen. It was covered by a kind of tarpaulin, and wherever it went it left a thin trail of blood. Mother had to hurry off to work, but it being Saturday and no school I decided to follow the stretcher, which I did, all the way to the Old Montague Street mortuary. I can remember it now as though it were yesterday." They must have made a strange cortege behind the dead body, the tall bearded constables in their blue uniforms and the little boy.

4

As the morning wore on, a crowd of several hundred people gathered outside No. 29, and "loud were the expressions of terror on all sides," according to *The Times*, which added that "neighbors on either side did much business by making a small charge . . . to view from the windows the yard in which the murder was committed." News of the murder spread quickly to other parts of London, and as the first edition of the afternoon papers appeared there was a run on them, with people queuing up outside the news vendors until fresh supplies were brought in. A Deptford man was so eager to get his copy of the *Evening Standard* that he aroused suspicion. According to the newsagent, who summoned Deptford police, "The man snatched the open paper from my hand, threw down a penny, rushed out of the shop. He could not wait to get home, but by the gaslight of a shop window he read the account of the tragedy eagerly and excitedly." By the time the police arrived he had "slunk off."

It was in the Whitechapel road, however, that the excitement reached its peak. It being Saturday, Whitechapel Road was thronged with Cockneys who talked of nothing else but the "'Anbury Street 'orror." Within hours of the murder a broadsheet titled "Lines on the Terrible Tragedy" had been rushed from the printer, and men with the broad sheets tucked inside their hatbands now sang the doggerel verse to the tune of "My Village Home" as they hawked the penny sheets among the crowd.

The proprietor of a small waxworks museum in Whitechapel Road thought he saw an opportunity to turn a swift shilling. Accordingly he dusted off three wax figures that had done duty on many previous occasions, daubed them with red paint and opened for business under the banner, "Horrible Whitechapel Murders — See the George Yard, Buck's Row, Hanbury Street victims." The resultant bonanza was cut short by the action of a police inspector, who closed the museum in the name of public decency. (The waxworks emporium did not stay shut long, for shortly afterward a correspondent who signed himself "John Law" complained to the *Pall Mall Gazette:* "There is at present almost opposite the London Hospital a ghastly display of the unfortunate woman murdered by what the slummers call 'that bloody demon' . . . An old man exhibits these things, and while he points them out you will be tightly wedged in between a number of boys and girls, while a smell of death rises into your nostrils, and you feel as if your throat were filled up by fungus.")

As the day advanced, wild rumors began to circulate, adding to the confusion and incipient hysteria. One was to the effect that the killer had scrawled this message on a wall in the backyard of No. 29 Hanbury Street: FIVE — 15 MORE AND I WILL GIVE MYSELF UP. Some went so far as to affirm that the message had been written in the victim's blood. Others, notably a Mrs. Fiddymount, wife of the proprietor of The Prince Albert pub, came forward with eyewitness stories equally lurid. Mrs. Fiddymount was typical of the notoriety seekers who were to plague the Ripper case. These people haunted inquests and identity parades. They throve on the newspaper interview when for a brief moment they became the envy of less inventive neighbors.

Mrs. Fiddymount was standing behind the bar on the morning of the murder talking to a woman friend, she told reporters, when in walked a man whose appearance frightened her. He had on a brown stiff hat pulled well down over his eyes, a dark coat and no waistcoat. He ordered a half pint of four ale, which he downed in one gulp. But the thing that struck Mrs. Fiddymount was that there were bloodstains on his right hand and dried blood between the fingers. Also, she noticed that his shirt was torn. Unable to leave the pub unattended, Mrs. Fiddymount had detailed one Joseph Taylor to follow the man when he left the bar, and Taylor was able to add further details of the man's appearance. He was five feet eight inches tall, rather thin, between forty and fifty years of age, had a ginger-colored mustache, and "eyes as wild as a hawk's," according to Taylor.

Before nightfall, Mrs. Fiddymount's story, as it passed from mouth to mouth, became distorted beyond recognition. In the new version, it was Annie Chapman herself who was seen in The Prince Albert pub at about 5 A.M. (pubs in the neighborhood of Spitalfields market opened early for the market porters). She was quietly having a gin when a man wearing a skull cap and with a horrible face poked his head around the door, beckoned her away to her doom.

5

Sunday, September 9, brought no letup to the spate of rumors and eyewitness stories. For example, an anonymous prostitute told police that she was accosted not far from No. 29 Hanbury Street on the morning of the murder by a man who, when she repulsed him, began to knock her about. She screamed, the man ran off, but not before he had tried to palm off two brass medals as half sovereigns. "She was asked to describe the man, but her description of him was not considered clear," noted *The Times.* Such interest as this unsupported story contains lies in the coincidence that two polished farthings were found neatly stacked at Chapman's feet. But the notion that a man would offer half sovereigns, even counterfeit ones, to a whore as desperate as Annie Chapman is ludicrous; Annie would have gladly gone with any man for the price of her bed. Besides, half sovereigns have milled edges, whereas farthings do not, and people such as Annie Chapman feel the edges of coins when they are proffered in the dark.

Nevertheless the polished-farthing business was to have an unusual sequel. In his memoirs Major (later Lieutenant Colonel Sir Henry) Smith, who in 1888 was Assistant Police Commissioner for the City of London, tells of putting the Metropolitan Police onto the track of a very promising suspect. "He had been a medical student," Smith writes. "He had been in a lunatic asylum; he spent all his time with women of loose character, whom he bilked by giving them polished farthings instead of sovereigns." Sir Charles Warren probably was not very interested in this report from a rival police force, and probably made no serious effort to find the man, but this did not deter Major Smith from looking for the suspect outside his, Smith's, own bailiwick. "I thought he was likely to be in Rupert Street, Haymarket, so I sent up two men and there he was," the Major declared. The denouement was swift: "Polished farthings and all, he proved an alibi without a shadow of a doubt."

6

The weekend of the murder heard the first mention of a mysterious personage known as "Leather Apron," a monster conjured by the collective will who was to dog the Ripper investigation to the point where Chief Inspector Abberline finally exploded in justifiable wrath. "Never let me hear that blasted nickname again." Leather Apron was more a recurrent symbol than a person; or rather, it was the nickname applied to a whole series of persons who automatically became suspect through mere possession of this talisman.

The Leather Apron hysteria was created by several factors. For one thing, the Nicholls murder, it will be recalled, occurred in the vicinity of a horse slaughterhouse in Buck's Row, which inevitably caused the public mind to dwell upon butchers and stockyards. For another, Dr. Llewellyn had given it as his opinion that the murder weapon was a short pointed knife such as was used by cork cutters and shoemakers. Leather aprons were articles of apparel common to slaughtermen, cork cutters and cobblers. Finally, it seemed obvious that the killer had worn protective clothing of some sort or his bloodstained appearance would have attracted notice as he sought to escape from the scene of his crimes.

The first public mention of Leather Apron, however, occurred in *The Times*, which added that "over 200 common lodging-houses have been visited by the police in hopes of finding some trace of the mysterious and much talked-of person, but he has succeeded in evading arrest." The *Daily Telegraph* was more explicit concerning Leather Apron, declaring that "a man who bears this nickname is believed to be guilty of at least two of the four murders." "He had been repeatedly described by women who have asserted that they have been accosted by him," the *Telegraph* continued. In fairness, it pointed out that all of the complaints did not necessarily refer to the same person. "It is not unreasonable to suppose that in a district where cabinet and shoe-makers constantly wear such aprons more than one man may have been called by the name."

Perhaps one should not be too harsh with the police for swallowing the Leather Apron bait; after all, they were under considerable pressure. The press never tired of repeating that four prostitutes had been murdered by the same fiendish hand since April, and that the police had failed not only to apprehend the killer, but to come up with a single positive clue. But as public criticism mounted, the police lost their heads and began to make indiscriminate arrests. Suspicious-looking foreigners, thieves, beggars, cockney workmen and the remaining dregs of the doss houses — all were rounded up for questioning, only to be released when not a shred of evidence could be found against them. Peak of the arrests came on Sunday, September 9, the day following the Chapman murder, when fourteen suspects were held at the Commercial Street police station alone, while others were brought to the Leman Street and Upper Thames Street stations for questioning. The reaction was inevitable. The police were accused of blundering, and from the extreme of being "arrest happy," these same law officers overnight became "arrest shy," and refused to take anyone into custody in connection with the Ripper case.

The most sensational arrest that Sunday was made in Gravesend when William Henry Piggott, aged fifty-two, was picked up by the police after having done just about everything he could to call down suspicion upon himself. First, he was seen wandering around in a dazed condition with bloodstains on his clothing and his hands badly cut up as though by a knife. Then, in The Pope's Head tavern, he was overheard to make derogatory remarks about women in a loud, belligerent voice. Finally, Piggott became something more than suspect when the local police, who were called upon to deal with him, found two bloodstained shirts in a bundle which he was carrying. Piggott's appearance "resembled in some respects that of Leather Apron," according to *The Times,* which noted that his scarecrow attire was crowned by a battered felt hat. The odd thing was that eight years earlier Piggott, as it later developed, had been prosperous enough to be able to pay £8,000 to open a pub in Hoxton.

The story Piggott told was rambling almost to the point of incoherence. He had been in the Spitalfields–Whitechapel area at the time of the murder; in fact, he had arrived in London from Gravesend on Thursday and had spent his last penny for a bed in an Osborne Street lodging house Thursday night. Then, hungry and broke, he had tramped the streets of Whitechapel all Friday night. While walking along Brick Lane at about four-thirty Saturday morning he saw a woman fall down in a fit, he claimed, but when he stooped to pick her up she bit his hand. Exasperated by this response to his Good Samaritan act, Piggott struck the woman, who, in turn, raised a fearful clamor. Seeing two policemen coming on the run, Piggott made off, and, without further adventure, that same day, Saturday, walked from East London to Gravesend, a distance of twenty-two miles.

Chief Inspector Abberline was dispatched to Gravesend to take Piggott into custody, and when the two arrived at London Bridge station at noon Monday the inspector commandeered a four-wheeler cab and made his prisoner crouch on the floor so as not to attract attention. These precautions were in vain, however, for in expectation of Piggott's arrival a group of idlers had hung about the Commercial Street station all morning. News of the actual arrival brought other gawkers, eager to catch a glimpse of the supposed murderer, on the run, and in no time Commercial Street was all but closed to traffic.

Inspector Abberline sent for all the women who claimed that they had been accosted by Leather Apron or by other suspicious strangers; but in the resultant identity parade none of these women, including the redoubtable Mrs. Fiddymount, recognized Piggott as her aggressor. Piggott was then questioned closely by police with curious, though not altogether unexpected results. But let *The Times* describe what happened: "After an interval of a couple of hours, the man's manner becoming more strange and his speech more incoherent, the divisional police surgeon was called in, and he gave it as his opinion that the prisoner's mind was unhinged." Piggott was still detained in custody while his movements were checked, then he was certified as insane and locked up in an asylum at Bow.

7

In addition to visiting over 200 doss houses in the Spitalfields area and questioning their inmates, Scotland Yard that weekend issued the first of several descriptions of the killer which were to circulate during the investigation. This one was vague and hopelessly ungrammatical: "Description of a man *who entered a passage of the house at which murder was committed* of a prostitute at 2 A.M. on 8th.—Age 37; height, 5 ft. 7 ins; rather dark beard and moustache. Dress—shirt, dark jacket, dark vest and trousers, black scarf, and black felt hat. Spoke with a foreign accent." (My italics.) I am inclined to believe that this description was entirely made up out of some policeman's head, for there is no record of any man having been seen entering the passage of No. 29 Hanbury Street at 2 A.M. on the morning of the murder. Certainly no witness ever testified to this effect. The physical description, itself, is vague enough to accommodate thousands of costermongers who lived in the East End. It appears to be made up in equal parts of Fiddymount and pure flannel. As for the "foreign accent," this, too, seems to be gratuitous if it is not simply pandering to local prejudice. In fact, this "Wanted" notice seems to have had no other purpose than to reassure the public that Scotland Yard was on the job.

Meanwhile, police had gone over the backyard of No. 29 Hanbury Street with a sable brush, so to speak, and had turned up what at first looked like a promising clue: a portion of an envelope stained with blood. The envelope had the crest of a Sussex regiment on it, and the postmark "London August 20," but the address portion had been torn off, with the exception of the single letter *M*. Nearby were two white pills. These clues subsequently turned out to be will-o'-the-wisps; for at the inquest a witness testified that Annie Chapman, as she sat by the fire in Donovan's kitchen the night of the murder, had retrieved the bit of envelope from the grate and had then wrapped the pills in it, those same placebos which she had been given at the infirmary to ease the pain in her empty belly.

One other clue was turned up by the police in their search of the backyard, a piece of evidence which they deliberately concealed from press and public until the inquest for fear that it might trigger off an ugly reaction. Under a water tap in the backyard they found a leather apron. It showed signs of having recently been scrubbed.

CHAPTER IV

LEATHER APRON CAPTURED

They've captured Leather Apron now, if guilty you'll agree;
He'll have to meet a murderer's doom, and hang upon a tree.

THIS BIT of doggerel graced a broadsheet which was hawked in Whitechapel streets on Monday, September 10, only a few hours after the event which it celebrated, the capture of Leather Apron. The doggerel was preceded by a notice to the effect that: "About nine o'clock this morning Detective Sergeant William Thicke, H-Division, who has had charge of this case, succeeded in capturing the man known as Leather Apron. *There is no doubt that he is the murderer, for a large number of long-bladed knives and several hats were found in his possession.*" (My italics)

The man whom the detective "captured" was John Pizer, aged thirty-three, a Polish Jew employed as a shoemaker, and *The Times* supplied further details concerning the arrest. Detective Sergeant Thicke had gone to Pizer's house in Mulberry Street, Whitechapel, in company of two or three officers, and Pizer himself had answered the door. Thicke at once took hold of the man saying, "You're just the man I want," according to *The Times*. He then charged Pizer with being concerned in the murder of Annie Chapman, to which the poor man made no reply. His resigned manner suggested that he had been patiently awaiting the arrival of the police to arrest him. After searching the premises, the police took possession of five sharp, long-handled knives such as were used in Pizer's trade, and of several old hats.

One can picture the wild jubilation that this news must have touched off in Whitechapel Road. How Dark Annie's sisters must have lifted their skirts and capered for joy. Leather Apron captured. Polly Nicholls and Annie Chapman avenged. The East End's terror reign brought to an end. Such at least was the prospect which Pizer's arrest held out, but like many another vista in the Ripper case, this one was to prove a mirage.

Meanwhile, the press had other strange occurrences in the East End to report for the weekend of September 8–9. For example, there was a curious item in the *Daily News* to the effect that Dr. George B. Phillips, the divisional police surgeon, and his assistant "were out of their beds nearly all Saturday night in attendance on cases of assault, *some of them of the most serious character, arising directly or indirectly out of the intense excitement occasioned by discussion of the Murder.*" (My italics.) Cases of assault? Excited discussion? The report makes it sound more like an encounter between Orangemen and Sinn Feiners on the anniversary of the Battle of the Boyne. What were these strange scufflings behind the scenes, these "noises off" about which the *News* was so reticent? East London streets, it will be recalled, were thronged with people on the Saturday night of the murder, September 8. Many of them had milled around in a frightened, aimless way, or had gathered in front of the Commercial Street police station to shout and hoot for the murderer of Annie Chapman.

The *East London Observer* lifts the curtain a bit further on these scenes in reporting that "the crowds began to assume a very threatening attitude *towards the Hebrew population* of the district." It was repeatedly asserted that no Englishman could have perpetrated such a horrible crime as that of Hanbury-street," the newspaper continued, *"therefore the crowds proceeded to threaten and abuse such of the unfortunate Hebrews as they found in the streets."* (My italics) Suddenly the picture comes into focus. These were not Irish Protestants and Catholics having an excited "discussion" on the streets of Belfast, for example. These were Gentiles beating up Jews on the streets of East London. It was the heads of these latter that were being patched up by Dr. Phillips and his assistant all that Saturday night.

Without mentioning Jews, *The Times* spoke editorially of the East End being thrown into a state of panic "as favorable to the escape of the assassin as it is dangerous to innocent persons whose appearance or conduct is sufficiently irregular to excite suspicion." The *Daily News* went further in warning that "there may soon be murders from panic to add to murders from lust for blood," and that "a touch will fire the whole district, in the mood in which it is now."

Suddenly the true nature of the Leather Apron hysteria becomes apparent: it was simply a cover for anti-Semiticism. And in John Pizer anti-Semiticism found its prefect victim. For in addition to being endowed with such supernatural qualities as "piercing eyes" and the ability to walk "noiselessly like a cat," Leather Apron was said to be a Jew of foreign extraction. Now Pizer was a Polish Jew and a shoemaker who was accustomed not only to wearing a leather apron but to handling sharp, pointed knives. Anti-Semiticism does not, of course, explain the readiness of Whitechapel prostitutes to swear that they had been accosted by men wearing leather aprons. For such an explanation one must turn to Freudian psychology where leather aprons figure as castration symbols. According to the Freudians, a man wearing such an article of apparel may appear emasculated to a hysterical woman and, as such, he may assume a threatening aspect. At least, this is the suggestion put forward to me by a qualified analyst. But it is time now to have a look at the man behind the apron.

2

Mulberry Street was so named because the eighteenth century Huguenot weavers planted mulberry trees along its length in the vain hope of founding a silkworm industry. By 1888 not only had the last of these trees withered, defeated in an unequal struggle with London soot, but the Huguenot weavers themselves had fled Mulberry Street before the invasion of Russians and Poles, most of whom were engaged in the shoemaking trade. John Pizer, who lived at No. 22 Mulberry Street with his seventy-year-old stepmother and his married brother Gabriel, was no ordinary cobbler. He made ballet slippers — that is, when he worked, for John fancied his health to be delicate and consequently he spent much time in bed nursing illnesses of his own invention. Ironically enough, in view of his arrest as Jack the Ripper, he complained continually that he had no strength in his hands.

He was a man of singularly repellent appearance, if the newspaper descriptions of him are to be believed. The *East London Observer*, for example, pictured him thus: "He was 5 ft. 4 ins. tall with a dark-hued face, which was not altogether pleasant to look upon by reason of grizzly black strips of hair, nearly an inch in length, which almost covered the face. The thin lips, too, had a cruel, sardonic look, which was increased if anything, by the drooping dark moustache and sidewhiskers . . . The head was large, and was fixed to the body by a thick, heavy-looking neck." Compare this description with the Cruikshank illustrations of Fagin in *Oliver Twist* and one can readily see where the reporter derived his inspiration. But this was not all. The reporter even had Pizer walking with a "splay-footed gait," and talking with a "thick, guttural, foreign accent."

It is perfectly true that Pizer was known to the neighborhood long before the Ripper murders as "Leather Apron," and that he was something of a figure of fun. Perhaps it was that splay-footed, Chaplinesque walk, or perhaps it was the combination of his forbidding looks and his mild, hypochondriac disposition, but Pizer seemed to invite ridicule. Small boys would follow him in the streets mimicking his movements and shouting, "Leather Apron, yah!"

Actually, this notoriety was to prove Pizer's salvation, for no sooner did the Leather Apron agitation start up in connection with the "Polly" Nicholls murder than Pizer, with knowledge no doubt acquired from Jewish ancestors in Poland who had survived pogroms, took to his room, and he did not emerge until his arrest, remaining indoors and out of sight from 10:45 P.M. Thursday, September 6, until 9 A.M. Monday, September 10. In other words, he had an unshakable alibi as far as the Annie Chapman murder was concerned. Furthermore, when Pizer was paraded with other Jews at the Leman Street police station, none of the women who had earlier told of encounters with the mysterious Leather Apron picked him out of the identity parade.

But the unfortunate Jew's ordeal was not yet over. He was held in jail another twenty-four hours, one imagines at his own request in order to escape mob violence, and the police took the extraordinary precaution of giving him a public clearance. Had they not done so, it is conceivable that Pizer might have been lynched the first time he ventured out alone. When the Annie Chapman inquest was opened on Wednesday, September 12, by Coroner Wynne E. Baxter, Pizer was duly called, sworn and gave his occupation as that of shoemaker.

Q (Coroner): Are you known by the nickname "Leather Apron"?

A: Yes, sir.

Q: Where were you on Friday night last?

A: I was at 22 Mulberry Road. I arrived there on Thursday, September 6th.

Q: From where?

A: From the West end of town.

Q: I'm afraid we shall have to have a better address than that presently. What time did you reach 22 Mulberry Street?

A: Shortly before 11 P.M.

Pizer then explained that he remained indoors until he was arrested by Sergeant Thicke on Monday, September 10, at 9 A.M.

Q: Why were you remaining indoors?

A: Because my brother advised me.

Q: You were the subject of suspicion?

A: I was the object of a false suspicion.

Q: You remained on the advice of friends?

A: Yes, I am telling you what I did.

Q: It was not the best advice that you could have had. You have been released, and are not now in custody?

A: No, I am not. (Pause) I wish to vindicate my character to the world at large.

Q: I have called you in your own interests, partly with the object of giving you an opportunity of doing so.

Coronor Baxter then questioned Pizer closely as to his movements on Thursday, August 30, eve of the "Polly" Nicholls murder. It was important that he should have an alibi for Whitechapel's other celebrated murder as well.

A (after considering): I was in the Holloway Road.

Q: You had better say exactly where you were. It is important to account for your time from that Thursday to the Friday morning.

Pizer then replied that he had stayed at a common lodging house called "The Round House" in Holloway Road, and that he fixed the date and place clearly by the fact that a big

London dock fire, which was visible all the way to Highgate, had occurred that night.

Q: Did you sleep the night there?

A: Yes.

Q: At what time did you go in?

A: It was about 2 or 2:15 Friday morning.

Q: When did you leave the lodging house?

A: At 11 A.M. on the same day. I saw on the placards "Another Horrible Murder."

Before turning in early Friday morning he had wandered as far afield as the Seven Sisters Road, where he first noticed the crimson reflection of the fire in the sky. Returning along Holloway Road he saw two constables talking with a doss-house deputy, and he asked one of the policemen where the fire was. "Down by the Albert Docks," he replied. It was then about 1:30 A.M., to the best of his recollection, Pizer said. He then returned to the lodging house.

Q: Did anyone speak to you about being out so late?

A: No, I paid the night watchman. I asked him if my bed was let, and he said, "They are let by eleven o'clock. You don't think they are let to this hour do you?" So I paid him fourpence for another bed.

Q: You got up at 11 A.M.?

A: Yes, the day man came, and told me to get up, as he wanted to make the bed. I got up and dressed and went down into the kitchen.

Q: Is there anything else you want to say?

A: Nothing.

Q: When you said the West End of town did you mean Holloway?

A: No, I stayed in another lodging house in Peter Street Westminster, until Thursday, September 6.

In telling Pizer to step down, Coroner Baxter remarked for

the record, "It is only fair to say that the witness's statements can be corroborated."

Pizer walked out of the coroner's courtroom and into the civil courts to bring libel suits against those newspapers that had been rash enough to identify him as the Whitechapel murderer. Rumors that the sums awarded to him as a result of these court actions ran to four figures were vigorously denied by the *East London Advertiser.* "The story that 'Leather Apron,' alias Mr. Piser [sic], is getting large sums from his libel actions is untrue," this weekly newspaper declared. "More than one of them has been compromised, and for moderate sums. Two or three of them are still outstanding. The report that he has already received £5,000 is preposterously wide of the mark; £500 would, I should say, be a serious exaggeration."

Not so fortunate was another Jew named Jacobs, who worked in a slaughterhouse, and who likewise was known as Leather Apron. Jacobs was perfectly harmless, but his life was made unbearable after the police had questioned him. Wherever he went he was pointed out as the Whitechapel killer, and more than once he had to run helter-skelter to the nearest police station in order to escape angry mobs which threatened him. Finally, he lost his reason altogether and was committed to an asylum.

In the beginning Scotland Yard took the Leather Apron rumors so seriously that detectives were disguised as butchers and planted in slaughterhouses in an effort to develop a lead on this mysterious fellow. But when Pizer was given a public clearance, the Leather Apron agitation was effectively knocked on the head. The *Spectator* made an interesting (and prophetic) comparison between mob hysteria in England and on the Continent. "In most continental towns such a series of crimes would have disorganized society throughout the quartier, and have ended in attempts to lynch some class or other of innocent persons. In Naples the doctors would have perished, and in Berlin the Jews." In East London the local cockney humor asserted itself in the end and, far from pursuing a vendetta against a mythical Leather Apron, the inhabitants bestowed this name upon a particularly tough molasses toffee of the jawbreaking variety.

3

"'DARK ANNIE'S' spirit," begins a *Daily Telegraph* editorial:

> still walks Whitechapel unavenged by Justice . . . And yet even this forlorn, despised citizeness of London cannot be said to have suffered in vain . . . 'Dark Annie's' dreadful end has compelled a hundred thousand Londoners to reflect what it must be like to have no home at all except the common kitchen of a low lodging-house; to sit there, sick and weak and bruised and wretched, for lack of fourpence with which to pay for the right of a "doss"; to be turned out after midnight to earn the requisite pence, anywhere and anyhow; and in the course of earning it to come across your murderer and to caress your assassin . . . "Dark Annie" will effect in one way what fifty Secretaries of State could never accomplish . . .

Not the least remarkable thing about this editorial is that it should have appeared in the *Daily Telegraph,* which only a fortnight earlier had characterized Dark Annie and her kind as "wild savages" who required an "iron hand to save them from themselves." It attests at once to the peculiar fascination which the Dark Annies exercised over the Victorian mind and to the ambivalence of this same mind in relationship to the errant sisterhood. At one moment Annie was being condemned harshly; the next, Dickensian tears were being shed over her plight. In the drawingroom she was referred to as an "unfortunate," a "Magdalen," or even as a "soiled dove"; but once caught in the toils of the law she was stigmatized as "a common prostitute," an "idle and disorderly person" or as an "incorrigible rogue."

"Prostitutes were to the Victorians what witches were to the medievals," writes Gordon Rattray Taylor in his entertaining *Sex in History*.[1] T. H. Lecky, an early nineteenth-century reformer, said much the same thing when he described the prostitute as "the eternal priestess of humanity, blasted for the sins of the people . . . On that one degraded and ignoble form," Lecky went on, "are concentrated the passions that might have filled the world with shame."

The Victorians may have been ready to shed tears over Dark Annie, but when it came to protecting her from being slaughtered they showed themselves to be hopelessly impractical. Among other wild schemes, it was suggested that every prostitute found on the prowl in Whitechapel after midnight should be arrested; or alternatively, that they should be provided with police whistles and instructed in a signaling system ("belling the cats," this last scheme was dubbed). It was Sir Robert Anderson who advocated the first course, arguing, "It would have been merciful to the very small class of women affected by it." But his superiors disagreed. The nightly roundup of Whitechapel's hetaerae, even if legal, would have been beyond the power of the police to cope. There was not enough jail space for them.[2]

As for police whistles, at least one streetwalker, a young woman named Eleanor Candey, took this suggestion seriously, with amusing results. Candey picked up a licensed victualer

[1] In an essay on Victorian pornography in *Partisan Review*, Spring 1964, Steven Marcus puts it another way. "Prostitution in Victorian England," he writes, "was the Red China of its day."

[2] Unfortunately, there are no reliable figures as to the number of prostitutes in Whitechapel in 1888, or in the whole of London, for that matter. Earlier in Victoria's reign the Bishop of Exeter had estimated that there were 80,000 prostitutes in London, a figure which Scotland Yard promptly denied. But Henry Mayhew thought the Bishop's estimate was "below the reality rather than above it."

named Joseph Woods in the Whitechapel Road one night, and in the course of conversation confided that since the Ripper murders, she never ventured out after dark without her police whistle. Woods, who was drunk, promptly replied, "And I, I never go out without my trusty little knife . . . If you want to know who I am," he added, "I am the Whitechapel murderer." Whereupon several things happened in rapid succession: Candey blew her whistle, Woods started to run, collided with a policeman, and was arrested for indecent assault.

The *Star* not only favored belling the cats, but thought that they should be cautioned to walk in pairs. "The unfortunates who are the objects of the man-monster's malignity should be shadowed by one or two amateur patrols," the newspaper added. That Scotland Yard should disguise some of its men as women and use them as decoys to trap the murderer was the suggestion of the *Daily News,* which interviewed a top police official on the subject. The official objected that none of his men was less than five feet seven inches tall, and that all or nearly all wore mustaches or beards, which they would be loathe to shave off. "Besides," he told the reporter, "you know how awkward a man in woman's clothes always appears on the stage. The military drill of our men could hardly be disguised. We would not only have to pick the men, but regularly train them for such work."

Undaunted, the *Pall Mall Gazette* came up with a startling suggestion. "There are numbers of well-trained pugilists in Shoreditch and Whitechapel who are, many of them, young, and as is the custom in their profession, clean-shaved," the *Gazette* pointed out. "Twenty game men of this class in women's clothing loitering about Whitechapel would have more chance than any number of heavy-footed policemen." This was topped by a proposal from Mr. W. H. Spencer-Howell, which the *Star* printed. "I would suggest," Mr. Spencer-Howell wrote, "that a few young men of somewhat feminine appearance should be got up disguised as females. They should wear around their necks steel collars made after the style of a ladies collaret, coming well down the breast and likewise well down the back. My reason for this is . . . that the assassin first severs his victim's windpipe, thereby preventing her raising an alarm."

What made this confusion tragic rather than comic was that a great many East End prostitutes, frightened out of their wits by the series of Ripper murders, were genuinely in need of help. Sir Melville Macnaghten tells of visiting an East End doss house at about this time, and of finding an unemployed man toasting a bloater by the kitchen fire. When his doxy returned he asked her if she had had any luck. "No bloody luck," she replied, and, the conversation soon afterward having worked itself around to Jack the Ripper, the woman cried despairingly, "Well, let him come — the sooner the better for such as *me.*"

CHAPTER V

DRUNKS, LUNATICS, PRANKSTERS

NEXT DOOR to the Whitechapel underground station is the Working Lads' Institute and Mission, much the same today as it was in 1888 when its rooms were used for the inquest into the sudden death of Annie Chapman. Facing it across the Whitechapel Road is the London Hospital, which has nursed the East End through every affliction from malnutrition to cholera, which has patched up eyes blackened by loving spouses and heads broken by police batons.

Working lads no longer lodge at the Institute (a marble plaque serves to remind that 160 of them perished in the first world war), but upstairs, by some miracle of preservation, the meeting room is almost exactly as it was on September 10, 1888, when the Chapman inquest opened. The gas lamps have given way to electric lights, but the room is still dominated by the big oak table around which the coroner and his veniremen sat to hear evidence. On walls now covered by the brown gravy of time is the same melancholy text which stared down upon Coroner Wynne E. Baxter as he opened the proceedings: "What doth the Lord require of thee, but to do justly, and to love mercy, and to walk humbly with this God?" The eleven jurors who assembled around the table were prepared to do just that, tempering justice with mercy, and certainly exhibiting their humility in the face of this fearsome, but as yet unexplained death.

The Chapman inquest was the longest of the Whitechapel murder inquests, lasting for five full sessions which were stretched over a period of fifteen days. Characteristically, it opened with a passage of arms between Coroner Baxter and the police, the former complaining that the latter had not furnished him with a map of the area or even a plan of the house at No. 29 Hanbury Street, in the backyard of which Annie Chapman was found. "If country police can do this for a coroner, surely the Metropolitan Police can do the same," the coroner testily observed. Police Inspector Joseph Chandler then promised that such plans would be produced at the next inquest session.

As one of the first witnesses called, Mrs. Amelia Richardson, the landlady, described the sixteen tenants who slept in the house at No. 29, Hanbury Street. The result was like a cross section of Mayhew's London. *Ground floor:* the front parlor was used as a cats'-meat shop by Mrs. Annie Hardyman, who sold bits of horseflesh on skewers at a farthing or a ha'penny each depending upon the size. Mrs. Hardyman and her eighteen-year-old son slept in the same room where she sold the pussy-food. The back parlor was used as a sort of prayer-meeting room by Mrs. Richardson, who had been badly bitten by the religious bug. *First floor:* Mrs. Richardson and her fourteen-year-old grandson slept in the front room; and a Mr. Waker, who made lawn tennis boots, occupied the back room with his son, who was feeble-minded. *Second floor:* Mr. Thompson, a carter, his wife and their adopted daughter occupied the front room; Mr. and Mrs. Copely, cigar makers, lived in the back. *Third floor:* John Davies, his wife and three sons occupied the front room, and Mrs. Sarah Cox had the back room on the same floor. "She is an old lady, and I keep her out of charity," Mrs. Richardson explained.

The witness testified that she had gone to bed at nine-thirty Friday night, but that she was wakeful half the night. "I woke up at three o'clock, and I only dozed after that," she said. She had heard no noise during the night, however.

Q (by the Coroner): Were the front and back doors of No. 29 Hanbury Street always left open?

A: Yes, all the houses along the street leave their doors open. They are all let out in rooms, and people are coming in or going out at all hours of the night.

Q: Did you ever see anyone in the passage at No. 29?

A: Yes, about a month ago I heard a man on the stairs. I asked Mr. Thompson, my second-floor tenant, to investigate, but the man said he was waiting for the market to open.

Q: At what time was this?

A: Between half past three and four o'clock.

Q: Coming now to the early hours of Saturday morning, September 8, did you hear anyone go through the passage at that time?

A: No.

Q: You heard no cries?

A: None.

Q: Supposing a person had gone through at half past three, would that have attracted your attention?

A: Yes.

Q: You always hear people going to the backyard?

A: Yes, people frequently do go through.

Q: People go there who have no business to do so?

A: Yes, I daresay they do.

Q (by a juror): Do they go there for an immoral purpose?

A: I would not allow such a thing if I knew about it.

All eyes focused on the next witness, John Richardson, for his movements on the morning of the murder, as reported by the press, had been most curious. Although he assisted his mother in her box-making business, Richardson, a market porter, did not in fact live at No. 29 Hanbury Street, but in nearby John

Street. He did, however, visit No. 29 on the morning of Saturday, September 8, between 4:45 and 4:50 A.M.

Q (by the Coroner): Why did you go to No. 29 at that hour in the morning?

A: I looked in on my way to work to see if the cellar was properly padlocked. Some months ago it was broken into and a saw and hammer were stolen. Since that time I have been in the habit, on market mornings, of stopping in at No. 29 on my way to work.

Q: Did you find the door of the passage leading from the front of the house open?

A: No, it was closed. I lifted the latch and went through the passage to the back door.

Q: Did you go into the backyard?

A: No, I opened the back door, looked out and saw that the cellar was locked. Then I sat on the doorstep.

Q: What did you do next?

A: I cut a piece of leather off my boot with a table knife, about five inches long.

Q: Do you usually carry this knife with you?

A: No, usually I keep it at home in John Street. But this morning I had been cutting up carrots to feed my rabbit, so I just slipped the knife into my pocket. I don't know what made me do it.

Q: What did you do after cutting the leather from your boot?

A: I put the knife back into my pocket, and left for work.

Q: Did you close the back door?

A: No, it closed itself. I shut the front door, however.

Q: How long were you there?

A: Not more than two minutes at most.

Questioned as to whether it was light enough for him to see into the backyard, Richardson replied that it was getting light, and that he could see all over the place. He could not have failed to notice the deceased had she been lying there near the steps, he testified.

Q: Did you sit on the top step?

A: No, on the middle step, so that my feet rested on the flags in the yard.

Q: You must have been quite close to where the deceased was found?

A: Yes, I would have seen her.

Q: You have been there at all hours of the night.

A: Yes.

Q: Have you ever seen any strangers there?

A: Yes, plenty, at all hours — both men and women. I have often turned them out. I have even found them on the first floor landing.

Q: Do you mean that they go there for an immoral purpose?

A: Yes, they do.

Richardson's nocturnal prowlings were strange, to say the least; but there was not a shred of evidence to connect him with the Chapman murder. Still one matter remained to be cleared up, and Mrs. Richardson was now recalled to the witness stand to testify concerning the leather apron which had been found in the backyard of No. 29. The Police, it will be recalled, had deliberately withheld news of this discovery from the press for fear that the news might create panic. Mrs. Richardson's testimony, therefore, was the first public intimation that this singular article had been found at the murder site, and provided the sensation of the day. She readily identified the apron, said that it belonged to her son John, who used it in his work.

Q (by the Coroner): It is rather a dangerous thing to wear, is it not?

A: Yes.

Q: Can you explain to us how the apron happened to be under the water tap in the backyard when it was found by police?

A: Yes, I can. Last Thursday I found the apron in the cellar, where it had gotten mildewed. My son had not used it for a month — so I put it under the tap intending to wash it, and left it there.

Q: The apron remained there from Thursday to Saturday?

A: Yes.

Q: Was this tap used?

A: Yes, by all of us in the house. The apron was on the stones.

Q: Had you an idea at any time that a part of the house was used for an immoral purpose?

A (emphatically): No, sir.

John Richardson, recalled, produced the knife — a much worn dessert knife — with which he had cut his boot. He added that as it was not sharp enough he had borrowed another one at Spitalfields market to finish the job of trimming the boot sole. He also flatly contradicted his mother concerning the nightly visitations to the house and yard. "My mother has heard me speak of people having been in the house," he said. "She has heard them herself."

Friday, September 14, the third day of the inquest, turned out to be everybody's day to grizzle. Again, attention was called to the East End's lack of mortuary facilities. Called upon to give the postmortem results, Dr. George B. Phillips, the police surgeon, complained that it was only under great difficulty that he had made his examination. Once again, the body of the deceased had been tampered with prior to the medical examination. Dr. Phillips testified that, upon arriving at the Old Montague Street workhouse after 2 P.M. Saturday, he was surprised to find that the body had been stripped and was lying ready on the table for his examination. This time, neither the epileptic, Robert Mann, nor his dim-witted assistant, James Hatfield, was the culprit. Mindful of the criticism which had attended the careless handling of the Nicholls cadaver, or perhaps acting from a newly acquired sense of delicacy, the workhouse had appointed two nurses, Mary Elizabeth Simonds and Frances Wright, to undress the body, which they did leaving the handkerchief knotted round Annie Chapman's neck. They then washed from her chest the blood that had flowed from the throat wound and in general tidied up the body. They had done this, they testified on the witness stand, on the instructions of Police Inspector Joseph Chandler, an accusation which Chandler hastily denied.

Dr. Phillips testified to certain pathological symptoms exhibited by Dark Annie which had been noted earlier. He said that her tubercular condition had even affected the membranes of the brain, but that this condition had nothing to do with the cause of her death. "There was no indication of the deceased having taken alcohol for some hours prior to her death," he pursued. "But there were signs of great deprivation, and I would say that she had been badly fed." Certain organs were missing from her body, he disclosed. Coming now to the murder weapon, the police surgeon said: "It must have been a very sharp knife, with a thin, narrow blade, and must have been at least six inches or eight inches in length, probably longer." In fact, the injuries could have been done by an instrument such as medical men use for postmortem purposes. Certainly the mode in which the missing organs were extracted showed some anatomical skill, he further testified.

It was when it came to discussing these missing organs that Dr. Phillips showed a sudden and strange reticence, arguing that to go into further details of the mutilations "could only be painful to the feelings of the jury and the public." Coroner Baxter knew perfectly well that by the Statute of Coronatore he was bound to enquire into the nature, character and size of every wound on the body of the deceased and to enter the same on his roll. Puzzled as he was by this unexpected reticence, Baxter decided, however, to humor the police surgeon at least for the time being, and he therefore dismissed Dr. Phillips, subject to recall later to complete his postmortem report.

Annie Chapman was quietly buried at Manor Park cemetery on Friday, September 14, some of her relatives attending the funeral. The following Sunday the Reverend W. Evans Hurndall of Bow preached to a crowded congregation on the Whitechapel murders, choosing as his text Deuteronomy 29:18. "A root that beareth gall and wormwood."

2

On a fine morning in September, 1888, two stockbrokers decided to play truant from their offices in the City and to go fishing near Dorking — an incident not unusual in itself except that these particular fugitives from the Royal Stock Exchange were arrested as Jack the Ripper suspects. According to the *Daily News* they were tailed all the way to Dorking by a pair of detectives from Scotland Yard. "On what grounds they were suspected and why they were allowed to proceed to Dorking has not been made public, though doubtless the records of this strange action have been filed," the *News* adds.

Undoubtedly this was the most bizarre of the arrests made in connection with the Whitechapel murders, which is a striking claim, for in the London area alone over a thousand people were either arrested or questioned by police in their house-to-house searches. In fact, a situation developed in the East End which was somewhat akin to the Terror that followed the French Revolution, with dozens of East Enders eager to inform on their neighbors in order to pay off old scores. As *The Times* pointed out, "It seems at times as if every person in the streets were suspicious of everyone else he met, and as if it were a race between them who could first inform against his neighbor." *Punch* criticized the police for acting on such information. The magazine ran a full-page cartoon captioned "Blind Man's Buff," showing a policeman blindfolded and being spun around by the criminal element. It also printed a skit in which a detective, after arresting everyone in sight, finally arrests himself as the Whitechapel killer.

I have analyzed thirty-four arrests made in the London area over an eleven-week period in connection with the Ripper investigation, and in none of these arrests was there a shred of evidence for the police to act upon, not a single hard clue. In fact, the majority of suspects were released almost immediately after their arrest, the police having nothing on which to hold them. The suspects included Irishmen, Germans, Poles and an American seaman, who threatened to "rip up" a prostitute who would not accompany him. Nearly half of those arrested were drunks who, in their alcoholic euphoria, shouted "I am Jack the Ripper," or playfully threatened to carve up various women "in the Whitechapel manner."

Quite a few of these drunken pranksters were Irish. John Brennan, an Irishman with his coat split up the back, emptied The White Hart pub in Camberwell by first discussing the Chapman murder in loud tones, then claiming that Leather Apron was a pal of his, and finally, that he had the murder knife in his pocket. The other customers nearly tore down the door in their haste to depart, while the landlady barricaded herself in her parlor leaving Brennan in full possession of the saloon bar. Another son of Erin, Edward Quinn, was arrested in a pub near the Woolwich arsenal for no other reason than that his face and hands were scratched and his clothing bloodstained. "Me murder a woman?" Quinn protested to the police court magistrate. "Why, I couldn't murder a cat."

Many of those arrested turned out to be certifiable lunatics, as we have seen already in the case of William Piggott. In fact, the number of homicidal maniacs at large, as revealed by the Ripper investigation, was so startling that a country doctor, writing to *The Times,* suggested that police check immediately the whereabouts of all such persons discharged as "cured" from metropolitan asylums in the past two years. Typical of these lunatics was the so-called "Mad Pork Butcher of Holloway," a Swiss named Isenschmid, who was detained by police on suspicion of being concerned in the Chapman murder. Isenschmid suffered from delusions of grandeur, styled himself "King of Elthorne Road," the modest street in Holloway where he kept his pork butcher's shop. But he also threatened persons he disliked, boasting that he would "put their lights out," and he had an unpleasant habit of sharpening a long butcher's knife while uttering these menaces. After questioning him, police had him certified to the Colney Hatch asylum.

But the drunken pranks of Irishmen and the menaces of madmen were as nothing compared to the wave of self-incrimination which the Whitechapel murders touched off. The number of men, drunk and sober, who walked into police stations to "confess" the murders, who confided "I am Jack the Ripper" to total strangers, or who scrawled these dreadful words on back fences is exceeded only by those who wrote self-accusatory letters to the police. With the Chapman murder the penitentes became a steady stream, and the fact that many of these were exhibitionists, or engaged in playing crude jokes does not detract from an overall impression that they felt themselves laden with guilt.

How some of these self-confessed "killers" escaped mob violence is as puzzling as the Ripper's ability to elude the police. As it was, some of the escapes were hair-raising. For example, a German was nearly lynched in the East End for merely looking at a woman. Apparently the woman had been so unnerved by recent events that the stare was sufficient to set her screaming "Jack the Ripper!" Immediately the German was surrounded by what *The Times* described as "an enormous mob of men and women, shouting and screaming in the most extraordinary manner." At the Commercial Street police station where he was taken for questioning, it was discovered that the German spoke not a word of English. Through an interpreter it was learned that he was stopping in London only forty-eight hours en route from Germany to America.

The Whitechapel murders seem to have lifted the lid on a Pandoran box of horrors, revealing the hidden violence of the times. Until the Ripper appeared on the scene a drunken brute might have been content to beat his wife or mistress, but now he threatened to "do her in," Ripper-fashion. The *Daily News* reported the case of a man who actually offered ten shillings to anyone who would rid him of his wife by the "Whitechapel process." The Whitechapel murders also provided a field day for the superstitious. As the *East London Advertiser* observed, "It is so impossible to account, on any ordinary hypothesis, for these revolting acts of blood that the mind turns as it were instinctively to some theory of occult force, and the myths of the Dark Ages arise before the imagination. Ghouls, vampires, blood-suckers . . . take form and seize hold of the excited fancy."[1]

Unfortunately, superstitious beliefs were not confined to occult circles. Thus a senior police official ordered the eyes of Dark Annie photographed in the hope that the retinas might retain the image of her killer. (William Stewart claims that the police photographed the eyes of not less than three of the Ripper victims in the course of their investigations. "For some years previous," Stewart writes, "there was a popular belief,

[1] In his book *Haunted Britain* Elliott O'Donnell tells of visiting Whitechapel in 1895 and discussing the murders with the local inhabitants. "They told me that in the streets where the murders had been committed," O'Donnell writes, "appalling screams and groans uttered by no living human being were sometimes heard at night, and that in Buck's Row, a huddled-up figure, like that of a woman, emitting from all over it a ghostly light, was frequently to be seen lying in the gutter."

which was started by a short-story writer, that when a person dies the last scene is indelibly imprinted on the pupils of the eyes.") Asked by the inquest jury foreman for his opinion as to the efficacy of this photographic operation, Dr. George B. Phillips commented dryly, "I was asked about it very early in the inquiry, and my opinion was that the operation would be useless, especially in this case."

3

Tim Donovan, the landlord at No. 35 Dorset Street, had testified earlier that there was one particular man whom Dark Annie used to bring back to the doss house regularly, who was her steady boyfriend, so to speak. He was known as "The Pensioner," and was a man of military appearance according to Donovan. At mention of this latter fact the public mind once more reverted to the torn bit of envelope with the crest of a Sussex regiment on it that had been found near Chapman's body. Now on the fourth day of the inquest, "The Pensioner" came forward reluctantly to take the witness stand.

He was Edward Stanley, a bricklayer living at No. 1, Osborne Place, Spitalfields, who passed himself off as an ex-soldier of an Essex Regiment who had seen better days. Stanley had an air of the bogus about him that became apparent immediately when he took the witness stand. He testified that he had known Dark Annie for about two years and admitted that he had visited her regularly on weekends at the Dorset Street establishment. The last time he had seen her, he claimed, was on Sunday, September 2, between the hours of 1 P.M. and 3 P.M. It was when Coroner Wynne Baxter started to question him concerning his military background that he began to squirm.

Q (Coroner): Are you a pensioner?

A: Am I bound to answer that question?

Q: You have to answer all questions affecting this case.

A: No, I am not a pensioner.

Q: Did you belong to an Essex regiment?

A: No, neither that nor any other regiment.

Then realizing that his ridiculous little game was up, he wailed disgustedly, "What I say will be published all over Europe." Turning on the coroner, he became indignant. "I have lost five hours in coming here," he said; adding illogically, "When you talk to me, sir, you talk to an honest man." Mercifully, the little bricklayer was allowed to leave the witness box, no doubt to face the scorn of his friends.

Next the coroner produced two surprise witnesses. The first, a carpenter named Albert Cadoche, who lived next door to No. 29 Hanbury Street, testified that he paid a visit to the outhouse in the back of his premises at 5:15 A.M. on the morning of the murder. As he passed the wooden fence which divided the two properties he heard a woman say, "No, no." On returning from the outhouse he heard a scuffle and then a sound as though someone had fallen heavily against the fence, which was about five feet six inches in height. Being of a singularly incurious nature, Mr. Cadoche went back into his house.

The second witness, and the most important one produced so far at the inquest, was Mrs. Elizabeth Long, the wife of a park keeper at No. 198 Church Row, Spitalfields. Mrs. Long told the jury that she was passing along Hanbury Street on her way to Spitalfields market at 5:30 A.M. on the morning of the murder when she saw a man and a woman standing in front of No. 29. They were talking quite loudly, and she overheard the man say, "Will you?" and the woman reply, "Yes." After viewing the remains at the mortuary, Mrs. Long positively identified Dark Annie as the woman she had seen and heard. She did not see the man's face, however, except to notice that he was dark. He looked to be over forty and was a little taller than Chapman. He wore a brown deerstalker hat, and she thought he had on a dark coat, but she was not certain. He appeared to be a foreigner and had a "shabby genteel" appearance. The couple were still standing there as she passed, and she did not bother to look back.

As a result of a casual glance in which she admits that she did not see the killer's face, Mrs. Long seems to have drawn a number of inferences concerning his appearance — namely, that he was a foreigner of shabby gentility. Still, to her goes the distinction of being the first witness since the atrocious murder cycle started who could claim with any degree of certainty to have seen the Ripper with one of his victims just prior to the crime. Certainly, the police drew heavily on her testimony at this stage in posting descriptions of the killer.

From the statements of Mrs. Long, Albert Cadoche and others at the inquest, the following timetable of murder can be drawn up:

2 A.M. Man seen entering passage of No. 29 Hanbury Street, according to the description circulated by the police (Who saw him was never disclosed).
4:45 A.M. Chapman's body was not in the backyard of No. 29, according to John Richardson.
5:20 A.M. Albert Cadoche hears sounds of scuffle in backyard.
5:30 A.M. Mrs. Long sees a man and woman standing outside No. 29.
5:55 A.M. Body discovered by John Davies.

If these times are correct the murder must have taken place between 5:30 and 5:55 A.M., a time when Hanbury Street would have been crowded with porters on their way to work at Spitalfields market. Among the unresolved problems, *The Times* poses this one: "He [the murderer] must have left the yard in Hanbury Street reeking with blood, and yet, if the theory that the murder took place between 5 and 6 be accepted, he must have walked in almost broad daylight along streets comparatively well frequented, even at that early hour, without his startling appearance attracting the slightest attention." Consideration of this point led *The Times* to abandon the theory that the killer came from the "wretched class" from which doss-house inmates were drawn. "More probably . . . he is a man lodging in a comparatively decent house in the district, to which he would be able to retire quickly, and in which, once it was reached, he would be able at his leisure to remove from his person all traces of his hideous crime. It is at any rate almost certain that the murderer would not have ventured to return to a common lodging-house smeared with blood as he must have been." Had the police acted upon such sound deductive logic the lives of three more "unfortunates" might have been spared.

4

Recalled to the witness stand to complete his postmortem report, Dr. George B. Phillips renewed his objection to giving evidence in open courts concerning the organs missing from Chapman's body, despite the firm insistence of the coroner that he do so. In fact, Coroner Wynne Baxter became quite sharpish about it.

DR. PHILLIPS: I still think it a great pity that I should have to give this evidence.

CORONER: We are here to decide the cause of death and therefore have a right to hear all particulars. Whether this evidence is made public or not rests with the press. I might add that I have never before heard of any evidence being kept back from a coroner.

DR. PHILLIPS: I am in the hands of the court. But what I was going to detail took place after death.

CORONER: That is a matter of opinion. You know that medical men often differ.

Thereupon the court was cleared of all women and boys, at

Dr. Phillips's request, and the police surgeon proceeded to give medical evidence which was "totally unfit for publication," in the opinion of *The Times*. In retrospect, Dr. Phillips appears to have been unduly squeamish. His request to clear the court was certainly in order, as would have been a similar request to the press to use discretion in reporting his findings (no Victorian newspaper was likely to print such details anyway): but in making such a fuss in the witness box the surgeon seems to have been playing with one eye to the gallery.

The suppressed testimony is to be found in *The Lancet*, the weekly medical journal, which describes the mutilation of Chapman's body as follows:

> The abdomen had been entirely laid open; the intestines, severed from their mesenteric attachments, had been lifted out of the body, and placed on the shoulder of the corpse; whilst from the pelvis the uterus and its appendages with the upper portion of the vagina and the posterior two-thirds of the bladder, had been entirely removed. No trace of these parts could be found, and the incisions were cleanly cut, avoiding the rectum, and dividing the vagina low enough to avoid injury to the cervix uteri.
>
> Obviously [the *Lancet* articles continues], the work was that of an expert—of one, at least, who had such knowledge of anatomical or pathological examinations as to be enabled to secure the pelvic organs with one sweep of the knife, which must therefore, as Dr. Phillips pointed out, have been at least five inches long . . .

Dr. Phillips entirely agreed with this conclusion as to the killer's expertise, estimated that he, himself, could not have performed the mutilations in under a quarter of an hour. If he had been removing these organs in a deliberate way, such as in the course of an autopsy, it would have taken him the better part of an hour, he testified.

CHAPTER VI

THE ASSASSIN HUNTERS

"ANNIE CHAPMAN lived in a Spitalfields lodging house where such as she are herded like cattle," Coroner Wynne E. Baxter began his summation; then, turning to the jurors, he continued, "but you are constantly called together to hear the sad tale of starvation, misery, immorality and wickedness which some of the occupants of the five thousand beds in the district have to relate every week at coroners inquests — you do not need to be reminded what life in a Spitalfields lodging house is like."

Next he turned to the murder itself. Using language which might have been more appropriate to Victorian melodrama, he spoke of the "Judas-like" manner in which the killer had approached his victim. "There was no evidence of struggle," he pointed out. "The clothes were not torn." The wretch must have seized her and pressed her throat until insensibility and suffocation were induced, then lowered her body to the ground. Annie's throat was then slashed and her body mutilated. "All of this was done with cool impudence and reckless daring," the coroner declared. "Nothing is more noticeable than the emptying of her pockets and the arrangement of their contents with businesslike precision near her feet."

Another feature which this murder shared with that in Buck's Row was that no cry had been heard. Sixteen people slept, fitfully or otherwise, in the house at No. 29 Hanbury

Street, whose partitions were of thinnest wood. None of them had heard a noise during the night. The coroner then remarked on the public manner in which the killer had advertised his crime by leaving the body exposed to the view of the first-comer. "This accords but little with the trouble taken with the rings, and suggests either that he had at length been disturbed or that as daylight broke a sudden fear suggested the danger of detection he was running."

Coroner Baxter, like the good showman he was, saved his *coup de théâtre* until the last, when he came to deal with the missing organs. These, he said, were not more than would fill a breakfast cup, and the fact that there were any organs missing might easily have been overlooked had not the medical examination been of a thorough and searching character. Dr. Phillips, who was present, blushed with suitable modesty. "But there was a market for the missing organs," the coroner announced, pausing for the full dramatic effect of his words to sink in. A few hours after medical evidence had been given at the last inquest session, an official of "one of our great medical schools" got in touch with Coroner Baxter saying that he had information which might help the inquiry.

Coroner Baxter at once hastened to the school where the sub-curator of the pathological museum told him the following fantastic story: Some months previously an American had called on him and asked him to procure a number of specimens of the organ that was missing in the deceased, offering to pay twenty pounds apiece for said specimens. The American said that he was writing a treatise on female disorders and that he planned to issue an actual specimen with each copy of the publication. Told that it was impossible to comply with his request, he still urged that the organs be given to him. He intended to preserve the specimens in glycerin, rather than in spirits of wine, so that they would remain in a "flaccid condition," he said, and he intended to have them sent to America direct. Coroner

Baxter understood that the American had approached another medical institution with the same request, and had been turned down. Naturally the coroner had passed this information on to Scotland Yard at once.

Coroner Baxter's disclosure burst like a bombshell in the press and elsewhere. At last a motive, albeit a bizarre one, had been supplied for the serial murders. The coroner's theory if correct, cancelled out all other theories which had been advanced concerning the killer. The maniac indulging a craze for human blood, the slaughterman run amuck, the devotee of the heathen sect which practiced human sacrifice — all of these must now cede pride of place to the new candidate.

What the police here had to deal with was a composite Burke and Hare in a mid-nineteenth century avatar, a latter-day "Resurrectionist" descended from those ghouls who sold specimens to the anatomists for a paltry few pounds.[1] At least this was the prospect held out by Coroner Baxter, and *The Times* fell for it readily enough. "The police," admonished a *Times* editorial, "will be expected to follow up with the keenest vigilance the valuable clue elicited through the coroner's inquest." "Since the lines of their investigation are plainly chalked out by information which they themselves failed to collect," it added with some asperity, "it will be a signal disgrace if they do not succeed."

Almost immediately the Bishop of Lichfield, the Rt. Rev. Charles H. Bromby, suggested to *The Times* that the remains of the other murdered women be exhumed in an effort to connect these homicides with the same "diabolical trade." Coroner

[1] From Vienna came a report that the uterus and other female organs were used to make *Diebslichter* or *Schlasslichter*, respectively "thieves' candles" and "soporific candles." According to an old German superstition, the light from such candles threw into a deep slumber any person upon whom it fell; hence they were considered to be valuable adjuncts to robbery. So much so that German criminal codes of the seventeenth and eighteenth centuries prescribed severe penalties for the mutilation of female corpses for the purpose of making such candles.

Baxter's theory however, was received with extreme skepticism by members of the medical profession, who sensed a slur intended for the profession as a whole. "That parts of the body carried off were wanted for any quasi-scientific publication or any other more or less legitimate purpose no one having any knowledge of medical science will for a moment believe," one doctor wrote to *The Times*. Such an insinuation was, in fact, "a gross and unjustifiable calumny on the medical profession . . . calculated to exert an injurious influence on the public mind and to defeat the ends of justice." *The Lancet* was even more outspoken. "We believe the story to be highly improbable," declared *Lancet*. "The public mind — ever ready to cast mud at legitimate research — will hardly fail to be excited to a pitch of animosity against anatomists and curators."[2]

In retrospect, it seems incredible that anyone could have been taken in by this story, which sounds more as though it had issued from the overheated imagination of the keeper of the Chamber of Horrors at Madame Tussaud's than from the curator of a reputable science museum. Certainly, it does little credit to Coroner Baxter to have been duped by it.

2

The storm of criticism which had been gathering slowly now broke over the head of the Home Secretary, Henry Matthews, and of his luckless Police Commissioner, Sir Charles Warren. The attack was led by the *Star*, a brash, Socialist-minded after-

[2] In his memoirs, *Doctor in the Nineties* (London: 1959), Dr. Halsted tells of the cloud of suspicion under which medical men walked in 1888, thanks to the Ripper. "Naturally those of us at the London Hospital were in the limelight," he writes. "The East End was alive with plain-clothes men. They were lurking in every alley-way, ready to pounce, and this more than anything gave us a sinister feeling . . . On more than one occasion I became aware that I was being shadowed by the plain-clothes men . . . I must be the only man living to have been suspected of being Jack the Ripper . . ." Dr. Halsted was ninety-four years old when his book was published in 1959.

noon sheet, which dubbed Matthews "a feeble montebank" and Warren, "our Maladroit Martinet"; but the *Star* was soon to get powerful if unexpected support from the *Daily Telegraph* and *The Times.* In an editorial on September 12 the *Telegraph* turned on Matthews. "The fact can no longer be disguised that the Home Secretary now in office is a source of miserable weakness and discredit to the present Administration . . ." A week later the *Telegraph* was at it again: "We have had enough of Mr. Home Secretary Matthews, who knows nothing, has heard nothing, and does not intend to do anything . . . It is high time that this helpless Minister should be promoted out of the way of some competent man."

As for the CID, "It is clear that the Detective Department at Scotland Yard is in an utterly hopeless and worthless condition; that were there a capable Director of Criminal Investigation, the scandalous exhibition of stupidity and ineptitude revealed at the East-end inquests, and the immunity enjoyed by criminals, murder after murder, would not have angered and disgusted the public feeling as it has undoubtedly done." (Sir Robert Anderson, the newly appointed CID head, who had left for a Swiss holiday on the day Annie Chapman was murdered, was still enjoying himself on the ski slopes, presumably.)

The attack, however, centered chiefly on General Sir Charles Warren. A rumor that Warren was about to be posted to Africa as a way of extricating the government from its present embarrassment brought a spate of comment, most of it satirical. The *Pall Mall Gazette* suggested that Warren be appointed Warden of the Marshes of the Upper Zambesi "defending the land of Ophir against Arab slave-traders on the one hand and Dutch filibusters on the other."

3

East Londoners, however, did not wait for Sir Charles to be transferred to the Upper Zambesi. With a suddenness which was all the more surprising because it was spontaneous, they now proceeded to take the law into their own hands, to organize vigilance committees and to patrol the streets of Whitechapel at night. Trade unionists, Oxford graduates who were doing settlement work at Toynbee Hall, Whitechapel costermongers — all were to be drawn into this patrol work.

Understandably, the loss of nighttime business, for women now refused to shop after dark, weighed heavily with the sixteen tradesmen, most of them Jews, who met in The Crown, Mile End Road on Monday, September 10, to form the Whitechapel Vigilance Committee. There were no firebrands among them. Their number included a builder, a cigar manufacturer, a tailor, a picture-frame maker, and a licensed victualer. A local vestryman, George Lusk, agreed to serve as their chairman, and Joseph Aarons, the licensee of The Crown, to be their treasurer.

They might have been small merchants meeting in the saloon of a frontier American town to decide how to stamp out lawlessness, and their method was just as unimaginative: to post a reward for the outlaw. The resolution which they adopted read: "Finding that in spite of the murders being committed in our midst the police force is inadequate to discover the author or authors of the late atrocities, we, the undersigned, have formed ourselves into a committee and intend offering a substantial reward to anyone, citizen or otherwise, who shall give such information as will be the means of bringing the murderer or murderers to justice."

The emphasis on a "substantial" reward was, as it turned out a tactical mistake, for not more than £200 was collected for this purpose, but in the beginning *The Times* reported, "The movement has been warmly taken up, and it is thought certain that a large sum will be subscribed within the next few days." *The Times* likewise reported that "meetings were held at various men's clubs and other organizations, political and social, at most of which the scheme was heartily approved." In the end, the committee put the limited funds raised to the more sensible purpose of hiring two private detectives and of paying about a dozen men, recruited from the ranks of the unemployed, to patrol the streets from midnight until 4 or 5 A.M. For this purpose Whitechapel was divided into beats, each man being assigned his round, and the committeemen themselves made inspection tours to see that the patrolmen were alert and on duty. The *Daily Telegraph* gives this graphic picture of the patrolmen: "Shortly after midnight these assassin-hunters are dispatched upon their mission. Their footfall is silenced by the use of galoshes and their safety is assured by the carrying of police whistles and stout sticks."

The patrolling was not without its comic incidents. As a rule the police and the amateur sleuths worked well enough together, but the *Daily News* reports one humorous mixup which might have been titled "The Comedy of the Watchers Watched." On this occasion, according to the *News*, "some of the plainclothes men who were strange to the neighborhood were watched by members of the Whitechapel Vigilance Committee, while they in their turn came under the scrutiny of the detectives."

4

In addition to the vigilance committees which sprang up, the Ripper manhunt attracted various lone-wolf operators. Of these Dr. L. Forbes Winslow, M.B., LL.D., Cantab., D.C.L. Oxon, to give him his full title, was by far the most intriguing. "I have breathed the atmosphere of lunacy for a period extending over sixty years," Dr. Winslow exults in his memoirs, referring to the fact that he grew up in a lunatic asylum in Hammersmith, London, where his father was resident physician.[3] The son, in turn became an alienist specializing in the criminally insane,

[3] L. Forbes Winslow, *Recollections of Forty Years*. London: 1910.

and his tall, dignified figure with the high, sloping forehead and full set of muttonchop whiskers was to be seen in the witness box at many a sensational murder trial, where he appeared as a medical witness.[4]

In the autumn of 1888 the Ripper murders engaged the attention of Dr. Winslow to the full, or, as he expressed it, "I gave my whole heart and soul to the study of the mystery." And not just academic study, either — the good doctor carried out "field research" on the spot in London's East End, reporting his findings to the police. So persistent was he in forcing his attentions upon the latter that they began to suspect Dr. Winslow of being Jack the Ripper, according to Donald McCormick. "All the detectives working on the case knew him and at one time his ubiquity at the scene of the crimes caused them to check up on his movements," McCormick writes.

Dr. Winslow himself tells us how he spent day after day and night after night in the Whitechapel slums, and how gradually he won the confidence of the poor creatures who were Dark Annie's sisters. "In terror," he recalls, "they rushed to me with every scrap of information which might to my mind be of value. To me the frightened women looked for hope . . . and welcomed me to their dens and obeyed my commands eagerly."

In the belief that the Ripper was a religious maniac, Dr. Winslow suggested that Scotland Yard insert an advertisement in the "Personal Columns" of London newspapers to the following effect: "Gentleman who is strongly opposed to presence of fallen women in the streets of London would like to co-operate with someone with a view to their suppression." But this suggestion, which had some merit, was turned down by Scotland

[4] Dr. Winslow's celebrity followed him to New York, where he chaired a lunacy caucus at an International Medico-Legal Congress in August, 1895. His views on every thing from phrenology to the suitability of ladies riding bicycles were quoted by the press. Indeed, the *New York Herald* considered him so important that it assigned a reporter to do nothing but trail the learned doctor and chronicle his daily adventures.

Yard, along with many other proposals emanating from the same source.

5

Toward the end of September the *Illustrated London News* paid a visit to a Spitalfields lodging house and reported that things were not as bad as they had been painted. For only fourpence a night one could "sleep as soundly as in the grandest hotel," this illustrated weekly assured its readers. "The dreams that visit poor weary people, often hungry people in such a dormitory," the article went on, "may be as bright and sweet as those of happy youth in a rural home where the morning sunlight, when it enters the cottage window, is accompanied by the twittering of birds . . ."

There was little to suggest such bucolic delights to the Toynbee Hall residents who patrolled the back streets and alleyways of Spitalfields at night. Toynbee Hall, the Universities Settlement set down in the heart of the East End jungle, had a vested interest in Jack the Ripper. For one of the murders attributed to him, that of Martha Tabram, had occurred in its backyard. So now, under the watchful eye of their warden, Reverend Samuel Barnett, the young Oxford and Cambridge graduates who were doing settlement work in the East End joined in the manhunt for the Ripper. Many of them were to distinguish themselves in later life as educators, social welfare workers, town planners, civil servants, and their ranks included at least one future Cabinet Minister, Hubert (later Sir Hubert) Llewellyn Smith, who was to organize Britain's first Labor Exchanges. But at the moment they were enthusiastic assassin hunters.

They penetrated courtyards which reeked of poisonous gases arising from an accumulation of filth. They climbed rotten staircases which threatened to give way at every step. They knocked at doors whose panels were cracked and whose locks were useless, doors that were kept closed by pieces of dirty rag. And what dramas they witnessed. Here it was a drunken free-for-all outside a pub; there it was a stranger who had been robbed and left bleeding; in a third spot two women, stripped to the waist, fought while a crowd of urchins looked on. "Never a night passes but what some new information is forthcoming," Thomas Hancock Nunn, Secretary of the Toynbee patrol committee, remarks in what must surely rate as the classic understatement of 1888.

The young Toynbee residents learned of the clannishness of the East Enders, how quickly they closed ranks whenever it was a question of "them" versus "us." One of the greatest difficulties the Toynbee committee encountered was in persuading an aggrieved party to take out a summons against his or her assailant. Time and again the patrollers came across husbands and wives seemingly murdering each other in the streets only to find that, when offered a means of redress, the injured party would quickly embrace his or her assailant. Here are some extracts from the Toynbee Street patrol reports:

> September 16: Man bleeding from stab wound in neck inflicted by woman. Great noise from crowd. Man refused to charge woman.
>
> October 9: Woman's head badly cut by man. Charge brought next day by Mr. X, but not being supported by woman was dismissed. [Note: "Mister X" was evidently a member of the Toynbee street patrol committee.]

During that dreadful autumn of 1888 the Toynbee Hallers found men and women sleeping out everywhere — in courts, alleys, passages, carts and vans. The women, mindful of Jack the Ripper, crouched in abject fear when the bull's-eye lanterns were shone on them, but the patrollers succeeded in persuading many of them to go along to Harlow House in Mile End Road, where they were offered a pint of coffee and shelter for the night. The committee also found children who had been turned on to the streets early in the evening because their mothers let the communal room for immoral purposes until long past midnight. All of this went into their reports.

Toynbee Hall continued its street patrols until February, 1889, by which time the members, "unable to bear the long hours and exposure involved in patrol work," had begun to drift away, according to the *Toynbee Record.* They therefore resolved themselves into a "Sanitary Aid Committee," to work under the direction of the Mansion House Fund. "The residents continued their patrols long after their working-class colleagues had given it up," writes J. A. R. Pimlott, official historian of Toynbee Hall. "There were some thrilling moments during the search for Jack the Ripper," he adds, "but afterwards the self-appointed task proved far from exciting."

6

Toward the end of September Dr. Thomas J. Barnardo had an encounter in a common lodging house at No. 32 Flower and Dean Street that he was not soon to forget. Dr. Barnardo, whose specialty was rescuing waifs from the sewers of the East End, was then at the height of his fame as the "Father of Nobody's Children" (before the century was out he was to wring £3,000,000 from the Victorians as "conscience money"), and it was undoubtedly in search of these human strays that he had wandered into the communal kitchen of the doss house at No. 32. There he was immediately struck by the despairing attitude of the female inmates whom he found gathered around the big open fire. They had been discussing the series of atrocious murders committed by Jack the Ripper and aimed exclusively at women of their class. "They seemed thoroughly frightened at the dangers to which they were exposed," Dr. Barnardo wrote to *The Times.*

One gaunt, sharp-faced creature, who had been drinking, was particularly bitter. "No one cares what becomes of us," she railed. "Perhaps one of us will be killed next." Dr. Barnardo was to remember this woman's face long after he left the doss house. He was to see her again, four days later — this time lifeless and laid out on a slab at the mortuary of St. George-in-the-East, Cable Street. Her throat had been slit from ear to ear.

CHAPTER VII

THE FOUR-PERCENTERS

As THOUGH Londoners had not already "supp'd full on horrors," fresh ones were now served with the breakfast coffee. On Tuesday, September 11, a grisly object was washed onto the foreshore of the Thames off Pimlico. It was a human arm, severed above the shoulder, to which the armpit was still attached. Rushed to the Millbank Street mortuary, it was examined by a Dr. Neville, a surgeon who had gained great experience in such matters during the Turkish war. Dr. Neville gave it as his opinion that it was the right arm of a woman, and that it had been in the water some two or three days. He thought that it had been cut off after death, for if it had been cut off in life the muscles would have been more contracted. As a bizarre note, the arm had a string tied lightly around it, as though to facilitate carrying it. Commented *The Times:* "It is impossible to form an opinion as to whether another revolting murder has been committed in London, or whether the arm has been placed in the water as a grim joke by some medical student."

Londoners were not to remain long in doubt. Three weeks later, the badly decomposed torso of a woman, wrapped in what appeared to be a black petticoat, was discovered in the foundations that were being dug for New Scotland Yard headquarters on the Thames Embankment. It had no head, arms or legs, and was altogether a revolting sight. "I have an arm which will fit that," announced Dr. Thomas Bond, police divisional surgeon; and, indeed, the Pimlico arm when joined to the Whitehall torso was found to be a perfect fit. The result, which became known as the "Whitehall Mystery," was added to the already existing "Whitechapel 'Orrors," and from now on the newspaper reader, reading his favorite daily over breakfast, was to be tossed between the Charybdis of full-bodied homicide and the Scylla of murder without head and without limbs, though these latter deficiencies were gradually atoned for.

Acting on a hunch, a Fleet Street journalist got permission from the police to search the area where the torso had been found. He then enlisted the aid of a Spitzbergen dog and a laborer named Hedge. No sooner had they arrived at the New Scotland Yard building site than the dog began to scratch and sniff. By digging just beneath the surface Hedge uncovered a left leg which had been cut off above the knee, and which Dr. Bond declared to be part of the human jigsaw.

At the inquest Dr. Bond came to the conclusion that the "Whitehall Mystery" was, in reality, a well-nourished woman between five feet eight inches and five feet nine inches in height, with dark hair and fair skin, and that she suffered from pleurisy. He fixed six weeks as the time that had elapsed since the body had been cut up, which would place the date of the murder at about August 20. (The postmortem examination, incidentally, was conducted under the most harrowing conditions for, in addition to the decomposed remains, the crowded mortuary contained the bodies of a woman who had been murdered by her husband in Westminster, a man who had committed suicide by hanging, and a woman who had been killed by a boiler explosion. In these circumstances, the standard fee of two guineas a body which was paid for these autopsies was derisory.)

In succeeding days other bits of anatomy, including a spare left leg which didn't fit, were washed ashore along the Thames, possibly as a result of medical school pranks. But hereafter the "Whitehall Mystery," which was never solved, was to provide a sort of contrapuntal background for the Ripper's Whitechapel fugue.

2

The Great Debate on "What is to be done?"—which had started with a discussion of prostitution and had progressed to such wild proposals as "belling" the streetwalkers and providing them with steel collarets, was now revived with a vengeance. The Victorians were having another of their *crises de conscience,* and suddenly everyone seemed to be talking at once. The Socialists were shrillest. "The real criminal," declared *Justice,* organ of H. H. Hyndman's Social Democrats, "is the vicious bourgeois system which, based upon class injustice, condemns thousands to poverty, vice and crime."

Others were not quite so rational in apportioning blame. Yellow-back French novels came in for their share of abuse as helping to create a climate of murder. "A flood of the most bestial works ever written by man is coming over from Paris," a *Times* reader warned, adding, "there is a larger consumption of putrid filth by the British people than ever since it became a nation." (In October, 1888, Henry Vizetelly, a London publisher, was fined £100 for bringing out an English edition of Zola's *La Terre,* which *The Times* described as "an outrage upon public decency.")

Another reader blamed crime thrillers glorifying the exploits of Highwaymen Dick Turpin, William Palmer, the Rugeley poisoner, and Charley Peace, the "King of Criminals." He cited the recent case of a lad of eighteen who, when arrested for larceny, bit the constable's thumb, saying, "I am as game as Charley Peace, and I will do as much as him before I die."

Nor did the theater escape condemnation. In deference to

public opinion Richard Mansfield withdrew his spine-chilling *Dr. Jekyll and Mr. Hyde* from the Lyceum in October after a run of only ten weeks. (Before closing, the American actor gave a benefit performance to raise funds for a night shelter for the homeless poor in the East End.) "Mr. Richard Mansfield has determined to abandon the 'creepy drama,' evidently beloved in America, in favor of wholesome comedy," crowed the *Daily Telegraph*. "The murderous Hyde will peer round the drawing-room windows and leap at his victim's throat for the last time during the forthcoming week . . . Experience has taught this clever young actor that there is no taste in London just now for horrors on the stage. There is quite sufficient to make us shudder out of doors."

Even the Salvation Army came in for criticism. "Such exciting revivalism as the Salvation Army movement may be responsible in a measure for the mind of the criminal," a *Daily Telegraph* reader suggested.

In despair, Reverend Samuel A. Barnett, the warden of Toynbee Hall, sought to get the discussion back on the rails again with a radical proposal that wealthy philanthropists should come forward and buy up some of the worst slum dwellings in Whitechapel. "In most of these dwellings there is lease under lease, and the acting landlord is probably one who encourages vice to pay his rent," Barnett pointed out in a letter to *The Times*. "If rich men would come forward and buy up this bad property," he pleaded, "they might not secure great interest, but they would clear away evil. Such properties have been bought with results morally most satisfactory and economically not unsatisfactory," he added. "Some of that which remains might now be bought, some of the worst is at present in the market, and I should be glad, indeed, to hear of purchasers."

The clergyman underrated the profits to be derived from such property. "I see more than 4 per cent in it," cried a reader who signed himself "Practical Philanthropist," adding, "but it is well to be moderate, and one need not excite too high expectations at first." No less amazing than its vociferousness was the speed with which the debate, having begun on a high moral plane, now descended to bickering over interest rates.

3

Always supposing him to be the megalomaniac of which his crimes gave every evidence, how the unknown killer must have chortled over this debate that he had inspired. Now he could contain his glee no longer. On Thursday, September 27, the Central News Agency, with offices in Fleet Street, received the following letter, written in red ink, and postmarked "London East Central":

> Dear Boss,
>
> I keep on hearing the police have caught me, but they won't fix me just yet. I have laughed when they look so clever and talk about being on the right track. The joke about Leather Apron gave me real fits.
>
> I am down on whores and I shan't quit ripping them till I do get buckled. Grand work, the last job was. I gave the lady no time to squeal. How can they catch me now? I love my work and want to start again. You will soon hear of me and my funny little games.
>
> I saved some of the proper red stuff in a ginger beer bottle over the last job, to write with, but it went thick like glue and I can't use it. Red ink is fit enough, I hope. Ha! Ha!
>
> The next job I do I shall clip the lady's ears off and send them to the police, just for jolly, wouldn't you? Keep this letter back until I do a bit more work, then give it out straight. My knife's so nice and sharp, I want to get to work right away if I get a chance. Good luck,
>
> Yours truly,
>
> Jack the Ripper

Don't mind me giving the trade name. Wasn't good enough to post this before I got all the red ink off my hands; curse it. No luck yet. They say I am a doctor now. Ha! Ha!

Thus did the sobriquet "Jack the Ripper" first see light of day. (Donald McCormick is of the opinion that without this nickname "in all probability the crimes he committed would have long ago been forgotten.") The origin of this composite nickname is not hard to divine. "Jack" was a popular name with many famous criminals of the past — Jack Shepphard, Spring-Heeled Jack, Sixteen-Stringed Jack, Three-Fingered Jack, and Slippery Jack, to mention but a few. "High Rip" gangs were those who preyed on prostitutes, either in robbing them or in exacting tribute from them.

The use of such Americanisms as "Boss," "Fix me," "Shan't quit," and "Right away" focused attention on the possibility that the assassin might be an American. In this connection the press recalled a series of brutal murders which had occurred in Austin, Texas, in 1885, in the course of which the victims, having been robbed, were hacked to death with an axe. A *Daily Telegraph* reader went so far as to declare that the Ripper's letter was "an exact reprint of the Texas rough's style."[1]

This is not the place to discuss the stylistic niceties of the letter other than to say that despite its obvious Americanisms it appears to be the genuine article and not a hoax. The important thing about this initial letter is the light it throws upon the Ripper's state of mind, the insight it gives us into his psychology. Note the supreme self-confidence of the writer, the absence of anything approaching panic. The police are no-

[1] Not so, replied a *Telegraph* reader who signed himself "Anglo-Texan," and who claimed to have spent the past three years in Texas railway camps. "The ghastly sangfroid which the perpetrator of these murders has proved himself to possess," he wrote, "is utterly contrary to the character of the 'Texas rough.' Beyond being addicted to an overindulgence in bad whisky and an unpleasant readiness with his six-shooter, the Texan has none of the qualifications which are indispensable to the stealthy assassin."

where near to catching him ("I have laughed when they look so clever"); in fact, they haven't a clue. He seems to feel himself immune to capture ("How can they catch me now?") as if by some magic power. It is this superhuman quality which must have struck terror into the hearts of the Victorians.

Only once, and then but briefly, does he drop his grinning mask and let us see the man crouched behind it. "I am down on whores," he says, "and I shan't quit ripping them till I do get buckled." It is like one of those Wagnerian leitmotifs which herald the approach of a principal character. In this case, it warns of the presence of a homicidal maniac. Why is he down on whores? He doesn't tell us. Instead, he reverts to his boorish humor. He becomes once again the Till Eulenspiegel of the stockyards, whose mania is killing. But not just ordinary homicide. No, Jack has an irrepressible urge to commit outrage. ("The next job I do I shall clip the lady's ears off.") In his dark, destructive power, the Ripper calls to mind that other serial killer, Joseph Vacher, the French peasant, whose boast was that he was "the anarchist of God."

4

The philanthropists continued to bicker over the dividends they could expect in return for taking over slum property in Whitechapel. "Ratepayer," writing to the *Daily Telegraph,* thought that such an investment would be sounder than English railway securities of average standing, and that "with subsequent good management 4 per cent might safely be taken as the minimum yield." Lest the charitable nature of the enterprise be lost sight of, "Gamma," writing to *The Times,* was sure that the public-spirited investors would be willing "to give their services as directors gratuitously until a 5 per cent dividend could be paid."

At this point the *Telegraph* joined the chorus with an editorial which reads more like the prospectus for a South Sea Bubble scheme. "A perfect gold mine exists in undeveloped London at our back door," the editorial gushed. "We purposely abstain from dwelling on the philanthropic aspect of the question," it continued, dismissing with contempt what it called "charity dribbles." "We want to see a freshet, a flood of capital spring from practical sources and taking the direction of this channel of Pactolus." The newspaper then gave as its considered judgment that, with proper management, Whitechapel slums could be made to pay "better than preference shares in the best railways, or Prussian stocks, or any foreign *rentes*. A net and safe 4 per cent is something to be desired . . . More than that — sometimes considerably more — has been and can be secured."

Indeed, the profits to be made from rent-farming in the East End were enormous. A landlord who owned six lodging houses in Thrawl Street, where Polly Nicholls dossed, did so well off his property that he could afford a country house in Hampstead, according to Henry Mayhew. Montagu Williams, the police magistrate, tells of other landlords who bought up condemned property on short leases from the railway companies, paying as little as £1 a week for a house, and who turned around and let their single rooms for 35*s*. to £2 a week. Very little capital outlay was required to set up as a rent farmer. One landlord bought enough beds to furnish four doss houses from a smallpox hospital which was being pulled down, all for the sum of £20. No one else would touch the furniture for fear of infection.

But, to return to the Four-Percenters, as September drew to a close they began to wrangle among themselves. In particular they turned on Reverend Samuel Barnett and accused him of alerting the owners of slum property as to their intention to buy, and thus encouraging the owners to charge "fancy prices." Indignantly, the clergyman denied giving any such encouragement. A new note was introduced into the debate by a correspondent who signed himself "One Who Knows" in *The Times.* Referring to the doss houses, he wrote, "The suppression of these haunts of crime and the dispersion of their lawless population should be the watchword and cry — the *Carthago delenda est* — of every social reformer."

"Dispersion of their lawless population" — there is nothing to indicate that Mr. Barnett had envisaged this in his original proposal. And if the inhabitants of Dorset Street, Flower-and-Dean and Thrawl Streets were to be dispersed where were they to go? Certainly, there were no more wretched streets in the whole of London than these. And with equal certainty, their inhabitants were entitled to hire shelter from the bitterness of the English night — the outcry occasioned by the murder of the Whitechapel outcasts implied a universal belief in this. If the Annie Chapmans were to be dispersed, they would be robbed of greater sums for accommodation; they would be forced to resort to ever more desperate expedients to make their doss money, with starvation the alternative.

Then there was the question of moral hygiene — were the Annie Chapmans to be allowed to spread their trade to streets hitherto untainted? Were these the results that Mr. Barnett was working for? If so the "mawkish twaddle" epithet with which the Social Democrats stigmatized the slum clearance program would seem to apply. The Socialist League was even more to the point. Referring to "the opening for profit made literally with the murderer's knife," Frank Fitz, the league secretary, prophesied that "The gutters of London and their terrible human wreckage shall be made to yield 4 per cent and 'even more.' "

5

Meanwhile, heedless of the discussion as to what constituted a safe return on investment, Jack the Ripper was sharpening his knife. "You will soon hear of me and my funny little games," he had warned the police, and now his name was to be blazoned in the headlines of the world, coupled with one of the most audacious crimes on record. This time it was to be a "double-header," two murders separated by three-quarters of an hour in time and ten minutes' walking distance apart. This double event was to mark an increase in ferocity and recklessness on the part of the Ripper, betokening the true megalomaniac. It was to drive the terror even deeper into the heart of East London.

But first he apparently found it necessary to advert the police as to his intentions, this time with a note postmarked Liverpool, Saturday, September 29, signed "Jack the Ripper," and reading as follows: "Beware, I shall be at work on the first and second in Minories at twelve midnight and I give the authorities a good chance, but there is never a policeman near when I am at work." The Minories is a street running north from the Tower of London. In the thirteenth century it was the site of a nunnery founded by the Poor Clares, or Minoresses, hence its name. But for the purposes of this narrative it was located hard by Mitre Square, which Jack was now to transform into a ghoulish dissecting theater.

The police no doubt were still pondering this message from Liverpool when, on Sunday, September 30, a postcard addressed to the Central News Agency was pushed through an East London letterbox. The handwriting on this postcard was identical with that of the Ripper's first, "Down on whores" letter, but it differed in that it had been written after the crime, and, as if to underline this fact, it bore a large, bloody thumb-print. "I was not codding, dear Boss, when I gave you the tip," the postcard read. "You'll hear about Saucy Jack's work tomorrow. Double event this time. Number One squealed a bit; couldn't finish straight off. Had no time to get ears for police. Thanks for keeping last letter back till I go to work again. — JACK THE RIPPER."

The postcard, I repeat, was mailed on Sunday when nothing had yet appeared in the press about the double murder. Only the killer could have known of the unsuccessful attempt to cut off the ears of one of the victims.

CHAPTER VIII

DOUBLE MURDER

LOUIS DIEMSCHUTZ heard the clock of St. Mary's Whitechapel strike one as he turned his pony cart into Berner Street and headed for the International Workmen's Educational Club, of which he was a steward.

Diemschutz was a hawker of cheap jewelry, or "swag" as it was known to the trade, and this Saturday night, September 29, 1888, he had set up his pitch at the Crystal Palace in Camberwell, south of the Thames. Choosing a spot directly in the path of the crowds that eddied to and from this many-splendored pleasure dome, the coster then let down the sides of his pony cart to form shelves. These he ranged with a large and varied assortment of gimcrack ware — brooches of colored glass in imitation of rubies and topazes, cameos, musical boxes, shirt studs, tea trays, sailors' knives and gutta percha heads.

Mostly the factory girls on their night out threw a quick glance at this cheap-jackery, then giggled and moved on — the night air was too chill for them to dawdle — but Diemschutz decided to stick to his post until the spectacle at the Crystal Palace, billed as "The Swiss Avalanche," had finished.

The spectacle was what was known as a "firework picture," and featured an Alpine landscape dotted with chalets and trains emerging from tunneled rock — "all to be overwhelmed by sudden ruin," as the billposters put it. Still marveling at these wonders, Londoners flowed into the streets at half past eleven. As it had begun to drizzle they did not tarry at the street traders' stalls, but made straight for nearby pubs to see how many pints they could down before closing time. Seeing that he would get no customers that night, Diemschutz packed up his wares and headed for the Berner Street clubhouse in the East End.

The International Workmen's Educational Club, an offshoot of William Morris's Socialist League, was a weird amalgam of Russian, Polish and German Jews, most of whom had fled to East London as the victims of persecution of one sort or another, and who were now endeavoring to carry on the Continental tradition of a combined social and political club in this alien atmosphere.

Their club premises occupied one side of a narrow court in Berner Street, the entrance to which was a pair of large wooden gates. On the opposite side were a number of cottages where tailors and cigarette makers lived, and the whole was encased by high walls which shut out all light except a faint glimmer from the clubhouse windows.

Saturday nights were open house at the club, and members were allowed to bring their wives and lady friends to the debates, which were usually followed by entertainment. "The Necessity for Socialism Among Jews" had been the topic this particular Saturday night, and the lively discussion had lasted until eleven-thirty, after which there was an impromptu sing-song.

Although it was now one o'clock, Diemschutz could hear the voices of a few stragglers raised in song as he turned his cart into the courtyard, whose gates were still open. Then an extraordinary thing happened: the pony shied violently, almost pitching Diemschutz onto his head. Thinking that there must be some sort of obstacle that he could not see, the coster poked around with his long-handled whip until it met an object that seemed soft and yielding. He then jumped down from the cart, struck a match and, by its flickering light, made out the form of a woman huddled close to the right-hand wall.

There was not the slightest doubt in the coster's mind as to the significance of his find. He knew almost instinctively that the woman was dead, and the dreadful name "Jack the Ripper" flashed through his mind as he rushed into the clubhouse to tell his friends. Zozebrodski, a member of the club, accompanied the coster when he returned to the court. Diemschutz's hand was so unsteady that the candle it held threatened several times to gutter out, but by its light they could make out the figure of the woman in more detail.

She was lying on her left side across the yard, with her legs drawn up and her feet against the wall on the right-hand side of the court. Her head was resting almost in line with the carriageway. Her clothes were wet, but when they moved the body the police noticed that the ground beneath it was quite dry.

As for Diemschutz he noticed only the dark trickle that issued from her neck. "There must have been quite two quarts of blood on the ground," he told the inquest jury later. He touched the body and was surprised to find that it was still warm. Obviously the woman could not have been dead many minutes before Diemschutz arrived.

2

Within an hour of Diemschutz's stumbling onto a body in the dark courtyard off Berner Street, a second murder was discovered, this time within the precincts of the financial tenderloin that is known as the City of London. This second murder, which occurred in Mitre Square, topped all the previous Ripper murders in the audacity of its execution. It was as though the killer had worked himself up into a mad crescendo of blood and violence.

I have timed myself in walking from Berner Street to Mitre Square, and in daytime traffic it took me exactly ten minutes to make the trajectory (this of course, was without taking advantage of shortcuts which may have been known to the killer). This means that the Ripper had approximately forty-five minutes to strike up an acquaintance with his second victim, to lure her into a dark corner of Mitre Square, to slit her throat, and then to perform the extensive mutilations which will presently be described. But the Ripper's timing was honed even finer than that. For Mitre Square, which is lined on two sides by the warehouses of Messrs. Kearley and Tonge, tea importers, *was patrolled every fifteen minutes by a policeman,* thanks to whose regularity it is possible to fix the time of the murder as between 1:30 and 1:45 A.M. In addition, there was a night watchman on duty in the tea warehouse at the time of the murder.

The Ripper ran even greater risks of discovery, for Mitre Square served as a shortcut for people going toward Bishopsgate; and after one o'clock on a Saturday night there were sure to be stragglers from nearby pubs cutting across it on their way home. Not only that, but there were three entrances to the square, leading from Mitre Street, from Duke Street, and from St. James's Place, which tripled the Ripper's chances of being caught red-handed by either pedestrians or police. The fact that he was not was one of those weird flukes which caused some people to attribute his crimes to a supernatural force.[1]

[1] According to a lurid pamphlet entitled *The Curse Upon Mitre Square,* this latest Ripper victim was found at exactly the same spot where, in 1530, a woman had been murdered by a mad monk named Brother Martin. In those days Mitre Square was the site of the Priory of the Holy Trinity, and Brother Martin coming upon this woman at prayer before the high altar had seized her

Police Constable Edward Watkins, City Police Badge 881, neither saw nor heard anything unusual when he passed through Mitre Square at 1:30 A.M. It was a quarter of an hour later that in making these same rounds his bull's-eye lantern picked out the form of a woman lying in what appeared to be a pool of blood in the southwest corner of the square. Constable Watkins seems to have shared with Diemschutz the gift of prescience, for he too had not the slightest doubt as to the import of his discovery. Not even bothering to ascertain whether the woman was alive, so sure was he that she was not, he ran across to the Kearley and Tonge warehouse, the door of which was slightly ajar, and shouted to the night watchman within, "Come quickly, for God's sake — there's another woman been cut to pieces!"

The watchman, as luck would have it, was himself a retired policeman, so he knew exactly what to do. Locking the warehouse, he ran up Mitre Street and into the Aldgate blowing a whistle, and he soon attracted the attention of two policemen, one of whom, P. C. Holland, was dispatched to fetch a doctor. Meanwhile, alone with the body, Constable Watkins screwed up his courage to examine it more closely.

The dead woman was lying on her back with her head inclined to the left side. She wore a pair of men's boots, and her left leg was extended, while her right was bent at the knee; both arms were extended, palms upward, as if in supplication. The throat was terribly mutilated, and there was a large gash across the face from the nose to the right angle of the cheek. The right eye appeared to have been smashed in, and a portion

---

by the throat. "The knife descended with lightning rapidity, and pools of blood deluged the altar steps. With a demon's fury the monk then threw down the corpse and trod it out of recognition." Brother Martin then plunged the knife into his own heart. Naturally, Mitre Square had remained unhallowed ground, according to the author; and just as naturally the Ripper murder was in fulfillment of the ancient curse, he maintained.

of the right ear was missing. A thimble was lying on the ground near the right hand.

3

At about the same moment that the policeman bent over the body to examine it, Major Henry Smith, Acting Police Commissioner for the City of London, was being summoned from a riverside police station in Cloak Lane where he had spent the night. And a very trying night it had been, too. The Cloak Lane station fronted onto a railway freight yard and backed onto a furrier's premises, so that, choked by the sickening stench of the fur skins and unable to open the windows because of the noisy freight trains, Major Smith had not slept.

He was still tossing about in his bed when, shortly after 2 A.M., the bell at his head was rung violently. "What is it?" he inquired irritably, putting his ear to the tube. "Another murder, sir," came the respectful voice; adding, "This time it's in the City, sir — in Mitre Square." The major was dressed and in the street in no time. He managed to squeeze both his frame and that of his 210-pound inspector into a hansom, and, with three detectives hanging on behind, set out for Mitre Square at a smart clip.

There was no love lost between Major Smith, who was responsible for law and order inside the ancient mile-square City of London, and General Sir Charles Warren, who commanded the much larger Metropolitan Police force. In fact, the major considered the general to be something of a Blimp, a judgment which was to be confirmed before this night of September 29–30 was out. In contrast to the general, who was inclined to panic, the major displayed coolness, imagination and wit (his memoirs are subtitled *The Story of Sixty Years, Most of Them Misspent*).

But Major Smith was also intensely interested in the Ripper

murders, and so, while Warren was making indiscriminate arrests, the major went about quietly making his own inquiries. For example, his men interviewed every butcher doing business in the City. Next, he put nearly a third of his police force into plainclothes, with instructions to do everything a constable, in ordinary circumstances, should not do. "It was subversive of discipline," he writes, "but I had them well supervised by senior officers . . . The weather was lovely," he adds, "and I have little doubt that they thoroughly enjoyed themselves sitting on doorsteps smoking their pipes, hanging about public houses, and gossiping with all and sundry." (In contrast, General Warren, who was a teetotaller, forbade members of his detective branch to enter public houses, even in the line of duty.)

The tragic part is that had Major Smith's subversive instructions been carried out to the letter, Catherine Eddowes (the woman whose body was found in Mitre Square) would not have fallen victim to Jack the Ripper. *For Catherine Eddowes had been in the major's custody at Bishopsgate police station less than an hour before she was found murdered.*[2] She had been arrested for drunk and disorderly conduct earlier that Saturday evening, and taken to Bishopsgate to sober up.

At twelve-fifteen Eddowes was awake and singing to herself. At twelve-thirty she asked when she was going to be released. "As soon as you are able to take care of yourself," she was told. A half hour later she was judged to be sober enough for release, and as the jailer was bringing her from her cell she asked the time. "Too late for you to get any more to drink," he told her. "Now off with you," he said, opening the door and shooing her into the night.

[2] Had she been arrested by Metropolitan Police, instead of City Police, she might still have escaped her sticky fate, for the former made a practice of holding drunks until morning, when they were formally charged before a magistrate, while in the City drunks were allowed to go free as soon as they had sobered sufficiently.

Now Major Smith's orders were that every man and woman seen together after midnight within the precincts of the City was to be accounted for. "The 'beat' of Catherine Eddowes was a small one," he recalls. "She was known to a good many of the constables, but known or not known, she was in the streets late at night, and must have been seen making for Mitre Square . . . Had she been followed, and men called to guard the approaches, the murderer would to a certainty have been taken red-handed."

This, however, was not the only frustration in store for Major Smith. All during this never-ending Saturday night the major was to find himself exactly one jump behind Jack the Ripper, who was fleeing for his life through the back streets of Spitalfields. In fact the major could trace the route that the killer had taken. From Mitre Square he had cut across Houndsditch and Middlesex Street to Goulston Street, where he left a tangible clue behind him, and then north to the notorious Dorset Street, where he paused long enough to wash the blood off his hands at a public sink set back about six yards from the street. (When Major Smith arrived not quite all of the bloodstained water had gurgled down the drain.) It shows his familiarity with Whitechapel that the Ripper knew about this sink, which was well set back from the street and located up a tiny close. From there on all trace of the killer was lost.

4

Meanwhile, another important clue had been turned up. Police Constable Alfred Long, H-Division, Whitechapel, was passing the Peabody "model dwellings" in Goulston Street at 2:55 A.M. when he noticed a bloodstained rag, which turned out to be a piece of Catherine Eddowes's apron whacked off with a knife. It was lying in a passage leading to the staircase of model flats Nos. 118 and 119 but it had not been there when he had passed the same spot at 2:20 A.M. Chalked on the black dado of the wall directly above the apron was this message written in a round, schoolboy hand: "The Juwes are the men that will not be blamed for nothing." Constable Long immediately searched the staircase and areas of the building, but found nothing. He then took the piece of apron to the Commercial Street Police station and reported his find to the inspector on duty.

The Eddowes murder inquiry at this point began to take on the aspect of a jurisdictional dispute, for the pursuit of their quarry had led Major Smith's City police deep into Metropolitan territory. But there was no turning back now, the major decided. He immediately dispatched City Police Inspector James MacWilliams with Detectives Halse and Hunt to Goulston Street with orders to photograph the wall writing. Meanwhile, Sir Charles Warren himself had arrived on the scene.

There now occurred the most astonishing episode in this long night of upsets and thrills. Warren not only refused to allow the wall writing to be photographed, *he ordered that it be rubbed out immediately.*[3] In vain did Inspector MacWilliams protest that it was "a great mistake" to destroy this evidence. The words, if photographed, might afford an important clue to the killer's identity, he argued. But Warren refused to rescind his order. (Major Smith says that Sir Charles wiped out the writing with his own hand, although this is not certain.) Sir Charles sought to justify his action by claiming the imminence of an anti-Jewish uprising. Goulston and its neighboring streets were already beginning to fill with

[3] Dr. Thomas Dutton, amateur criminologist and expert in microphotography, contradicts this. Dr. Dutton claims that he actually photographed the wall writing at the request of the police, and that the prints were destroyed on Warren's orders. "The micro-photograph which I took definitely established that the writing was the same as that in some of the letters," the doctor adds.

costermongers who were busy setting up stalls for the regular Sunday morning open air market known as Petticoat Lane. The sight of this wall writing might, he feared, have stirred them to a miniature pogrom.

Major Smith did not subscribe to Warren's views. The latter's action was "an unpardonable blunder," in the opinion of the major, who added this harsh comment: "The writing on the wall may have been written — and, I think, probably was written — to throw the police off the scent, to divert suspicion from the Gentiles and throw it upon the Jews. It may have been written by the murderer, or it may not. To obliterate the words that might have given us a most valuable clue, more especially after I had sent a man to stand over them till they were photographed, was not only indiscreet, but unwarrantable." Even Sir Robert Anderson, who as CID head was Warren's stooge, condemned the erasure of the wall writing as "an act of crass stupidity" but was careful to shield his boss from the blame. "It was done by the officers of the uniformed force in the division upon an order issued by one of my colleagues," says Anderson, without naming the colleague.

5

Major Smith was not alone in experiencing frustration. As though two murders in one night were not enough, Sir Charles Warren now discovered that a burglary of a particularly impudent character had been committed in the vicinity of the murders, or right under his nose, so to speak. While the unknown killer was busy turning Whitechapel and environs into a shambles, burglars were busy breaking into the Aldgate post office, which was located not a stone's throw from Mitre Square. They entered the post office through a trapdoor in the roof, and proceeded to rifle the office safe, making off with £300 in money and stamps. They did this moreover at a time when Whitechapel was swarming with Metropolitan police, vigilantes and amateur detectives, some of whom no doubt were trailing one another.

Meanwhile, the body of Catherine Eddowes having been examined on the spot by both Dr. Frederick Gordon Brown, the City police surgeon, and Dr. George W. Sequeira, of Jewry Street, who had been summoned to the scene, it was conveyed to the City mortuary in Golden Lane, where it was stripped and photographed before and after the postmortem examination. The inventory of her clothing and effects is so extraordinary that I print it in full as it appeared in *The Times:*

> She wore a black cloth jacket with imitation fur collar and three large metal buttons. Her dress is of dark green print, the pattern consisting of Michaelmas daisies and golden lilies. She also wore a thin white vest, a drab linsey skirt, and a very dark green alpaca petticoat, white chemise and brown ribbed stockings mended at the foot with white material. Her bonnet was black straw, trimmed with black beads and green and black velvet.
>
> She wore a pair of men's laced boots; and a piece of old white coarse apron and a piece of riband were tied loosely around the neck. There were also found upon her a piece of string, a common white handkerchief with a red border, a match box with cotton in it, a white linen pocket containing a white bone handle table knife, very blunt (with no blood on it), two short clay pipes, a red cigarette case with white metal fittings . . . a check pocket containing five pieces of soap, a small tin box containing tea and sugar, a portion of a pair of spectacles, a three-cornered check handkerchief, and a large white linen pocket containing a small comb, a red mitten and a ball of worsted.

This inventory stamps Catherine Eddowes indelibly as a doss-house inmate, for these homeless creatures carried most of their worldly goods on their backs. What they could not actually sleep in they tucked under their heads at night for use as a pillow. Indeed, if the American hotelkeeper's rule that "Guests found in bed with their boots on will die that way" had been enforced in the common lodging houses Whitechapel would have been reduced to a shambles.

Police found near Eddowes's body a small object which was to lead swiftly to her identification. It was a tin box containing two pawnbroker's tickets, made out in the names of Emily Birrell and Anne Kelly, which related to pledges made for a man's flannel shirt, and a pair of men's boots. These two items had fetched 1*s.* 6*d.* apiece in a Spitalfields hock shop.

6

Berner Street, too, the scene of the night's first murder, was in a ferment of excitement. The narrow courtyard and clubhouse were soon teeming with police from H-Division, Whitechapel. They shut the two wooden gates, as much to keep spectators out as to keep the inmates in, posted guards on all possible exits, and then began to interrogate the twenty-odd Russian and Polish members of the workmen's club who had remained behind when Diemschutz discovered the murder. Their hands and clothing were examined minutely for bloodstains, their names and addresses taken down, but when the police ransacked the clubhouse itself in a search for clues, the socialists began to feel that they were being persecuted. To add to the confusion many of them spoke only broken English. It was not until 5 A.M. that they were allowed to go to their homes.

In addition, the police questioned the tenants — tailors and cigarette makers, for the most part — who lived in the row of cottages on the lefthand side of the court facing the club — but not one of them had heard any cries or unusual noises, though these, of course, could easily have been drowned by the singing in the club.

William West, a socialist printer with premises at No. 40 Berner Street, told the police that he had attended the club meeting until 12:30 A.M. at which time he went into the court. He noticed that the gates were open, but was sure that there was no body in the court then. Morris Eagle, another club member, said he left the club about midnight to return at 12:40 A.M. but he saw nothing unusual. Neither had Joseph Lave, a Russian, who passed through the court about a quarter of an hour before the body was found. Had there been a body there then he could not have missed it, he said. "The court was very dark, and so I had to grope my way along the right-hand wall. I would have stumbled over the body if it had been there at the time."

The Berner Street victim, although her identity was not established immediately, was Elizabeth Stride, otherwise known as "Long Liz," a forty-five-year-old widow of Swedish origin (she was the only one of the Ripper's victims who was foreign born). A big, rawboned woman, her body was wasted away by hunger, as the two surgeons, Dr. George B. Phillips and Dr. Frederick Blackwell, discovered in making their gross examination on the spot. Her features were sharp and pinched, and her mouth, slightly ajar, revealed that all the teeth were missing from the lower jaw.

There was a silk scarf around her neck, the bow of which was pulled tightly to the left side. Following the lower edge of the scarf so closely as to fray the silk, a knife had been drawn over her neck so as to completely sever the windpipe and the left carotid artery. Stride had died of the resulting hemorrhage. The Ripper, however, had had no time to perform his usual hideous mutilations on the body. Indeed, there was every indication that he had been interrupted at his ghoulish task by the arrival of Diemschutz and his pony, the clop-clop of whose hoofs would have been heard at some distance.

Stride wore a black worsted jacket trimmed with fur over a dress of rusty black sateen, elastic-sided boots and white stockings. Her bonnet, which had fallen from her head, was of black crepe. There is some dispute as to what she clasped in her hands. *The Times* reported that she held a bunch of grapes in her right hand, while her left hand was closed over some sweetmeats; but at the inquest mention was made only of a small packet of cachous wrapped in tissue paper in her left hand. Both the jacket and bodice beneath were unbuttoned at the top but otherwise her clothing was not disarranged. "The linen was clean and in tolerably good repair," *The Times* conscientiously reported. In her pockets police found two handkerchiefs, a brass thimble and a skein of black darning worsted.

Despite the fact that it was not yet daybreak, a large crowd had gathered in Berner Street, and about sixty thrill seekers now fell in behind the covered corpse as it was wheeled through the wooden gates. Thus, followed by this strange cortege, Long Liz made the journey to the mortuary of St. George's-in-the-East, Cable Street.

CHAPTER IX

WARREN'S OFFENSIVE

LONG LIZ STRIDE was a mythomaniac, her particular mythomania being to invent for herself a romantic past in which she figured as the tragic heroine. The young widow bereft by sudden disaster, the necessitous mother of orphans, the helpless victim of life's turbulence, these were the roles in which she cast herself. How much they owed to fact, and how much to the melodramas which played at the Pavilion in Whitechapel Road we shall presently examine. But the fact is that with Long Liz everything had to be slightly larger than life size. She was a born actress.

Her best performances were reserved for the Thames police court, where she frequently appeared charged with being drunk and disorderly. Whenever so charged, she would begin by indignantly denying that she had so much as touched a drop, pleading that she suffered from "queer spells." Then, as evidence was being adduced against her, she would slump to the floor of the dock and begin to twitch and moan until carried from the courtroom in a seemingly insensible condition. Sometimes the magistrate, wearying of these performances, would sentence her summarily; but more often than not Long Liz escaped to drink another day, much to the envy of her less talented sisters.

Born at Forslander, near Göteborg, Sweden, Long Liz did not come to England until she was in her early twenties, and then it was to work as a servant for a family living at Hyde Park. (At the time of her death she still spoke English with a heavy Swedish accent.) When she was twenty-six Long Liz escaped from this domestic servitude by marrying a man nearly twice her age, John Stride, a ship's carpenter from Sheerness. According to one version of her life story which she confided to cronies over drams of gin, she then proceeded to bear nine children, most of whom were farmed out to a school run by the Swedish Church. But a clerk of that church by the name of Sven Olson, who had known Stride for seventeen years, told the coroner's jury, "I do not remember hearing she ever had any children." Neither did the Swedish Church run a school, according to Olson.

John Stride, as a joiner, helped to build the *Great Eastern,* Isambard Kingdom Brunel's ill-fated leviathan. (Long Liz claimed that she herself worked on the ship, making cushions and fittings for the ship's salons, but this can be discounted: she was a girl of fifteen and still in Sweden when the *Great Eastern* was launched in 1858.) At any rate, her husband's connection with ships suggested to Long Liz the great myth of her life, which was woven around a ship disaster.

On September 3, 1878, the pleasure steamer *SS Princess Alice* sank in the Thames after colliding with a cargo vessel, and carried to the bottom 700 passengers. Among those drowned, according to Long Liz, were her husband and two of her children, one of whom died in its father's arms. Long Liz, who had accompanied her husband on the outing, escaped only by climbing up a rope as the vessel was sinking, according to her story. A man who had climbed onto the rope ahead of her slipped and kicked her accidentally in the mouth, knockink out her front teeth, she said. It was a legend which she never tired of repeating in the dramshops of Whitechapel.

I have examined the list of 527 passengers upon whom an inquest was opened at Woolwich Town Hall, and found no one named Stride among them. Whole families went down with the *Princess Alice,* but the only case of a father and two children under the age of twelve drowning was that of an accountant named Bell and his two sons, aged ten and seven respectively. Moreover, a large public fund was raised for the families made bereft by the *Princess Alice* disaster, but there is no record of Elizabeth Stride, who was destitute most of the time, ever applying for her share. While it is true that all of Long Liz's lower teeth were missing, the postmortem examination disclosed no mouth injury such as might have been occasioned by a man's boot.

Somerset House does, however, record the death of a John Stride, a joiner aged sixty-five, of heart disease at the Poplar Workhouse on October 24, 1884, or about four years before Long Liz met her own terrible death. It may be that Stride, as a ship's carpenter, had had something to do with the building of the *Princess Alice,* and that this fact had suggested to Long Liz a convenient, if spectacular, way of blotting him out, while giving herself the status of a tragic widow. However that may be, it is safe to venture that Stride was separated from her husband long before his death. In fact, she had been living off and on for three years with a wild Irishman named Michael Kidney, who worked as a stevedore.

None of Stride's background was known, of course, that Sunday as she lay in the parish mortuary of St. George's-in-the-East. In fact her identity had not yet been established.

2

"All the talk on the train was about the two murders," George Bernard Shaw, returning from an open-air meeting on Plumstead Common, noted in his diary for Sunday, September 30. And not only railway carriages, but pubs all over the metropolis buzzed with this topic as Londoners drained their midday pints. In the Whitechapel Road the Cockneys, dressed in their Sunday best, stopped each other with "Isn't it 'orrible?" or "Have you 'eard?" This latter question was largely rhetorical, for the gutter poets were already on the street with broadsheets containing this bit of doggerel:

Has anyone seen him? Can you tell us where he is?
If you meet him you must take away his knife.
Then give him to the ladies. They'll spoil his pretty fiz.
And I wouldn't give you tuppence for his life.

At the murder sites, themselves, in Mitre Square and in Berner Street, there was such a press of morbid sightseers that the police finally had to cordon off both areas. At the latter site John Nogent, a Dublin revenue commissioner on holiday in London, was "limbered" of his gold watch, after being jostled by three or four villainous-looking fellows. But the magistrate at the Worship Street police court had scant sympathy for this Irish visitor. Those who toured the scene of the Ripper's depredations might reasonably expect to lose their time pieces, the magistrate observed.

Curiously enough, the double murder aroused less terror than it did indignation, which now proceeded to fall with full fury upon the luckless head of Sir Charles Warren. Warren's scalp was demanded at four separate meetings held that Sunday at Mile-End Waste. At one of these meetings a Social Democrat orator threatened "to string him up to the nearest lamppost" if Sir Charles so much as showed his face in the East End. At another meeting held that same afternoon in Victoria Park and attended by nearly a thousand persons the resignations of both Warren and Henry Matthews, the Home Secretary, were demanded.

The socialists were not alone in expressing their indignation. Hurt by the loss of evening trade resulting from the Ripper panic, Whitechapel merchants complained bitterly of police inefficiency. "Acts of violence and robbery have been committed in this neighbourhood almost with impunity," declared a petition signed by two hundred Whitechapel tradesmen and addressed to the Home Secretary. "The universal feeling . . . is that the government no longer insures the security of life and property in the East of London, and that in consequence respectable people fear to go out shopping, thus depriving traders of their means of livelihood."

Nightfall brought no lessening of the crowds which gathered like vultures at the murder sites, where some ghoulish scenes occurred. In Berner Street a woman did brisk business selling swordsticks, crying, "Here you are, sixpence for a swordstick — just the sort to do 'em in." In Mitre Square the police cordon was withdrawn at midnight, but a crowd of thrill seekers still lingered, according to the *Star*. Here is the *Star's* description of the scene at that late hour:

> A keen-eyed little Jew was explaining to a half-dozen women the position the body had occupied, and was pointing out some water marks as blood-stains, when the baby of one of the women began to cry. The mother, ever thoughtful of her offspring, drew the child from beneath her shawl and brought it forward a step or two. "Does it want to see the blood, bless its heart? So it shall. Take a good look at it, my pet. You may see enough of it if this sort of thing keeps up." Thus comforted, the child quieted down.

The following day, Monday, Michael Kidney turned up at the parish mortuary to identify the Berner Street victim as Elizabeth Stride. The Irish dock worker, who appeared grief-stricken, told police that he had not seen Long Liz since Tuesday, September 25. "It was drink that drove her away," he cried.

Another visitor to the mortuary was Dr. Thomas Barnardo, whom we have encountered earlier. He recognized instantly in the horribly mutilated features of Stride as she lay on the mortuary slab the drunken woman whom he had seen four days earlier in the doss-house kitchen at No. 32 Flower-and-Dean Street. As he gazed down upon the remains, he no doubt recalled her words, "Maybe one of us will be killed next . . ."

3

Stung by the widespread criticism of his administration, General Sir Charles Warren now launched an all-out offensive which was designed to prevent the Ripper committing further atrocities, if not to effect his capture outright. As a starter, he summoned home from his Swiss holiday the missing head of Scotland Yard's Criminal Investigation Division, Robert Anderson. Warren was not the only one to note Anderson's absence from the investigation of which he was supposed to be in charge. The *Pall Mall Gazette* had this to say: "The chief official who is responsible for the detection of the murderer is as invisible to Londoners as the murderer himself. You may seek Dr. Anderson in Scotland Yard, you may look for him in Whitehall-place, but you will not find him. Dr. Anderson, with all the arduous duties of his office still to learn, is preparing himself for his apprenticeship by taking a pleasant holiday in Switzerland!"

Arriving in London on Monday, October 1, Anderson was immediately closeted with the Home Secretary, Henry Matthews who informed him, "We hold you responsible to find the murderer." But Anderson was too full of ca'canny to have any of this. "I hold myself responsible to take all legitimate means to find him," he quietly remarked, by way of emendation.

Next, Warren assigned seven top police officials full time to the Ripper investigation, with orders to send every available policeman into the East End to reinforce the 546 constables, 29 inspectors and 44 sergeants already attached to H-Division,

Whitechapel. This, of course, was in addition to the City police and detectives who had been drawn into the manhunt by the fact that Catherine Eddowes had been found murdered on their doorstep.

Unfortunately, Warren's offensive was doomed from the start by the hostility that any police investigation was bound to call forth in the East End. "The hatred of a costermonger for a 'peeler' is intense," observed Mayhew; adding, "I am assured that in case of a political riot every 'coster' would seize his policeman." Nevertheless the peelers persisted in their house-to-house search of the Spitalfields area, which lasted nearly three weeks, and during the course of which they questioned nearly all the inhabitants of dossland. They also distributed 10,000 handbills headed "Police Notice to Occupier" and urging those who knew "any person to whom suspicion attached" to communicate at once with the nearest police station.

The vague wording of this handbill was self-defeating, for what doss-house inmate was not suspect of something or other? What it did was to loosen a flood of rumor and gossip which hindered the investigation rather than helped it. In one month Scotland Yard received no fewer than 1400 letters in response to this appeal, according to *The Times,* which adds that "although the greater portion of these gratuitous communications were found to be of a trivial and even ridiculous character, still each one was investigated."

As though the policeman's lot were not difficult enough, Michael Kidney, the wild Irishman with whom Long Liz Stride had spent the last years of her life, staggered into the Leman Street police station one night shortly after he had identified her body at the mortuary. He was blind drunk. His clothes were torn, his face bruised and tearstained, as though he had been on the losing end of half a dozen pub brawls, but there was about him the dignity of the gladiator who had just been mauled by lions. Seizing the sergeant on duty by his lapels, the Irishman now gave vent to one of the strangest expressions of grief on record. "If Long Liz had been murdered on my beat," he shouted, "I'd bloody well go out and shoot myself."

4

Coroner Wynne E. Baxter again presided when the inquest into Elizabeth Stride's death opened at the Vestry Hall in Cable Street. Dr. Frederick W. Blackwell gave the report of the autopsy, which had been held at 3 P.M. Monday, October 1. He said that when he arrived in Berner Street at 1:10 A.M. the body of the deceased was not yet cold; the neck and chest were quite warm, the face and legs slightly so. The right hand was lying on the chest and was smeared inside and out with blood. The left hand was partially closed and contained a small packet of cachous wrapped in tissue paper.

Dr. Blackwell gave as cause of death hemorrhage through partial severance of the left carotid artery. The incision in the neck, he said, commenced on the left side about two and one half inches below the angle of the jaw, cut the windpipe in two and terminated on the right side, but without severing the right carotid artery. "I formed the opinion," Dr. Blackwell told the inquest court, "that the murderer first took hold of the silk scarf deceased was wearing from behind and pulled the woman backwards. Whether the throat was cut while the woman was still standing or after she was pulled backwards I cannot say."

Dr. George B. Phillips, who had assisted Dr. Blackwell, testified that decomposition of the skin had already begun by the time the postmortem examination was made, with dark brown spots appearing on the anterior surface of the left chin. The autopsy revealed lung adhesions to the chest wall, indicating a history of tuberculosis at one time. Both lungs were unusually pale. Also the right leg was slightly deformed as the result of being set imperfectly after a fracture. The stomach was large and at time of death contained partly digested food. There was no trace of drugs of any sort in the stomach contents. (Some people had held that the Ripper drugged his victims first before cutting their throats.)

The Stride inquest produced its share of surprises. First, there was testimony concerning a knife found in Whitechapel Road. The knife was nine to ten inches long, dagger-shaped, sharpened on one side, and covered with dried blood. A bloodstained handkerchief was folded and then twisted around the handle. It was found lying on the doorstep at No. 252 Whitechapel Road by Thomas Coram, an employee of a coconut warehouse, who was returning home from visiting friends at 12:30 A.M. Monday morning, October 1. Coram did not touch the knife, but called it to the attention of a policeman who happened to be passing. It was examined by Drs. Phillips and Blackwell both of whom thought the knife was too blunt to have been the murder instrument, although the wounds could have been inflicted with this knife, they admitted to the coroner.

But even more important than this discovery was the fact that Long Liz had been seen talking to a man shortly before her murder by three different witnesses who now came forward with their evidence. Their descriptions of the man varied, but all three were positive in their identification of Stride.

The first was William Marshall, a laborer of No. 64 Berner Street, who said he saw Stride talking to a man at about 11:45 Saturday night. They were standing about three doors away. "Are you quite sure that this is the woman?" Coroner Baxter asked. "Yes, I am," the witness replied. "I did not take much notice of them. I was standing at my door, and what attracted my attention first was her standing there some time, and he was kissing her. I heard the man say to her, 'You would say anything but your prayers.' He was mild-speaking and appeared to be an educated man." Marshall added, "But there was no lamp near, so I could not see his face."

Pressed for a more detailed description of the man, Marshall said that he seemed to be middle-aged; that he was about five feet six inches tall, rather stout, and wore a black cutaway coat. The witness thought that he was clean-shaven. "He was decently dressed and had more the appearance of a clerk than anything else. He wore gloves but carried no stick or anything."

Police Constable William Smith, Badge No. 452, whose beat included part of Berner Street, next took the stand. He was passing along Berner Street at twelve thirty-five Sunday morning when he saw Stride talking to a man, he testified. The man was of medium height, about twenty-eight years of age, clean-shaven and of respectable appearance. He wore a dark overcoat, a hard felt deerstalker hat of dark color and carried a newspaper parcel measuring about eighteen inches in length. (This description was so clear that it was circulated immediately by Scotland Yard). When P.C. Smith later saw the deceased lying in the courtyard in a pool of blood he recognized her at once, and he reported this fact to his superiors.

Stride and her man friend were seen together even later that night, at 12:45 A.M. to be exact, or little more than a quarter of an hour before she was murdered. James Brown was on his way home to supper at that hour when he noticed the couple standing against a wall in Fairclough Street, which intersects Berner Street close to the scene of the murder. "As I passed them I heard the woman say, 'No, not tonight, some other time,'" Brown testified. "That made me turn round and look at them. The man had his arm up against the wall, and the woman had her back to the wall facing him. The man had on a long coat which came very nearly down to his heels. I cannot say what kind of hat he had on — the place where they were standing was rather dark. He was about five foot seven, I would say, and he appeared to be of a stoutish build. Both the man and woman appeared to be sober." The witness added that he had not even finished his supper when he heard screams of "Murder!" and "Police!" "That was about a quarter of an hour after I got in," he said.

5

As might be expected in a sensational case of this kind, the psychic brethren were not backward in their offers of "help" to the police. In Cardiff, Wales, a medium who was described as "a respectable-looking elderly lady" told police that she had successfully summoned the ghost of Elizabeth Stride during a séance held on October 6 and attended by five other persons. The ghost of Long Liz had not only given the name of her middle-aged assassin, but his address in Commercial Road, Whitechapel, and said that he was a member of a gang of twelve. But the Ripper was a farmer, according to another medium, this time in Bolton, who claimed that he had a dark mustache and scars behind his ears. He would be caught in the act of committing another murder, this medium predicted.

Students of black magic were not long, either, in claiming the Ripper as one of their own. He had been ordered by the secret Master of his Lodge, they said, to kill seven women in such a manner and place that their bodies would form a "Cross of Seven Points," with the head of the Cross to the west. One occultist claimed that if a line were drawn on a map of Whitechapel connecting the various murder sites the outline of a dagger would be disclosed. By following the direction to which the dagger pointed, the police might anticipate the location of the next murder, he thought.

Speculation grew so wild that *Light,* which described itself as "A Journal of Psychical, Occult and Mystical Research," finally thought it necessary to call a halt. "No good end can be served by the discussion of the hideous crimes which have recently been perpetrated," *Light* declared, adding that the dead should not be called upon to do Scotland Yard's work for it. "Besides," the editorial pointed out, "any clairvoyant who should offer aid to the police would run the risk of being locked up."

The most extraordinary of the mediums attracted to the Ripper case undoubtedly was Robert James Lees, author of *An Astral Bridegroom, The Car on Phoebus, The Life of Elysian,* etc. Lees conducted a Spiritualist Center at Peckham, and is said to have been consulted frequently by Queen Victoria. Lees, it seems, came to the Queen's notice in the late 1860's after he had been in communication with the Prince Consort in the spirit world. The medium, who was then only in his teens, was immediately summoned to Windsor Castle and asked to conduct séances there.

He was a "pale young man" with "fine dark eyes and broad intellectual forehead," according to one writer. He was also of a "retiring nature," and anxious to avoid publicity. These qualities apparently endeared him to Queen Victoria, for she asked "if he would be willing to be in close attendance on her at all times." Lees regretfully declined this offer on the grounds that "his spirit guide would not allow it."[1]

Lees, who died in 1931 at the age of eighty-one, showed no reticence when it came to taking credit for running Jack the Ripper to earth, however. In fact, he took such a clamorous interest in the Ripper case that he made a thorough nuisance of himself at Scotland Yard. His first brush with Scotland Yard came after he had seen the murder of Annie Chapman enacted in a precognitive dream, and saw, too, that he, Dr. Lees, would be instrumental in "stopping these murders." When he awakened the following morning he found the dream written down

[1] E. E. P. Tisdall, *Queen Victoria's John Brown* (London: 1938). Tisdall apparently got his information concerning Lees' connection with Queen Victoria from the medium's daughter, Miss Eva Lees.

on a pad by his bedside, though he had no recollection of having written it.

His second mystical experience occurred some months later on top of an omnibus bound for Notting Hill Gate when, glancing up, he saw the man who had previously figured in the dream as Jack the Ripper suddenly take flesh and prepare to alight from the vehicle. Without hesitating Dr. Lees jumped down from the omnibus and followed this character to the gates of a West End mansion which bore the nameplate of a distinguished physician. Maurice Barbanell, editor of *Psychic World*, takes up the story from there. "Police," he writes, "then found evidence that this physician, who led a Jekyll and Hyde existence, was responsible for the dreadful Ripper crimes. The physician was placed in a private asylum for the insane in Islington, where he was simply known as No. 124. To account for the doctor's disappearance a sham death and burial was staged, with an empty coffin being placed in the family vault. In recognition of his services to the authorities in solving this mystery, Lees received a pension from the Privy Purse for many years." I need hardly add that there is no record of any such pension having been paid from the Privy Purse.

6

After the Spiritualists, the occultists, the students of black magic came the transvestities and their efforts to trap the killer. The Ripper manhunt seems to have brought out the epicene in a number of seemingly normal men, or at least a desire to get themselves up in women's clothing.[2] Although Scotland Yard

[2] The advantages of using a policewoman in the Ripper investigation are self-evident, but in 1888 there were no policewomen. One Amelia Brown of Peckham, however, claimed that she was used by the police as a decoy during the Ripper manhunt, and that she had been furnished with a police whistle for her protection. This story appeared in the *Sunday Chronicle* in 1949. Mrs. Brown was then aged eighty-two.

affected to spurn such disguises, there is evidence of at least one detective being used as Ripper bait.

He was Detective Sergeant Robinson, of G-Division, Clerkenwell, who, heavily veiled and wearing petticoats and skirt, took up his stand in Phoenix Place, St. Pancras, after midnight on October 9. He was accompanied by Detective Sergeant Mather in ordinary dress, and the two of them kept a sharp watch on a man who was courting a woman in a darkened doorway "in a highly suspicious manner."

This scene might have passed off uneventfully had not the two detectives been mistaken for voyeurs by a cab washer named William Jarvis, who happened along at this point. "Wot yer muckin' about 'ere for?" Jarvis enquired, stepping up to the lawmen menacingly, whereupon Sergeant Robinson removed his bonnet with the veil and calmly announced that he was a police officer. "Oh, a rozzer, eh?" cried Jarvis, and with this he hauled off and belted the officer in the eye.

Another who took to the streets at midnight in female attire in order to play amateur detective was a young journalist living in Bow. Although he trailed his cloak in the Whitechapel Road, the reporter had little success until his masculine stride attracted the attention of a Police Constable Ludwig. "Just a minute," cried Ludwig, stopping the reporter. "You're a man, aren't you?" The impersonator admitted that such was the case, whereupon the constable enquired, "Are you one of us?" "I don't know what you mean," the young man evasively replied. "But I'm not a copper, if that's what you are referring to." It took the journalist nearly two hours to talk his way into being released from the Leman Street police station, where his story was meticulously checked.

Meanwhile, a *Daily News* reporter made a suggestion to a police inspector that appeared at first to have merit. Might not the Ripper have used the sewers as a means of making his escape? "Have you ever been down a sewer?" the inspector asked. When the reporter replied that he had, the inspector declared, "Ah, then you must know something of the difficulty of getting up again. The killer would require a key to get down, and he must shut down the grating and iron plate after him; and then, even with a key, he could not get up again. If he could, he would be more likely to be observed creeping up out of a sewer than by walking quietly off through the streets."

7

The *Evening News* dug up a new witness who swore that he had seen Elizabeth Stride with a man immediately prior to the murder. He was Matthew Packer, a greengrocer with a small shop at No. 4 Berner Street, a few doors down from the International Workers Educational Club. At about 11:45 P.M. Saturday the woman whom he identified as Stride came to his shop window with a stout, middle-aged man, Packer claimed. (Note that the shop was so tiny that dealings were carried on through the window in which the fruit was displayed.) "How much are the grapes?" the man asked, and was told that the black ones were sixpence, the green ones fourpence a pound. "Well then, give us half a pound of the black," the man ordered. With their purchase the couple then crossed the road and stood on the pavement almost directly opposite the shop for more than half an hour.

"I noticed them because it was a wet night," Packer told the *Evening News* reporter. "I said to my wife, 'What fools these people are to stand in the rain.' At last they crossed the road again and came and stood in front of the club as though listening to the music inside. Then I lost sight of them. It was then ten or fifteen minutes past midnight and time to close the shop. I noted the time by the fact that the pubs had closed."

Packer agreed that it was a dark night and that the only light was that afforded by an oil lamp which he kept burning inside his window, but he maintained that the couple had stood in front of the window long enough for him to get a clear view of their faces. The following is his description of the man he saw talking to Stride: "He was middle-aged, perhaps thirty-five, about five feet seven in height; stout, square built; wore a wide-awake hat; had the appearance of a clerk. He had a rough voice and a quick sharp way of talking." To test his veracity police first showed him the body of Catherine Eddowes, which he failed to recognize; he identified Stride readily, however, when shown her remains.

The significance of Packer's story lies in the fact that a grape stalk *was* found near Stride's body, although it may have had no connection with her but have been tossed there by a passer-by. (A Mrs. Rosenfield, of No. 14 Berner Street, stated that early Sunday morning she passed the spot where Stride's body had lain and observed on the ground nearby a grape stalk stained with blood. This story was corroborated by her sister, Miss Eva Harstein.)

The grape stalk became a part of East End folklore, and thus more than seventy years after the murder I found myself sitting in the kitchen of a council flat in Stepney and listening to Mrs. Annie Tapper tell how, as a girl, *she* had sold the grapes ("Almiras, they was — them pale green ones") to Jack the Ripper. Annie used to mind the fruit shop while Packer and his wife ("whether she was his wife or not I really couldn't say") had their supper. She was thus engaged on Saturday night, September 29, 1888, when in walked a dark, bearded stranger who bought a pound of grapes, told Annie to keep the change from sixpence. "He looked just like he was dressed for a wedding," she reminisced.

I have no doubt that this is how Mrs. Tapper remembers it, though how closely her memory corresponds with the events of seventy-odd years ago is another matter. I found myself more interested in what Mrs. Tapper did with those extra pennies which the man had given her as baksheesh for good weight. "I bought myself a ha'porth of red cabbage and a ha'porth of chips and sat right down and ate them," she recalled, her mouth watering with the memory. "I thought at the time that heaven could hold no greater delights."

CHAPTER X

EAST-END STIGMA

Meanwhile, the body of the Mitre Square victim lay cold and stiff in the mortuary in Golden Lane until Tuesday, October 2, when a market porter named John Kelly came along to claim it. Kelly gave the police a detailed description of the victim's clothing right down to a hole in her boot which he himself had mended with a piece of leather. He was then shown the corpse, which by that time had been tidied up by the autopsy surgeon, and he unhesitatingly identified it as being that of Catherine Eddowes, alias Kate Conway, alias Kate Kelly, aged forty-three, the woman with whom he had been cohabiting for the past seven years.

Kelly, white-faced and stunned with grief, remained a long time gazing down on the remains, then he stole over to a table where her clothes were laid out and ran a practiced finger inside the lining of the black straw bonnet trimmed with black beads. "Here's where she kept her money," he explained to the police. There was none there, however.

The market porter told City police what few details he knew concerning Kate Eddowes's life. She had been born in the Midlands, the daughter of a tinplate worker, but soon afterward the family had moved to London, where Kate was educated at a charity school. At nineteen she had run away with a soldier named Thomas Conway, whose initials were tattooed on her forearm. She had lived with Conway for twelve years and had borne him three children. No, the couple had never married, not at least to Kelly's knowledge, though she was sometimes known as Kate Conway.

Kelly could not trace all the steps of Kate's descent into the Spitalfields hell, but they must have been frightful, judging from her condition at the time of her death. The autopsy surgeon found her body so ravaged by Bright's disease that she could not have had more than a few years to live at best. Alcoholism added to disease made this tiny, birdlike woman appear ten years older than her actual age.

Despite the serious nature of her illness, Eddowes had gone hop-picking with Kelly at the beginning of September, 1888, near Maidstone in Kent in order to earn a few shillings. Walter Besant, in *East London*, paints an idyllic picture of "hopping," as the Cockneys call it. "The hoppers," he says, "come home with a pocket full of money; they have left their pasty cheeks in the country and they bring back rosy cheeks and freckled noses and sun-burned hands." As proof of the hoppers' financial solvency, Besant pictures the road to London as being "strewn with the old boots discarded by the hoppers when they bought new ones on their way home."

This hardly squares with the facts as Jack London, the American author, found them when he, too, went hopping in Kent in order to investigate the conditions at first hand. London describes the slum recruits as "an army of ghouls . . . dragging their squat, misshapen bodies along the highways and byways [like] some vile spawn from underground." Pickers, he said, were paid a shilling for seven bushels of hops, but not even the nimblest among them could expect to earn more than fifty shillings for a month's work. In bad summers like that of 1888 when the crop yield was low, the workhouse of Dover overflowed with vagrants who could not even pay their fare back to London. The American writer could not stick it more than a few days.

2

Ironically enough, it was not the poor pay, but the expectation of sudden wealth that caused Eddowes and her consort to cut short their hop-picking jaunt and return to London on Thursday, September 27, according to Kelly. They were after the reward money offered for information concerning Jack the Ripper. Kate Eddowes had a bee in her black straw bonnet that she knew the Ripper by sight. "I think I know who he is," she told her helpmate, little realizing that by entertaining this bizarre notion she was to seal her own doom. This, at any rate, was Kelly's story.

Upon arriving in London the couple had just enough left from their earnings after the train fare to get drunk on cheap gin and to pay a night's lodging at No. 55 Flower-and-Dean Street. Far from flinging their boots away in the euphoria of newly found prosperity that Besant describes, Kelly gave Eddowes his boots to pawn for half a crown the following day, and he stood barefoot outside the pawnshop door while she completed this transaction.

The half-crown having shriveled to sixpence in a pool of gin, the couple parted that Friday night. "Here, you take fourpence and go to the doss house in Flowery Dean," Eddowes told Kelly. "I'll chance my luck at the casual ward in Mile End." This seemed like a sensible arrangement to both, for had Kelly, an able-bodied man, gone to the Mile End workhouse as well, he would have been put to work picking oakum or reducing great lumps of granite to two-inch cubes in payment for his night's lodging and a plate of thin gruel.

On the following day, Saturday, September 29, the couple reached the end of their road together. They tramped the streets of Houndsditch all morning looking for odd jobs, but it was of no use. Perhaps it was their scarecrow appearance that frightened people off, or the fact that their eyes were bleary from drink. But nobody wanted them, not even for the most menial of jobs.

Finally, at about two o'clock, they decided to separate, Eddowes to go to Bermondsey to try to borrow money from her daughter Annie, who was married to a lampblack packer, and Kelly to strike out on his own. They stood together, cold and hungry, on a street corner, too miserable to look each other in the eye. "Watch out for Spring-heeled Jack," Kelly called after her as they parted, trying to sound jocular. "Don't worry about me," Eddowes replied, "I can take care of myself." This was the last he had seen of her alive, Kelly told police.

The next six hours in Eddowes's life were lost ones. Whether she actually went to Bermondsey in search of the daughter whom she had not seen in two years, or whether she picked up with another man immediately after leaving Kelly, will never be known. What is known is that at eight o'clock that evening she was arrested by two City policemen for being drunk and disorderly. She had been standing in the middle of the road imitating a fire engine. At the Bishopsgate police station, she gave her name as Mary Ann Kelly and her address as No. 6 Fashion Street.

As luck would have it, Eddowes was seen in police custody on her way to the Bishopsgate station by a lodger at No. 55 Flower-and-Dean Street, who passed this information on to Kelly. Therefore when Eddowes did not return to him on Sunday, Kelly concluded that she was safe in jail sleeping off her hangover. He even treated himself to a visit to Mitre Square that Sunday afternoon, mingling with the other onlookers who sought to trace the bloodstains on the pavement, little dreaming that the tragedy touched him personally. It was not until he read in the Tuesday papers about the pawn tickets found near Eddowes's body that the horrible truth dawned upon Kelly. He then hurried to the police.

The East Londoner's home is the sidewalk. Here a group of prostitutes take the sun in front of a doss house in Flower and Dean Street, Spitalfields, while children play at their feet. In 1881 a House of Lords Select Committee investigating child prostitution in London was told that in no other city in Europe was it so prevalent. *Reproduced by permission of Cassell and Company Ltd.*

The Whitechapel murders shocked the Victorian conscience as nothing else had. The very day after this cartoon appeared two more hapless women fell victims to Jack the Ripper. *Reproduced by permission of* Punch.

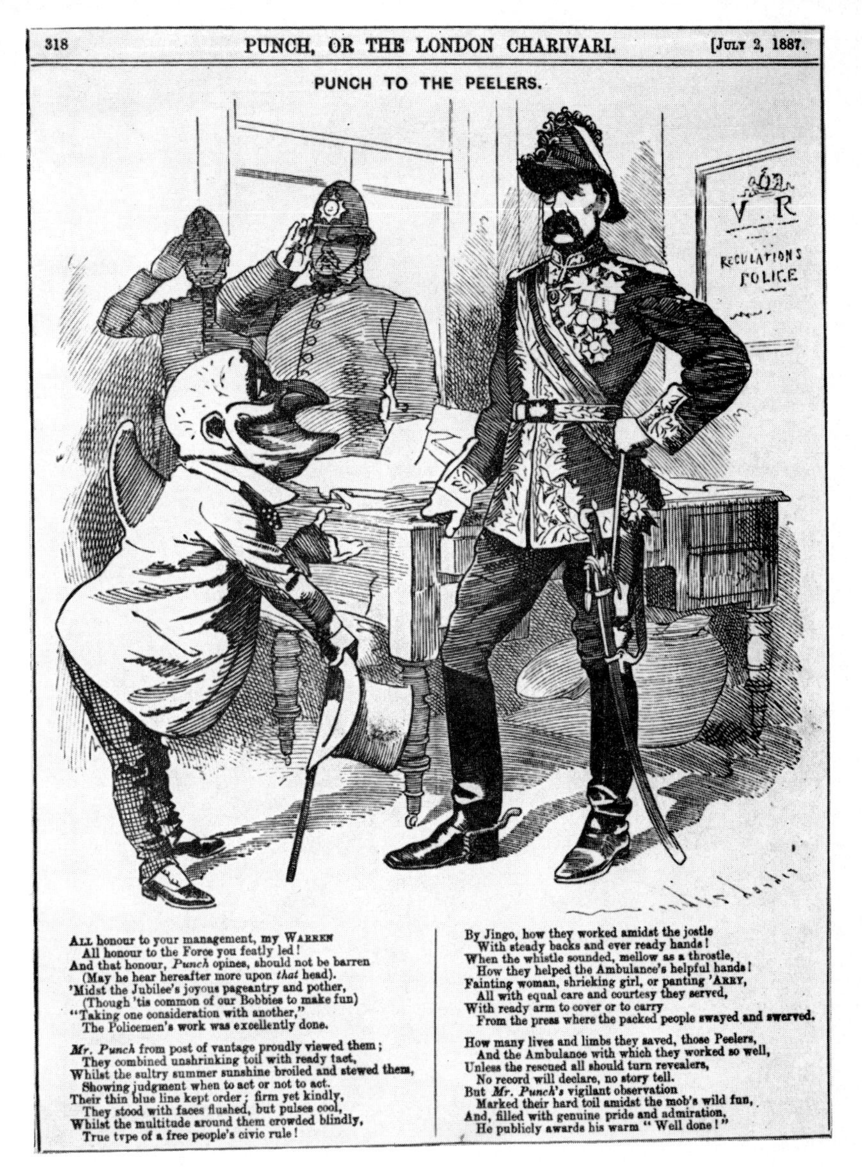
318 PUNCH, OR THE LONDON CHARIVARI. [JULY 2, 1887.

PUNCH TO THE PEELERS.

ALL honour to your management, my WARREN
All honour to the Force you featly led!
And that honour, *Punch* opines, should not be barren
(May he hear hereafter more upon *that* head).
'Midst the Jubilee's joyous pageantry and pother,
(Though 'tis common of our Bobbies to make fun)
"Taking one consideration with another,"
The Policemen's work was excellently done.

Mr. Punch from post of vantage proudly viewed them;
They combined unshrinking toil with ready tact,
Whilst the sultry summer sunshine broiled and stewed them,
Showing judgment when to act or not to act.
Their thin blue line kept order; firm yet kindly,
They stood with faces flushed, but pulses cool,
Whilst the multitude around them crowded blindly,
True tvpe of a free people's civic rule!

By Jingo, how they worked amidst the jostle
With steady backs and ever ready hands!
When the whistle sounded, mellow as a throstle,
How they helped the Ambulance's helpful hands!
Fainting woman, shrieking girl, or panting 'ARRY,
All with equal care and courtesy they served,
With ready arm to cover or to carry
From the press where the packed people swayed and swerved.

How many lives and limbs they saved, those Peelers,
And the Ambulance with which they worked so well,
Unless the rescued all should turn revealers,
No record will declare, no story tell.
But *Mr. Punch's* vigilant observation
Marked their hard toil amidst the mob's wild fun,
And, filled with genuine pride and admiration,
He publicly awards his warm "Well done!"

Punch doffs its hat to General Sir Charles Warren, the Metropolitan Police Commissioner, for his handling of Queen Victoria's Golden Jubilee celebrations. A year later the magazine had joined in the chorus criticizing Warren for ineptitude. *Reproduced by permission of* Punch.

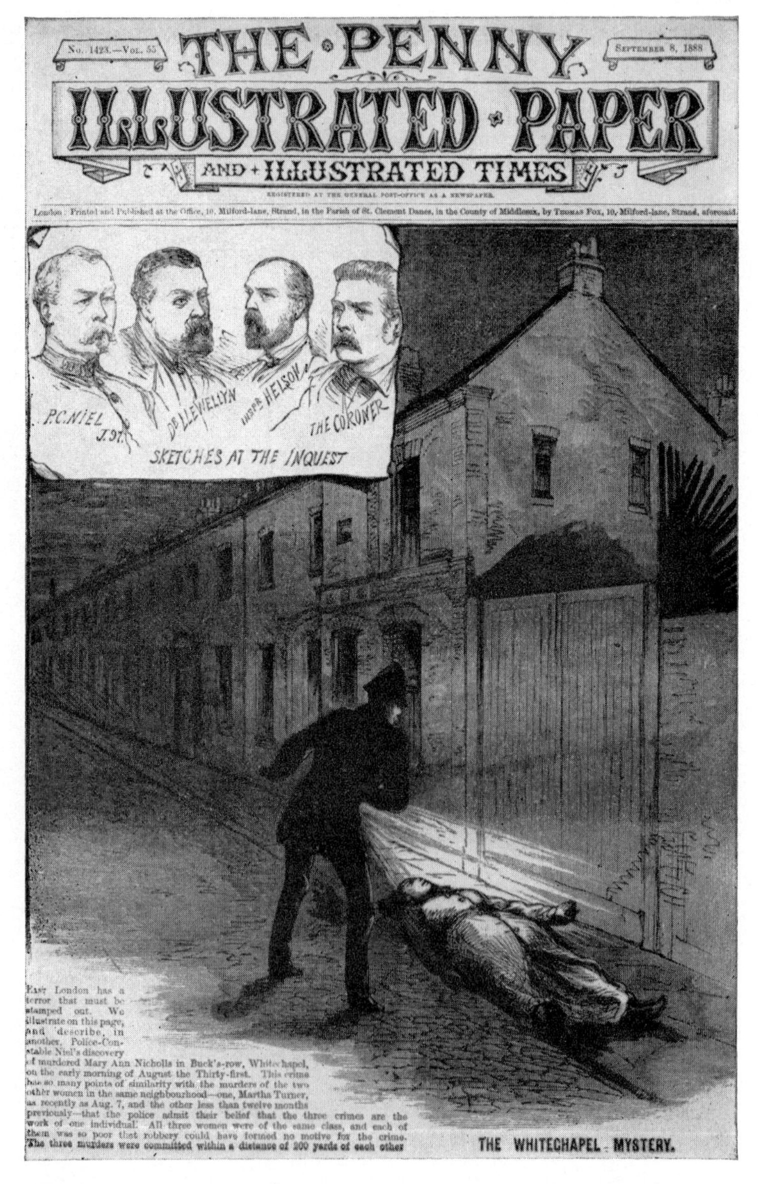

No. 1423.—Vol. 55

THE PENNY ILLUSTRATED PAPER AND ILLUSTRATED TIMES

September 8, 1888

REGISTERED AT THE GENERAL POST-OFFICE AS A NEWSPAPER.

London: Printed and Published at the Office, 10, Milford-lane, Strand, in the Parish of St. Clement Danes, in the County of Middlesex, by Thomas Fox, 10, Milford-lane, Strand, aforesaid.

East London has a terror that must be stamped out. We illustrate on this page, and describe, in another, Police-Constable Niel's discovery of murdered Mary Ann Nicholls in Buck's-row, Whitechapel, on the early morning of August the Thirty-first. This crime has so many points of similarity with the murders of the two other women in the same neighbourhood—one, Martha Turner, as recently as Aug. 7, and the other less than twelve months previously—that the police admit their belief that the three crimes are the work of one individual. All three women were of the same class, and each of them was so poor that robbery could have formed no motive for the crime. The three murders were committed within a distance of 200 yards of each other

THE WHITECHAPEL MYSTERY.

Police Constable John Neil discovers the body of Mary Ann Nicholls in Buck's Row. She was the first victim of Jack the Ripper, who was to leave a scarlet trail in London's East End.

The double murder of September 30. The bearded gentlemen in the upper sketch are Russian and Polish emigrees who were attending a social at the International Workmen's Club on Berner Street, on whose doorstep Elizabeth Stride was murdered. This gave rise to the fantastic theory that the murders were the work of Czarist secret police agents seeking to discredit Russian anarchists who had taken refuge in East London.

GHASTLY MURDER

IN THE EAST-END.

DREADFUL MUTILATION OF A WOMAN.

Capture of Leather Apron

Another murder of a character even more diabolical than that perpetrated in Buck's Row, on Friday week, was discovered in the same neighbourhood, on Saturday morning. At about six o'clock a woman was found lying in a back yard at the foot of a passage leading to a lodging-house in a Old Brown's Lane, Spitalfields. The house is occupied by a Mrs. Richardson, who lets it out to lodgers, and the door which admits to this passage, at the foot of which lies the yard where the body was found, is always open for the convenience of lodgers. A lodger named Davis was going down to work at the time mentioned and found the woman lying on her back close to the flight of steps leading into the yard. Her throat was cut in a fearful manner. The woman's body had been completely ripped open, and the heart and other organs laying about the place, and portions of the entrails round the victim's neck. An excited crowd gathered in front of Mrs. Richardson's house and also round the mortuary in old Montague Street, whither the body was quickly conveyed. As the body lies in the rough coffin in which it has been placed in the mortuary—the same coffin in which the unfortunate Mrs. Nicholls was first placed—it presents a fearful sight. The body is that of a womon about 45 years of age. The height is exactly five feet. The complexion is fair, with wavy dark brown hair; the eyes are blue, and two lower teeth have been knocked out. The nose is rather large and prominent.

Broadsheet announcing (prematurely, as it turned out) the "Capture of Leather Apron." Ha'penny broadsheets of this type were hawked about Whitechapel all during the Ripper's reign of terror. *Reproduced by permission of the Trustees of the British Museum.*

TWO MORE HORRIBLE

MURDERS

IN THE EAST-END.

Broadsheet reporting the double murder of September 30. The printer has used a stock woodcut of a scene from Victorian melodrama in order to beat his competitors to the streets with the first news of the "Whitechapel 'Orrors." *Reproduced by permission of the Trustees of the British Museum.*

Dorset Street, Spitalfields, as it was at the time of Jack the Ripper. A short thoroughfare known to familiars as the "Do As You Please," it had the reputation of being the most evil street in the whole of London. Police kept away from it, unless they came in numbers. *Reproduced by permission of Cassell and Company Ltd.* Below: Families evicted from one of the foul courts in Spitalfields to make way for slum clearance. Ironically, families like these were not to benefit from the new "model" dwellings erected on the site. The "models" were rented to artisans who agreed to pay higher rents. *Reproduced by permission of Cassell and Company Ltd.*

3

In addition to sacking Sir Charles Warren as Police Commissioner, there was one other step which the government might have taken to enhance the chances of capturing Jack the Ripper. That was to offer a substantial reward for information leading to his arrest. This the government obstinately refused to do, despite the fact that such a course of action was urged upon it by agencies as diverse as the *Daily Telegraph* and the foremen of both the Polly Nicholls and Annie Chapman inquest juries.

Samuel Montagu, the Member of Parliament for the Whitechapel division, offered £100 toward such a reward, to which Henry White, a Middlesex magistrate, added another £50. But to all such pleas the government turned a deaf ear. "The practice of offering rewards for the discovery of criminals," a Home Office under-secretary loftily declared, "was discontinued some years ago because experience showed that such offers of reward tended to produce more harm than good."

This was not strictly true. Six years earlier a £10,000 reward had been offered by the Lord Lieutenant of Ireland, on behalf of Her Majesty's Government, for information leading to the conviction of the murderers of Lord Frederick Cavendish and Thomas Henry Burke. Lord Cavendish was stabbed to death on May 6, 1882, while strolling in Phoenix Park, Dublin, with Burke, who was the real target of the assassins' knives. The fact that Lord Cavendish was the scion of the powerful house of Devonshire, a brother of the Marquis of Hartington, as well as being Gladstone's nephew, may have had something to do with the government's decision to post the reward; at any rate, it lost no time in doing so.[1]

[1] The assassinations were the work of a Fenian gang known as "The Invincibles." A group of them were rounded up in Dublin in January, 1883, tried,

Contrasting the Phoenix Park murders with those in Whitechapel, George Lusk, of the Whitechapel Vigilance Committee, pointed out in a letter to *The Times* that a similarly prompt and generous offer "would convince the poor and humble residents of our East End that the government authorities are as much anxious to avenge the blood of these unfortunate victims as they were the assassination of Lord Cavendish and Mr. Burke." The Home Office would not be budged on the issue.

But with the murder in Mitre Square the whole reward question had become a political one. By simply stepping over the border and into that ancient enclave known as the City, Jack the Ripper had, unwittingly, raised it to such a level. For City officials were not bound by Home Office rulings in such matters. Indeed, they were at loggerheads with the Home Office over the handling of the Ripper investigation, as was evident when Major Henry Smith, the Acting City Police Commissioner, clashed with Sir Charles Warren over the rubbing out of the wall writing.

The Lord Mayor of London now proceeded to widen the breach by offering on behalf of the City Corporation a £500 reward for "such information as shall lead to the discovery and conviction of the murderer or murderers." As though they had been waiting for just such a lead, various organizations and individuals rushed forward to supplement the reward. The Tower Hamlets battalion of the Royal Engineers, for example, not only added another £100 to the reward, but volunteered fifty men "either for the protection of the public or for finding out the criminals," according to Colonel Sir Alfred Kirby, the battalion commander.

---

and five of them were hanged, thanks largely to the testimony of James Carey, a Dublin Councilor, who turned informer. As a sort of poetic justice, Carey himself was shot in July, 1883, at Cape Colony by an Irishman named O'Donnell who traveled out with him on the same boat from England for the express purpose of killing the informer.

The Lord Mayor's offer posed a cruel dilemma for those City merchants and bankers who were Tory by conviction. They did not want to do anything that would embarrass the government, but they were thoroughly disgusted by the government's niggardly attitude toward offering a reward. This egregious example of meting out one sort of justice for the Cavendishes and another for the Dark Annies of Whitechapel Road filled many of them with shame. So they compromised. Sums totaling £300 and contributed by several City donors were forwarded to the Home Secretary with the request that he offer this reward *in the name of the government.* The *Financial News* acted as go-between in this transaction. But the £300 check must have burnt the Home Secretary's fingers, for it was returned to the editor by the next mail. "I am directed," a Home Office underling wrote, "to thank you, and the gentlemen whose names you forwarded, for the liberality of their offer, which Mr. Matthews much regrets he is unable to accept."

Perhaps it was the sight of so much money, though one would like to ascribe a more disinterested motive, but representatives of the various waterfront trade unions now came ambling forward with an offer to form a Workingmen's Vigilance and Patrol Committee "to assist the police in their present arduous duties." And a colorful lot they were as they assembled at The Three Nuns tavern, Aldgate, for their first meeting. Stevedores, lightermen, ship painters, scrapers, engineers, these were the men who were to bring the whole of London to a standstill a year later with the Great Dock Strike of 1889.

Almost the first thing the committee did was to approach the *Financial News* with a request for £150 to finance their patrol work. One can picture the look of utter astonishment on the editor's face when the waterfront deputation, headed by Thomas H. Kelly of the Dock Laborers' Society, waited upon him. One would like to think of these men as wearing the ancient and ceremonial costumes of their calling — the watermen's representative, for example, in pink stockings and with a huge pewter badge on his breast. But they were togged out in their best blue serge, of which their muscles seemed about to burst the seams.

As chairman, Kelly explained the purpose of their visit. "We propose to place seventy trained workingmen on the streets of Whitechapel from 10 P.M. until 7A.M.," he declared. "Men who are acquainted with every nook and cranny of the district. Seventy such men, full of courage and endurance, might well prove to be the means of capturing the villain," he added. Naturally, the committee would need money to defray its expenses. Workingmen could not be expected to tramp the streets all night without a cup of coffee and a bun. The editor, in turn, explained that the £300 had been entrusted to him for a specific purpose; namely, to offer a reward in the government's name. He would, however, be glad to open a subscription for the £150, and, to start the ball rolling, he offered £25 from his own pocket.

There is no record as to whether the £150, or any part of it, was raised by the *Financial News*. Nor is there any further record of the Workingmen's Vigilance and Patrol Committee. Whether they were discouraged by the lack of financial response, or by the patrolling in bitterly cold weather, they just disappeared from the scene.

4

So far it was the men of the East End who had taken the initiative in organizing the vigilance committees and in pressuring the government to offer a reward, though their womenfolk felt the tragedies more keenly, if anything. But on her breakfast tray one morning early in October, Queen Victoria received a petition signed by 4000 women of Whitechapel (the signatures had been gathered in three days). The petition, addressed to "Our Most Gracious Sovereign Lady," reads like a true social document of the times — pious, subservient, and yet with the faintest flicker of rebellion underlying it. I quote it in full:

> Madam, we, the women of East London, feel horror at the dreadful sins that have been lately committed in our midst, and grief because of the shame that has befallen our neighbourhood. By the facts which have come out in the inquests, we have learnt much of the lives of those of our sisters who have lost a firm hold on goodness and who are living sad and degraded lives.
>
> While each woman of us will do all she can to make men feel with horror the sins of impurity which cause such wicked lives to be led, we also beg that Your Majesty will call on your servants in authority and bid them put the law which already exists in motion to close bad houses within whose walls such wickedness is done and men and women ruined in body and soul.
>
> We are, Madam, your loyal and humble servants.

The petition was largely the work of Henrietta Barnett, wife of Reverend Samuel A. Barnett of Toynbee Hall, which explains its pious tone. But this does not entirely account for the resentment expressed at the lack of law enforcement in the East End. The truth was that Whitechapel was smarting from the unwanted notoriety that Jack the Ripper had foisted upon it by his crimes. The grief and shame that the Whitechapel women expressed were real.

In 1888 the East Ender had not yet been transformed into the Lovable Cockney Sparrow of a million music hall jokes, the one who could be counted upon to do a "Knees Up Mother Brown" at the drop of an haitch. In 1888 the East End was terra incognito to the gentlefolk of Balgravia and Knightsbridge, who never in their wildest dreams ventured farther east than the dividend and transfer department of the Bank of England in Threadneedle Street.[2] To these gentlefolk the inhabitants of East London, far from being lovable, were savages and as such to be feared. ("I have seen the polynesian in his primitive condition . . . he was not half so savage, so unclean, so irreclaimable, as the tenant of a tenement in an East London slum," cried Thomas Huxley.)

The Ripper murders added the last straw to the load of disrepute already borne by the East Ender, and he was quick to disown the murders and to express his resentment at the unwanted publicity. "We, in East London, are not so black as we are painted," the Reverend J. Farnsworth reminded listeners at an overflow meeting in the Unitarian Chapel, Spitafields. "We scorn the outrages committed in our midst," he added. "The murderer certainly does not belong to Whitechapel." What was remarkable about this meeting, which ended by expressing "no confidence in the present management of the police," was the large attendance of East End women, who ordinarily left politics to their menfolk.

The Whitechapel women's petition, with its 4000 signatures, had an interesting sequel. Toynbee Hall had made extensive use of the "old boy network" in order to smuggle the petition into Windsor Castle and to the attention of the Queen. In fact, Beatrice Webb's brother-in-law, Leonard Courtney, an influential Liberal politician, had undertaken this task. "Her Majesty has been graciously pleased to receive the petition," a Home

[2] In the first paragraph of his 366-page book *East London,* published in 1899, Sir Walter Besant dismisses East London's pretensions to historical interest thus: "But with East London there is no necessity to speak of history. This modern city . . . has no concern and no interest in the past . . . there are no monuments to recall the past; its history is mostly a blank." The *Encyclopaedia Britannica,* 1959 edition, adopts the same patronizing tone. In commenting upon the gulf between West London and East London, it has this to say: "The two regions speak the same language, if with different accents, and obey the same laws; to a large extent they are unknown to each other." This same authority goes on to speak of "the noise and vulgarity wherein resides the essence of the Cockney."

Office under-secretary wrote by way of acknowledgment. But Queen Victoria did not let the matter rest there. She had been kept informed of Whitechapel's ordeal by Charles Ritchie, the Member of Parliament for the Tower Hamlets division in East London. And now, through Ritchie, the Queen got word to the Reverend Samuel Barnett. "The answer that Mrs. Barnett will receive is an official one, and from the Home Office, not from the Queen, hence its dryness," Ritchie explained. "Because of this, the Queen spoke to me and seemed desirous that those interested should know how much she sympathized with them."

5

The Ripper murders sparked off a wave of hooliganism without parallel in the history of London crime. The mischiefmakers ranged from a seventeen-year-old-clerk who, by means of an umbrella handle, extinguished the streetlamps in Black Raven Avenue, East London, in order to throw the neighbors into a panic, to roughnecks who sprang from behind bushes at old ladies. One such old lady who lived in The Boltons, off Brompton Road, described how a man darted out of a dark corner "with a loud cry and flashing a knife." She also told of a young girl being followed by a man who shouted: "Stop! I am not Leather Apron."

In Cable Street an American was arrested after threatening to "rip up" a prostitute who would not go with him. Taken to the Leman Street police station, he demanded of the inspector in charge, "Are you the boss?" (the word "boss," it will be recalled, had acquired an almost talismanic significance ever since Jack the Ripper had used it in a letter).

Not even within the sanctuary of a church were women safe from ruffians, according to the rector of St. Mary Woolnoth in the City. This cleric told of finding his female caretaker in a semiconscious state in the vestry. "She told me a man had just entered the church, and finding her all alone . . . took out a pocket handkerchief and dashed it in her face," he wrote to *The Times*. "The strong smell of whatever liquid it had been steeped in dazed and stupefied her," he added. Only the entry of some workmen who were repairing the roof saved her from worse disasters, presumably.

In Islington a young man in a corduroy suit approached a policeman and begged to be arrested. "If you don't I shall murder someone this very night," he cried, producing a pocketknife. A bibulous glassblower from Clerkenwell likewise boasted in a pub that he was the Whitechapel murderer. "I guess I'll have to swing for it from a bit of hemp," he said cheerfully. Not so amiable was the man who walked into the police station in King Street, Chelsea, to report the loss of a black bag. He stayed to chat about the Whitechapel murders and ended by threatening to chop off the desk sergeant's head.

After a while the East Ender's response to any arrest became almost Pavlovian. For example, a man suspected of having stolen a barrel of oil was chased by a policeman into Baker's Row, where the suspect resisted arrest so violently that the constable had to whistle for help. The whistle brought hundreds of people running to the spot, where the opinion gained ground that Jack the Ripper was being arrested. "Men hooted the prisoner and women shrieked at him," reported the *East London Observer*, "but none offered to help the unfortunate constable who was being liberally kicked, beyond the advice to 'Catch hold of his legs.'" At last assistance arrived, and the thief was taken to the Bethnal Green police station.

6

Frustrated time and again in their efforts to apprehend the killer, the police in the end became "arrest shy," refused to book even those whose behavior might legitimately have excited suspicion.

In this connection, Robert Clifford Spicer of Woodford Green, Essex, a former policeman, told a remarkable story to the *Daily Express* in 1931. Spicer claimed that as a uniformed constable, aged twenty-two, "I had the pleasure of capturing Jack the Ripper and taking him to the Commercial Street police station after he had committed two murders."

It was shortly after the double murder that Spicer, in strolling his Spitalfields beat at 1:45 A.M., came upon an ill-assorted couple seated on a brick dustbin at the end of Henage Court. The shabbily dressed woman Spicer recognized instantly as "Rosy," a prostitute known to the police, but the man puzzled him. He wore "a high hat, a black suit with silk facings, and a gold watch and chain," according to Spicer's description. He also had a brown bag. "As soon as I saw him I felt sure that he was the Ripper," Spicer recalled. "What are you doing here at this hour?" the constable demanded. "That's none of your business," the stranger snapped peevishly; whereupon Spicer took the pair in custody.

Their progress to the Commercial Street police station was not without witnesses, for Whitechapel never sleeps. On the way "women peered out of bedroom windows and shouted and cheered," according to Spicer, "and some were so excited that they ran half-naked into the street," which is not altogether surprising in view of the number of brothels in the neighbourhood. As he marched his quarry into the station what dreams of glory must have flashed through Spicer's mind that he, a rookie, should singlehanded have captured the killer whom every London policeman sought. No doubt, in imagination he was already sewing the stripes of a sergeant to his unadorned sleeve.

But Spicer's reception was far different than he had anticipated. As luck would have it, eight inspectors, all assigned to the Ripper case, were on duty at the Commercial Street station that night, and these top officials now heard Spicer's story in a silence that was heavy with disbelief. In response to routine questions, the man in the top hat identified himself as a doctor with a Brixton address. Questioned in turn, Rosy, to whom the man had given two shillings, had no complaint to make, and her attitude seemed to decide the issue. So convinced were they that the man was not the Ripper that the inspectors didn't even ask him to open his brown bag.

As for Spicer, instead of being promoted, he was transferred to another beat, and resigned from the force five months later. "I was so disappointed when the man was allowed to go," he explained, "that I no longer had my heart in police work."

CHAPTER XI

"FROM HELL, MR. LUSK"

THE FIRST commandment of the East End jungle was "Thou shalt not nark" — meaning thou shalt neither "split," nor "grass," nor otherwise bear witness against thy neighbor in the presence of "Them." This class solidarity, born of bitter skirmishes with the law, was never more evident than when the inquest on Catherine Eddowes was opened in the Golden Lane mortuary on October 4, with the City Coroner presiding. Many of the inquest witnesses may have despised Kate Eddowes when she was alive, but now that she was dead none could be found to speak an ill word of her. There was an almost visible closing of the ranks.

For example, Eddowes's sister, Mrs. Eliza Gold, testified that the decedent was a woman of "sober habits," a conclusion piously echoed by Fred Wilkinson, the deputy of the doss house at No. 55 Flower-and-Dean Street where Kate and her paramour Kelly kipped when they had the money. This couple had lived together on very good terms, according to Wilkinson. Eddowes was "very jolly" and could often be heard singing, this woman who was far advanced in Bright's disease. As for Kelly, the Irish market porter, he was a paragon of virtue, and had never been known to touch a drop.

Compare this testimony with Major Smith's flat assertion that Eddowes was a known prostitute ("The beat of Catherine Eddowes was a small one . . . She was known to a good many constables") and the extent to which the sister, Mrs. Gold, and the doss-house keeper were lying immediately becomes evident. In the case of Wilkinson, he had his livelihood to consider: to admit that his tenants were other than models of rectitude would have been to risk being accused of running a "disorderly house" and having his license revoked.

Despite the efforts made to cover up for her character, it is plain that Kate's family spent much of their time dodging her. Had Kate on the last afternoon she was alive sought help from her daughter in Bermondsey, as was her intention, she would have knocked on the door in vain. The daughter, Mrs. Annie Phillips, had moved to Southwark, being careful to leave no forwarding address in case her mother followed and tried to hound her for money. Mrs. Phillips also told the coroner's jury that her father, Thomas Conway, had left Eddowes eight years earlier because she had taken to drink. There were two brothers, aged fifteen and twenty, whose whereabouts were also kept from the mother in view of her cadging proclivities, the witness testified.

The fact was that Thomas Conway, now retired on an Army pension, was so eager to help the police in their inquiries into the Eddowes murder that he waited two whole weeks before turning up at the City police headquarters in Old Jewry Street. Conway told police that he had been drawing his pension from the 18th Royal Irish Regiments under the name of "Thomas Quinn," in order to prevent Eddowes from tracing him.

It is not at all certain that Conway and Eddowes were, in fact, married. Even the daughter was in doubt on this point. But then marriages were sometimes entered into lightly in the East End. The vicar of St. James the Great in Bethnal Green, for example, did a thriving business in "sevenpenny hitches," which were regarded as a kind of lark. Arthur Morrison describes these bargain basement rites in his *Child of the Jago.* "There was a church in Bethnal Green," writes Morrison, "where you might be married for sevenpence, and no questions asked . . . You just came in, drunk if possible, with a batch of some scores, and rowdied about the church with your hat on, and the curate worked off the crowd at one go, calling the names one after another. You sang, or you shouted, or you drank from a bottle, or you flung a prayer-book at a friend as the fancy took you; and the whole thing was not a bad joke for the money, though after all sevenpence is a half gallon, and not to be wasted."

A clergyman who had officiated at 7500 marriages wrote to the *Daily Telegraph* at the time of the Ripper murders that some married couples were so unsuited to one another that "they could not hide their incompatibility of temper even in the church, but commenced jangling in the vestry. I have known more than one couple so uninfluenced by their marriage vows, and so depraved, that they fought each other publicly in the street on their wedding day," he added.

2

Kate Eddowes was seen talking to a man in Mitre Square just ten minutes before her mutilated body was discovered by the City police constable, according to the next witness. He was Joseph Lawende, a commercial traveler of German descent, who told of leaving the Imperial Club in nearby Duke Street with two companions at 1:35 A.M. They were passing Church passage, which leads into Mitre Square, when their attention was riveted by a woman's laughter, and they saw a couple standing at the entrance to the square. The woman was facing the man, who had his back half turned toward Lawende, and she wore a black jacket and a black bonnet. As he watched them he saw the woman place a hand on the man's chest.

"What sort of man was he?" the coroner asked. But before he could reply, Lawende was interrupted by the City Solicitor, a Mr. Crawford, who was keeping a watching brief on the proceedings. "Unless the jury wish it," Crawford declared, "I have special reason why no description of this man should be given at this time." The City Solicitor, obviously, was trying to forestall an attempt on the part of the killer to alter his clothing and appearance.

The missing details of the man's appearance, as supplied by Major Smith, were that he was about thirty years old, five feet nine inches in height, "with a small, fair moustache, dressed in something like navy serge, and with a deerstalker's cap — that is, a cap with a peak fore and aft." The description circulated by City police added that he wore a red neckerchief. Major Smith attached great importance to this description as being one of the few accurate tallies of the Ripper. As the major remarks, "It was bright moonlight, almost as light as day, and he [Lawende] saw them distinctly. This was, without doubt, the murderer and his victim."

The commercial traveler's testimony underlines the enormous gamble the Ripper took in choosing Mitre Square as his operating theater. He must have timed Constable Watkins's rounds and have known that the policemen passed through the square every quarter hour. And yet, in the interim, the Ripper risked being caught by late-night revelers such as Lawende entering the square from any one of three sides.

William Stewart, a commercial artist, carried out some fascinating experiments in Mitre Square in 1938 designed to show how great were the risks the Ripper had run. Stewart, in the company of friends, descended upon Mitre Square one midnight, and proceeded to test its acoustics. Among other things he tore up an apron to see if the sound would have carried to the watchman on duty at the Kearley & Tonge warehouse the night of the murder. He was startled to find how distinctly the noise could be heard from one end of the square to the other. In fact, the hubbub of the City having died away, Mitre Square at night became a veritable soundbox amplifying the slightest noise.

3

It was only when Dr. Frederick Gordon Brown gave his post-mortem that it became clear to what horrifying extent Kate Eddowes's body had been mutilated. It had been laid open by a very sharp-pointed knife, the surgeon testified, and the intestines had been pulled out and draped over the right shoulder, a piece of the intestines being detached and placed between the left arm and the body. The liver had been punctured as if by the point of the knife, and the left lobe of the liver was slit through by a vertical cut.

The face was horribly disfigured, the killer even going so far as to nick the lower eyelids with his knife. The lobe of the right ear was cut obliquely through. There was a quantity of clotted blood on the pavement, Dr. Brown declared, most of it coming from the hemorrhaging blood vessels on the left side of the neck. But the body was quite warm when he had arrived at 2:18 A.M., which was just over a half hour after the murder had taken place, by police estimate.

The surgeon also revealed for the first time that one of the organs was missing. It was the left kidney, which had been deftly excised. He was of the opinion that the killer had shown "a good deal of knowledge as to the positions of the organs in the abdominal cavity and the way of removing them" — in particular, knowledge of the location of the kidney, which is covered with a membrane and hence is easily overlooked. Concluding, Dr. Brown said he felt sure that there had been no struggle; therefore, he would expect to find very little blood on the person of the killer.

This matter of anatomical skill was hotly disputed by Dr. George Sequeira, who had been the first doctor to arrive at the scene of the murder, and by Dr. William Sedgwick Saunders, who was present at the postmortem. Both of these medicos were of the opinion that the mutilations indicated no particular knowledge of surgery.

The missing organ was not long in turning up. On Tuesday, October 16, Mr. George Lusk, chairman of the Whitechapel Vigilance Committee, received a parcel of a revolting nature through the mail. It was a cardboard box containing what appeared to be a portion of kidney, and the letter enclosed with it read: "From hell, Mr. Lusk, sir, I send you half the kidne I took from one woman, prasarved it for you, tother piece I fried and ate it; was very nice. I may send you the bloody knif that took it out if you only wate while longer. Catch me when you can, Mr. Lusk."

For some obscure reason the press was inclined to scoff at this latest development. Perhaps the press had burned its fingers once too often on developments in the Ripper case. Perhaps it was peeved at Sir Charles Warren. Whatever the reason the attitude it now adopted was one of skepticism. "The kidney was that of a dog" wrote one journalist. "A medical student's prank," pronounced a second, who held that the kidney had been removed from a cadaver used for dissection.

Major Smith of the City police appears to have had few doubts as to whom the kidney belonged; nevertheless he forwarded it to Dr. Openshaw, pathological curator of the London Hospital museum, for an analysis. In his report Dr. Openshaw identified the grisly object as a portion of human kidney and stated that it had been placed in spirits within a few hours of its removal. Furthermore, it was a "ginny" kidney, the curator declared, meaning that it had belonged to someone who punished alcohol heavily. It had belonged to a woman aged about forty-five, and had been removed from her body within the last three weeks, he concluded.

As a clincher, Major Smith pointed out that the renal artery is three inches long. Two inches of renal artery were discovered in the corpse of Catherine Eddowes; one inch was attached to the kidney portion mailed to Mr. Lusk. Major Smith added, "The kidney left in the corpse was in an advanced stage of Bright's disease. The kidney sent to me was in an exactly similar state."

Meanwhile, the Master Anatomist, himself, watched these developments with fiendish enjoyment. "Old Boss," he wrote to Major Smith, "have you see the devle with his mikerscope and scapul a-looking at a kidney with a slide cocked up?" At the same time, he seemed to be somewhat annoyed with Mr. Lusk for having run to Major Smith with the kidney. "Say Boss, you seem rare frightened," he scribbled on a postcard to Lusk. "Guess I like to give you fits, but can't stop long enough to let you box of toys play copper games with me, but hope to see you when I don't hurry too much. Goodbye, Boss." This sounds like a man who is being chased through hell by his own private demon.

4

It might be well to say a few words here about the voluminous correspondence connected with the Ripper murders. In one month alone Scotland Yard received 1400 letters bearing upon the case, and indeed the letters containing bogus "confessions" and accusations have continued down the years in a dwindling but steady stream.[1] Here, however, attention will be narrowed to the hundred or so letters written at the time of the murders, signed "Jack the Ripper," "The Ripper," or simply "Jack" and purporting to come from the killer himself. The majority of them, of course, were written by crackpots or practical jokers

[1] The latest I have been able to trace was the letter cited earlier sent to *Reynolds News* in February, 1959, from a retired blacksmith in Worthing and naming his cousin Frank as the murderer.

of various kinds. It is a known fact that every poison-pen letter tends to call forth a dozen imitators, and most of this correspondence consists of pale carbons of the original Jack and is not in the original Jack's handwriting.

A woman hoaxer was caught in Bradford by the police. She was Maria Coroner, aged twenty-one, whom *The Times* described as being "a respectable-looking young woman" employed as a mantle maker. Maria was charged in Bradford borough court with having written two letters signed "Jack the Ripper" which "tended to cause a breach of peace." One of the letters, which announced that the Ripper had arrived in Bradford "to do a little business," was sent to the Chief Constable; the other, to a local newspaper. Maria's defense: it was all intended as a big joke.

By far the most important of these letters is the original one postmarked September 27 and mailed to the Central News Agency, in which the writer announced that he was "down on whores," forewarned the police of his intention to commit murder, and signed himself for the first time "Jack the Ripper."

Yet, even this original letter was a hoax, according to Sir Robert Anderson, head of the CID at the time of the Whitechapel murders. In his memoirs written years after these events Sir Robert described the letter as "the creation of an enterprising journalist." He was tempted to identify the journalist, he added, "but no public benefit would result from such a course, and the traditions of my department would suffer." If the letter was a hoax, as Sir Robert maintains, then Scotland Yard was completely taken in by it, for the letter was reproduced in facsimile on hundreds of police handbills and posters which were distributed throughout London. Indeed, the letter occupied a place of honor in Scotland Yard's "Black Museum" of crime curios for many years, it being kept in a glass case to the left of the door as one entered.

But was this original letter a hoax? The answer would seem

to lie buried in the internal evidence of the letter, itself. For example, if it could be shown that the letter contained information which could have been known only to the killer, this would establish it as authentic — i.e., as having been written by the authentic article, the Ripper himself. But did it contain such information? Let us take a closer look at the letter. "*The next job I do I shall clip the lady's ears off and send to the police officers, just for jolly, wouldn't you?*" wrote this macabre jester. (My italics.)

Now, in Berner Street, as has already been indicated, the murderer was interrupted by the arrival of Louis Diemschutz in his pony cart. Was he thus thwarted in his avowed purpose to "clip the lady's ears off"? Was it in fulfillment of this boastful promise to the police that the Ripper, throwing caution to the winds, sought out a second victim that night? Certainly, the murder of Catherine Eddowes has the air of being unscheduled, which would account for the fearful risks the killer ran of being caught in the act.

Dr. Frederick G. Brown, who performed the autopsy on Catherine Eddowes, testified that "the lobe of the right ear was cut obliquely through," indicating that the killer had tried to keep his promise to the police. But again he appears to have been interrupted. Perhaps it was the heavy tread of Constable Watkins approaching on his rounds, or perhaps it was the voices of Lawende and his companions leaving the Imperial Club in Duke Street that caused the killer to leave off his fiendish task.

This brings us to the postcard of September 30 signed "Jack the Ripper" and in the same handwriting as the original letter: "I was not codding, dear old Boss, when I gave you the tip. You'll hear about Saucy Jack's work tomorrow. Double event this time. *Number one squealed a bit.* Couldn't finish straight off. *Had not time to get ears for police.* Thanks for keeping last letter back till I got to work again." (My italics.) Note that this postcard, which shows evidence of having been written in haste, was mailed on September 30, which was a Sunday, and that nothing had yet appeared in the press concerning the double murder.

Note also that the writer knows perfectly the contents of the earlier letter, which had not, of course, been made public. Indeed, he is resuming a crazy monologue which had been broken off by an interval of murder. Only the Whitechapel killer could have known that an attempt had been made "to clip the lady's ears off." Therefore the Whitechapel killer and the letter writer must have been one and the same person. (The information that Elizabeth Stride "squealed a bit" is tossed in gratuitously. Her squeals would, in all likelihood, have been drowned out by the community singing which emanated from the International Workmen's Educational Club in Berner Street, and which several witnesses testified to hearing at the time of the murder.)

5

I am indebted to Donald McCormick's fascinating book on Jack the Ripper for information concerning a detailed analysis of the Ripper letters made by Dr. Thomas Dutton. Dr. Dutton, who was thirty two years old at the time of the Whitechapel murders and living in Westbourne Villas, Bayswater, London, was a close crony of Inspector Abberline, of Scotland Yard, with whom he discussed the murders often. (Dr. Dutton's housekeeper was of the opinion that he had assisted at the postmortem on one of the Ripper victims, but I can find no record of this.) When the doctor died in 1935 at the age of seventy nine he left behind him three volumes of handwritten "Chronicles of Crime" which he had compiled over a sixty-year period. It was upon these that Mr. McCormick drew heavily in gathering materials for his own book, *The Identity of Jack the Ripper*. Prior to the Whitechapel murders Dr. Dutton had been a keen student of microphotography, as well as being a leading figure in the Chichester and West Sussex Microscopic Society, and it was this specialized knowledge which he brought to bear on the Ripper correspondence.

Dr. Dutton made microphotographs of 128 specimens of the "Jack the Ripper" correspondence, which had been sent to the police, to the Central News Agency and to individuals. Of these he satisfied himself that at least thirty four were in the same handwriting.[2] Jack the Ripper was no skilled forger, in Dutton's opinion; he made the error of forming his C's, H's, R's, and T's in a variety of ways, whereas a practiced forger would have been content with few variations. "Possibly he wanted the police to think that not all his letters were written by the same person. If so, he certainly succeeded in foxing some of them." The doctor blamed the police for treating the letters lightly. "They [the police] assumed that several hoaxers were at work and therefore regarded every new letter or warning received as of no significance."

Analyzing the thirty four letters which he felt to be the genuine article, Dr. Dutton notes that the handwriting was sometimes disguised to appear as that of a semi-literate person, on other occasions it was the neat script of an office clerk. The

[2] Not all the specimens Dr. Dutton examined were in prose. Typical of Jack's efforts at versifying is the moritat reproduced below. Note the reference to Gladstone, which was the crying scandal of the day; note also the knowledge of the East End shown by the reference to Henage Court:

> Eight little whores, with no hope of heaven,
> Gladstone may save one, then there'll be seven.
> Seven little whores begging for a shilling.
> One stays in Henage-court, then there's a killing.
>
> Six little whores, glad to be alive.
> One sidles up to Jack, then there are five.
> Four and whore rhyme aright, so do three and me,
> I'll set the town alight, ere there are two.
>
> Two little whores, shivering with fright,
> Seek a cosy doorway, in the middle of the night.
> Jack's knife flashes, then there's but one.
> And the last one's the ripest for Jack's idea of fun.

same with the language, which sometimes bristled with slang and such self-conscious Americanisms as "Boss." Sometimes Jack would deliberately misspell a word, such as "Juwes," which he scrawled on the wall in Goulston Street; but the word was spelled correctly at other times. (Dr. Dutton, incidentally, claims that he photographed the wall writing at the request of the police; he was thus in a position to compare it with the handwriting of the letters.)

That the Ripper may have kept on the move between murders is indicated by the fact that Dr. Dutton identified two letters from Liverpool and one postmarked Glasgow as being in the handwriting of the original letter. The first of the Liverpool letters was dated September 29 and read: Beware, I shall be at work on the 1st and 2nd inst. in Minories at twelve midnight and I give the authorities a good chance, but there is never a policeman near when I am at work." Its interest lies in the fact that Mitre Square is located not far from the Minories in East London. Although the writer has erred by a day or two as to the date of his next killing, still one would not expect him to pinpoint the exact date of the crime, any more than one would expect him to tip off Scotland Yard as to the exact place and time.

The second Liverpool letter gave a Prince William Street address and stated simply: "What fools the police are. I even give them the name of the street where I am living." From Glasgow Jack wrote: "Think I'll quit using my nice sharp knife. Too good for whores. Have come here to buy a Scotch dirk. Ha! Ha! That will tickle up their ovaries." Dr. Dutton adds: "The only mention in the press of a specific organ being removed from the Ripper's victim concerned the kidneys. Though the ovaries were on one occasion cut out of a body, the press merely referred to the removal of 'a certain organ.' "

In the end, the Victorians rejected the Ripper correspondence *in toto* as a series of poison pen hoaxes, a conclusion with which the police were inclined to agree. As Donald McCormick observes, "Subconsciously, the Victorian psychological viewpoint manifested itself; that is to say, they could not imagine a mad man making a joke about his crimes. A maniac, they argued falsely, must be a person without a sense of humour."[3]

6

Catherine Eddowes, alias Kate Conway, alias Kate Kelly was buried on Monday afternoon, October 8, with something approaching military honors. By one o'clock not more than a score of people had gathered in front of the City mortuary in Golden Lane, but a quarter of an hour later the number had swelled to several hundred, this being the lunch hour for City clerks and office workers.

Meanwhile, Eddowes's remains had been placed in a coffin of polished elm with oak moldings and black furniture, which had been donated by an undertaker in nearby Banner Street, and which bore a metal plate with the inscription: "Catherine Eddowes, Died September 30, 1888, Aged 43 Years." The coffin, in turn, was placed in an open glass car drawn by a pair of horses and escorted by a strong force of City police under Superintendent Foster as far as the boundary of the ancient City of London, where the escort was taken over by Metropolitan police under Inspector Barnham. The irony was, of course, that these same City police who now paid their respects to the dead woman had had her in their custody scarcely a week before as "drunk and disorderly." Eddowes was followed to her grave by her four sisters, all dressed in black, and by the man she had lived with, John Kelly. (The press made no mention of her daughter Annie nor of Thomas Conway, alias Thomas Quinn, the reluctant army pensioner, and his two sons,

[3] Donald McCormick, *The Identity of Jack the Ripper*. London: 1959.

though they may have attended the funeral.) A third coach contained newspaper reporters.

The cortege passed St. Mary's, Whitechapel, and moved along Mile End Road, where the sidewalk was lined five-deep with spectators, and so through Bow and Stratford-atte-Bow. "Many bystanders uncovered their heads as the hearse passed," the *East London Observer* reported. "Along the whole route great sympathy was expressed for the relatives." At Ilford cemetery nearly 500 people had gathered to witness the interment. The service was conducted by the Reverend T. Dunscombe, the cemetery chaplain, and was brief, no reference being made to the murder. In startling contrast, Elizabeth Stride was hustled into a pauper's grave as quickly and as secretly as possible.

CHAPTER XII

THE APPROACHING STORM

"IN THE LONG history of crime it has very, very seldom happened that a woman has betrayed one who has taken refuge with her," writes Mrs. Belloc Lowndes in her novel *The Lodger* which is based on Jack the Ripper. "So far, perhaps because she is subject rather than citizen, her duty as a component part of civilized society weighs but lightly on woman's shoulders." Mrs. Lowndes offers this curious, almost Oriental, reasoning as an explanation why the landlady heroine of her book cannot bring herself to turn over to the police the lodger, Mr. Sleuth, whom she suspects of being a serial murderer. As for Mr. Sleuth, he is pictured as a religious fanatic who spends his days poring over the Bible with a copy of *Cruden's Concordance* at his elbow, and his nights prowling the streets of London in search of women upon whom to wreak God's vengeance. To the skirts of his victims he pins a triangular piece of paper with the words, "The Avenger," printed in red ink.[1]

Mrs. Lowndes was not alone in believing that Jack the Ripper was not to be found among the ragtail and bob-ends of the

[1] Mrs. Lowndes's novel, which was first published in 1913, was to make not only her fortune, but the fortunes of several film companies which made celluloid versions of it. As for Mrs. Lowndes making the Ripper a religious zealot, Mrs. Susan Lowndes Marques, her daughter, writes from Estoril, Portugal: "My mother had a 'plot mind,' and I think she suddenly thought of that particular explanation as being a reasonable one in the case of these murders. She did this in other novels such as *Letty Lyton,* which is based on the case of Madeleine Smith."

doss houses. Others, too, held the view that the Ripper was hidden in the bosom of some respectable family who looked upon him trustingly as a paying guest.

For example, Walter Sickert, the painter, used to dine out on the story that he had once lived in digs in North London formerly occupied by the Ripper. He knew positively the identity of the killer, Sickert told Sir Osbert Sitwell. Jack was, in reality, a consumptive veterinary student given to nocturnal prowling. "The landlord and landlady would hear him come in about six in the morning, and then walk about in his room for an hour or two until the first edition of the morning paper was on sale, when he would creep lightly downstairs and run to the corner to buy one. Quietly he would return and go to bed; but an hour later, when the old man called him he would notice, by the traces in the fireplace, that his lodger had burnt the suit he had been wearing the previous evening."[2] Before they could make up their minds to call the police, the lodger's health had suddenly taken a turn for the worse; and his mother, a widow, had come to fetch him home to Bournemouth. From that moment the murders ceased.

Sickert scribbled the name of the lodger in pencil in the margin of a copy of Casanova's *Memoirs* belonging to Sitwell, but when Sir Osbert came to look for it he found that the book had been destroyed in the Blitz.[3] The painter evidently told the same story to Max Beerbohm, for in one of Beerbohm's notebooks, auctioned at Sotheby's in December, 1960, he had written after Sickert's name: "Extreme of refinement . . ." There followed a long arrow leading to a marginal note: "Love of squalor. Lodged in Jack the Ripper's house."

[2] Sir Osbert Sitwell, *Noble Essences,* being the fifth and last volume of his autobiography, *Left Hand, Right Hand.* London: Macmillan, 1950.

[3] When I wrote querying him concerning Sickert's address at the time in question, Sir Osbert Sitwell replied that he could not recall it. His brother, Sacheverell, writes, however: "Mr. Sickert was living in Mornington Crescent, London, N.W. I do not know the number of the house."

2

Nearly six weeks had gone by now without a sign of Jack the Ripper. No longer were the dark courts and alleyways of Whitechapel the scene of Grand Guignol. No longer were the peaceful citizens awakened from their sleep by the sound of police whistles and the terrible cry of "Murder!" Had the Ripper committed his last crime? Or was he merely lying in wait of a more propitious time to strike? Londoners had no way of knowing. All they knew was that he had apparently gone to earth; and, as a consequence, they began to breathe freely once more, and those who lived east of Aldgate to take to the streets at night.

Then, just as it began to appear that the whole business had been nothing more than a terrible nightmare, the following item appeared in the Paris edition of the *New York Herald,* under date of November 7, 1888: "A woman found stabbed on the Boulevard de la Chapelle last night stated that a man attacked her and stabbed her with a knife, saying he was 'Jack the Ripper' and had already killed ten women in London and two in Paris. He is believed to be mad and is still at large." It was like the distant roll of thunder which heralds the approaching storm.

For events now moved swiftly to bring the bloody career of Jack the Ripper to a climax, and, with it, to encompass the downfall of his opponent, Sir Charles Warren. All too soon Londoners were to be witness to one of the most fiendish murders in British crime annals. Unlike the Whitechapel murders that had gone before, this one was to take on an almost ritualistic character. Was Jack the Ripper entirely a free agent? One sometimes gets the impression that he was an actor in some primordial drama whose sacerdotal meaning has been obscured if not lost in time. Curiously, the other important figure in this drama was to be none other than the Lord Mayor-elect of

London. These two, the Cain-like figure with the knife and the Lord Mayor in his sable-trimmed robes, take on an almost archetypal significance, like Gog and Magog, or the Dame and the Principal Boy in the Christmas pantomime.

Yet the Rt. Hon. James Whitehead, the Lord Mayor-elect, was a personage in his own right. A Bradford merchant who had made his way in the City, he was noted for his charities and his interest in prison reform. He was chairman of the Board of Visitors to Borstal, founded the Penny-a-Week Collection for Metropolitan Hospitals. He opposed the government of the day on the Irish question, being a Gladstone Liberal and in favor of Home Rule.

It is as a symbol, however, that we are here concerned with Alderman Whitehead. Certainly it would be difficult to imagine anything more splendidly symbolic than the Lord Mayor's office which he had been elected to fill, and which dated back to the thirteenth century. For example, as Lord Mayor, Alderman Whitehead's symbolic status was only that of an earl; yet in that magic square mile known as the City, he took precedence over every subject of the Crown, not accepting members of the Royal Family.

The rites connected with the election of a Lord Mayor are as prescribed and formal as those connected with the succession of the priesthood of Diana at Arisia. They reach their climax on November 9 when the incoming Lord Mayor is sworn in by the Lord Chief Justice at the Royal Law Courts in the Strand. It is with this bit of pageantry, known as the Lord Mayor's Show, that presently we will be concerned. For Jack the Ripper chose to commit his final and most spectacular crime on this glittering occasion. The crime was to be remembered long after the Lord Mayor's Show of 1888, and the Lord Mayor himself were forgotten.

3

Meanwhile Sir Charles Warren suddenly found himself in serious trouble over an article he had written for *Murray's Magazine* without the prior approval of his immediate superior, the Home Secretary. In this article Sir Charles succeeded in the seemingly impossible task of uniting all of his enemies, and of throwing into their camp many of his well-wishers and friends as well. Above all, he antagonized the Gladstone Liberals who were then sitting in Opposition in Parliament.

Painting a lurid picture of London as being in the grips of a "mob stirred into spasmodic action by restless demagogues," Warren wrote: "It is deplorable that successive governments have not had the courage to make a stand against the more noisy section of these people, and *it is still more to be regretted that ex-Ministers, now in Opposition, have not hesitated to embarrass those in power by smiling on the insurgent mob.*" (My italics.) "If we search history during the present century," the police chief continued, "we shall find that down to 1886 the mob or rabble exercised a decided influence over the destinies of London." (It was in 1886, it will be recalled, that Sir Charles became Metropolitan Police Commissioner.)

The trouble with Londoners, Sir Charles opined, was that they were fickle in their attitude toward the police. "This violently fickle conduct is endangering the discipline of the force, encouraging the mob to disorder and rapine . . ." The Police Commissioner thought that they ordered these things better on the Continent. "Across the Channel the police are masters of the situation," he wrote with ill-concealed admiration. "The public give way before them, and the press does not venture to discuss their operations, to embarrass and hinder their inquiries, or to publish their results."

The police chief saved his biggest bombshell for the last. Back in August, Warren, it will be recalled, had forced the resignation of James Monro as Chief of the Criminal Investigation Division, Scotland Yard. He had done this by placing his own resignation on the Home Secretary's desk with the ultimatum, "Either Monro goes or I go." On this occasion Warren had prevailed, but Home Secretary Matthews continued to consult with Monro on the sly about police matters, including the organization of the CID itself. Warren was aware of these backstairs consultations, and it was this which rankled with him.

There had always existed a sharp division of power between the Metropolitan Police Commissioner and the CID head, the two bureaus being entirely separate. Warren now asserted the supremacy of the former over the latter. "It was clearly intended that he [the CID head] should be subordinate to the Commissioner of Police," he wrote, "and everyone who knows anything of police duties must be aware that it was quite impractical for police work to be done efficiently under two heads, the one independent of the other." Coming from a senior civil servant, this assertion in cold print amounted to heresy and was bound to cause repercussions in Parliament. But before Nemesis finally caught up with Sir Charles he was to figure in a richly comic episode which started innocently enough with an editorial in *The Times.*

4

"Twelve years ago," *The Times* editorial began, "a murder at Blackburn was traced out by the help of a bloodhound, and thanks to the sagacious instinct of the dog, the murderer was convicted." If it worked at Blackburn, why not in Whitechapel? So reasoned the newspaper which was sometimes called The Thunderer.

Times readers needed no more than a hint. The Master of Foxhounds of a Sussex hunt immediately demanded that he be given a clear field in Whitechapel and environs, guaranteeing that he would soon "root out this dastardly fiend." And, indeed, it looked for a time as though the East End would resound to the clatter of the pink coat and stirrup-cup set. Fortunately, the hunting gentry were persuaded to confine their activities to the letters columns of the daily press.

Bloodhounds not only excited strong passions in the breasts of foxhunters — they were a positive menace to dairymen, according to a breeder of York Hill, Loughton, writing to the *Pall Mall Gazette*. "If a country-trained hound were allowed to make casts in, say High-Street, Whitechapel," he wrote, "I should expect to find it next minute in some innocent butterman's shop intent, not upon the murderer, but upon the margarine it scented from afar." In fact, bloodhounds were inclined to get intent upon just about everything with the possible exception of blood, the sight of which was enough to stop them dead in their tracks, according to another *Times* reader. Consequently, fugitives had been known to spill some of their own blood in order to put these sapient beasts off the scent.

The merits and demerits of the so-called "clean shoe" method of tracking were likewise discussed in *The Times*. The advantage of the "clean shoe" method according to Edwin Brough, of Scarborough, was that a hound so trained could "follow the trail of a man whose shoes have not been prepared in any way by the application of blood or aniseed" (not that the Ripper was likely to smear his boots with either).

Mr. Brough, who identified himself as a dog breeder of twenty years' standing, was willing to back the English breed of bloodhound against all comers, including the Cuban bloodhound, which had been used for slave-hunting. "Our English bloodhound," he wrote, "is infinitely superior to this or to any other breed in natural scenting power, for, luckily, our breeders have developed the long, narrow, peaked head and immense flews, always associated with this faculty, to an extent never known before."

Mr. Brough argued his case so convincingly that Sir Charles Warren, to his undying regret, invited him to come up to London and to bring with him a couple of the hounds of the "sagacious instinct" and the "immense flews." The Scarborough breeder promptly accepted and arrived in London with Barnaby and Burgho, whom *The Times* described as "two magnificent animals," Burgho having a head that measured twelve inches in length.

Trials were started immediately in Regent's Park, with Sir Charles Warren as an interested spectator. Despite a thick coating of hoarfrost on the ground, the hounds, on this first occasion, were able to track for nearly a mile a young man who had been given a fifteen-minute head start. In Hyde Park that same night the dogs were hunted again, but this time on a leash — "as would be the case if they were employed in Whitechapel," *The Times* noted. In all, half a dozen runs were made with inconclusive results.

The genius who persuaded Sir Charles Warren to allow himself to be tracked by Barnaby and Burgho will probably never be known (rumor has it that it was one of his enemies in the Home Office); however, it is a matter of record that on two occasions Sir Charles himself played the role of the hunted man. Nor was this all. On October 19 *The Times* carried the following item: "Sir Charles Warren's bloodhounds were out for practice at Tooting yesterday morning and were lost. Telegrams have been dispatched to all the Metropolitan Police stations stating that if seen anywhere, information is to be immediately sent to Scotland Yard."

Mr. Watkin W. Williams, Sir Charles Warren's grandson, defends the use of bloodhounds. "The use of tracker dogs by the police was at that time an innovation which had so far only been tried out in the country districts," Williams explains in a recent letter to me. "Although my grandfather doubted whether they could effectively be used in Whitechapel, he felt that the experiment must be tried." The Ripper's "murderous activities ceased during the period that the hounds were in London, and recommenced only after their return to their owner," he points out. But Sir Melville Macnaghten's comment is characteristically blunt. "It should have been obvious that bloodhounds were useless in Whitechapel," he remarks. "I cannot conceive of a more impossible locality in which to expect hounds to work."

Unfortunately, the last had not yet been heard of these beasts. Burgho and Barnaby, or rather their ghosts, were to raise their long, narrow heads with the immense flews once again in the Ripper case, and to disastrous effect. But this is getting ahead of the story.

5

In deference to the mood of the unemployed, who had been cutting up rough of late, the Lord Mayor-elect, Alderman Whitehead, decided to curtail drastically the pageantry of the Lord Mayor's Show, and to donate to charity the money thus saved. *The Times* sought to put a gloss on the matter: "Alderman Whitehead is opposed to the introduction of the circus element and allegorical displays, which neither accord with his tastes nor, in his opinion, with the dignity of the city." But the truth was that the Lord Mayor-elect feared that there would be serious disturbances along the route of the procession.

Alderman Whitehead's decision to do away with the "circus element" in the Lord Mayor's Show did not go down well with the press. *Punch* opined that there were to be "no gals in tights seated on globes as Britannia," while The *Daily Telegraph* warned that allegorical tableaux illustrating incidents from the lives of Dick Whittington and Wat Tyler were "not to be sneered at as theatrical." *Reynolds News* had some timely suggestions for allegorical figures: Sir Charles Warren followed by a bevy of detectives blindfolded, an effigy of Jack the Ripper, and a *tableaux mort* composed of the Victims of Whitechapel. The paper also suggested that the banners bear such devices as *Waste, Dirt, Misery, Extravagance, Disease* and *Jobbery.*

On Guy Fawkes Night there was a brief clash between merrymakers and police on Clerkenwell Green, during which the latter confiscated a scarecrow figure. It turned out to be an effigy of Sir Charles Warren, complete with chimney-pot hat, which a group of Socialists were planning to burn. *Justice,* organ of the Social Democratic Federation, charged that Warren employed spies to circulate among workingmen and ferret out such information "They (the police) may not be able to find Jack the Ripper, but they were able to discover the fell design of the wicked Socialists to burn their great chief in effigy."

But worse was in store for the unhappy police commissioner. On November 8 he was rebuked by the Home Secretary for the indiscreet article which he had written for *Murray's Magazine.* To make the insult appear more calculated, Henry Matthews, the Home Secretary, did not deign to write to Warren directly, but had one of his underlings do it in a letter which began, "Sir, Mr. Secretary Matthews directs me to state —" The letter enclosed a copy of a Home Office circular of May 27, 1879, forbidding officers of the department to publicize any work relating to the Department without the Home Secretary's permission. It closed with the cold warning, "I am accordingly to request that, in the future, the terms of this order may be strictly compiled with." It was brutal, and Warren had little option but to resign. He decided, however, to go down with all guns firing, and in his letter of resignation he openly defied the Home Secretary:

> Sir, I have received a pressing and confidential letter stating that a Home Office circular of May 27, 1879 is intended to apply to the Metropolitan Police Force.

Had I been told that such a circular was in force, I should not have accepted the post of Commissioner of Police. My duties and those of the Metropolitan Police are governed by statute *and the Secretary of State for the Home Department has not the power under the statute of issuing orders for the police force.* (My italics.)

The circular, if put in force, would practically enable everyone anonymously to attack the police force without in any way permitting the Commissioner to correct false statements, which I have been in the habit of doing, whenever I found necessary, for nearly three years past.

I desire to say that I entirely decline to accept these instructions with regard to the Commissioner of Police, and I have again to place my resignation in the hands of Her Majesty's government.

The Home Secretary's reply was brief:

In my judgment the claim put forward by you as Commissioner of Police is altogether inadmissible, and accordingly I have only to accept your resignation.

It took two days, however, for this acceptance to be transmitted through channels, so that on the eve of the Lord Mayor's Show Sir Charles was left dangling in an official limbo. But Jack the Ripper could not wait for Warren's resignation to take effect. Already this mysterious assassin, who had been idle for six weeks, was on his way to No. 13 Miller's Court off Dorset Street to keep a rendezvous with Mary Jane Kelly, known to some as "Black Mary."

CHAPTER XIII

BLACK MARY

MARIE JEANETTE KELLY was not like most of the street women in the East End of London. They were old and ugly. She was young and good-looking . . . She did not have to walk the streets to earn food and lodging, as the others had to do." Thus does Leonard Matters, an Australian-born journalist and onetime Labor Member of Parliament, begin his highly romanticized account of the Ripper's ultimate victim, May Jane Kelly, aged twenty-five.[1]

And having begun in this vein, Matters finds it necessary to invent a phony French background, including French parents for Kelly. ("Probably she had some knowledge of French, and when she went to France with a 'gentleman' . . . she felt quite at home even though she said she preferred London to Paris.") Conveniently he has her born in Cardiff, Wales, because Cardiff was "a port of almost international character." "From Cardiff to London," Matters explains, "was a natural step for a young, smart girl who had discovered that she was very attractive to men."

Once arrived in London, the next obvious step for such an attractive young girl was to set herself up in a brothel in the fashionable West End, according to Matters. Immediately we are transported into the gay world of casinos, oyster rooms and supper clubs that abounded off Piccadilly. We have visions of

[1] Leonard Matters, *The Mystery of Jack the Ripper.* London: 1928.

Marie Jeanette being toasted in champagne. But when next we hear of her, two years later in the Matters account, she has unaccountably plummeted from West London to the East End in what must surely be one of the most rapid descents on record. ("From the luxury of the West-end she plunged straight down to the squalor of Whitechapel. From Piccadilly she took one stride on to the Ratcliffe-highway.") But even in Whitechapel "Marie was still almost an aristocrat among the street women," her chronicler claims. "Everybody knew she had only lately 'come down in the world,' that her recent past had been as luxurious as it had been vivid." Of such stuff are legends born.

Before examining the reality behind it, it is only fair to point out that Kelly herself was partly responsible for propagating this legend. She did it, no doubt, to compensate for the drabness of the present and the even dingier prospect of the future. I have already remarked on the propensity of the Ripper victims, Elizabeth Stride in particular, to invent for themselves existences that were larger than life. But of all the mythomaniacs we have encountered so far, Mary Jane Kelly, or Black Mary, as they called her, was the most pronounced. She seemed incapable of stating a fact without embroidering upon it. What Leonard Matters has done is to accept her story uncritically and to pass it on with a few embellishments of his own.

On only two points are those who knew Black Mary in agreement: she was a striking-looking woman, unlike the crones whom Jack the Ripper picked as his other victims; and she loved her gin, a trait which she shared with those other sisters in extremis. Kelly was blue-eyed, had a fine head of hair which reached nearly to her waist. In spite of the drink, she seems never to have lost the fresh-colored, outdoor complexion which she had brought with her from Ireland. I talked to a retired market porter named Dennis Barrett who, as a boy, knew Black Mary by sight. "She was a handsome woman," Barrett recalled, "tall and rather stout. She had her pitch outside The Ten Bells pub in Commercial Street, and woe to any woman who tried to poach her territory — such a woman was likely to have her hair pulled out in fistfuls." In short, Black Mary was a bit of a terror.

2

Mary Kelly was born in Limerick, not in Cardiff, and her parents were Irish Catholic and not French, as Matters would have it. Her family did move, when Mary Jane was quite young, to Carmarthenshire, Wales, where her father, John Kelly, became foreman in an ironworks. At the age of sixteen she married a collier named Davies, but the marriage came to a tragic end a year or two later when Davies was killed in a mine explosion. There were no children as far as I have been able to make out. The mine owners stalled for eighteen months before paying her a miserable pittance by way of a widow's compensation; and it was this delay, according to her friends, which drove Black Mary onto the streets, first in the "Tiger Bay" region of Cardiff, and later in London.

In London she seems to have made a beeline for the East End and its stews. There is absolutely no evidence to support the assertion that she had installed herself in a West End brothel, or that she had ever enjoyed the gay night life of the Haymarket and Piccadilly. This, like the interlude which she is supposed to have spent in Paris with a "gentleman," appears to be complete invention. Instead, she seems to have hustled in the notorious Ratcliffe Highway for a time, then to have lived with a number of rough types in Stepney and Bethnal Green, before ending up with Joseph Barnett, a fish porter at Billingsgate with whom she remained for nearly two years. When found murdered she was three months pregnant.

Black Mary seems to have lived in fear of Jack the Ripper, according to Barnett. "I used to buy newspapers and read her all the details of the Ripper murders," he claimed. It was a fear she shared with all the other drabs of Dorset Street, among whom she stood out as a sort of Amazon Queen. For one of the murder victims, Annie Chapman, had lived in Dorset Street for a time, and Hanbury Street, the scene of the Chapman murder, was located only two hundred yards away.

3

Dorset Street (now Duval Street), on which the shadow of Christ Church, Spitalfields, falls, was a law unto itself in the sense that its inhabitants respected none of the laws that ordinarily govern men. Long ago they had run up the Jolly Roger on society in general, and they defied anyone to make them haul it down.

"It was a toss-up whether it or Ratcliffe Highway could claim the honor of being London's worst crime street," writes Detective Sergeant Leeson in his memoirs. "Dorset Street was known to local people as the 'do as you please,' and it quite justified its title," he adds. Many a constable, hot in pursuit of some fugitive from justice, had been known to stop dead in his tracks when the miscreant made for the shelter of Dorset Street. To carry the pursuit further, unless in the company of strong police reinforcements, might have been worth a policeman's life.

Dennis Barrett, the retired market porter whom I talked to, knew Dorset Street well, and he described to me some of its characters. The old man came from a long line of costers, his mother having had a fruit stall at the Royal Exchange. When I talked to him he was living in a council flat at Stoke Newington, and he proudly showed me a framed telegram from the queen congratulating him on his diamond wedding anniversary.

"One of the worst characters in Dorset Street," he recalled, "was Mad Jack O'Brien, an Irishman with shoulders like a boxer. He never wore a shirt, and he would fight anyone. He would go from pub to pub, and the owners would stand him free drinks just to get rid of him." Then there were Tommy No-Legs and Mrs. Flower-of-the-Flock. Tommy, who had two wooden stumps for legs, sold matches outside the Bank of England, and when he got roaring drunk, as he frequently did, he would unstrap one of his wooden extremities and use it to smash up a pub.

As for Mrs. Flower-of-the-Flock — "God knows how she came by that name, for she was the terror of Whitechapel," Barrett explained. "Even the police were afraid to arrest her when she was drunk. She used to make toy whips for children, and she always carried a knife in her bodice. I saw her use that knife once," the porter continued, sobering with the recollection. "She pulled it on a man standing outside The Golden Hart. Slashed him right across the face, she did."

It was among such flotsam that Mary Kelly drifted on Thursday night, November 8, borne along by the tide, yet remaining curiously aloof as befit an Amazon Queen. Occasionally she stopped for a quick one at one or another of the pubs along Commercial Street where with one swift glance she took in the trade possibilities at the bar counter. Finding no likely customer, Kelly moved on.

Somewhere in this same sea of humanity another pair of eyes watched for the main chance. The anonymous killer who signed himself Jack the Ripper, too, was adrift in Whitechapel and being borne slowly, but irresistibly toward Black Mary, his compass being set on collision course, so to speak.

Not far away, in Cheapside, sign painters were feverishly putting the finishing touches to the banners that would form part of the Lord Mayor's procession on the morrow. The palimpsests were emblazoned with such devices as *Labour Omnia Vincit, Honour and Probity, Mercantile Success,* as descriptive of the qualities which the Rt. Hon. James Whitehead, the Lord Mayor-elect, embodied.

At Scotland Yard, too, the lights blazed late into the night. There Sir Charles Warren, whose resignation had not yet been accepted, was making last-minute preparations to cope with the socialist uprising which he, alone, anticipated on the morrow. To forestall this uprising Sir Charles had issued the following order: "No person, unless forming part of the Lord Mayor's procession, shall be allowed to deliver any public speech, or to carry placards or banners, in any street or thoroughfare through which the Lord Mayor's procession passes."

But Warren, who was inclined to see an anarchist under every bed, took no chance that this order would be disobeyed. He had detailed forty mounted police to augment the City police along the line of march, while Trafalgar Square was to have "a strong body of police, mounted and on foot," according to *The Times.* Now, as he stuck his colored pins into a map showing the route of the march, and twiddled with his bits of string, Sir Charles seemed to have foreseen every contingency but one — murder.

4

Mary Ann Cox, a widow who had taken to whoring, lived in Miller's Court, a narrow, evil-looking passage leading off of Dorset Street and containing six cribs which were known collectively as "M'Carthy's Rents." (They were owned by one John M'Carthy, who had a ship chandler's shop in Dorset Street.)

It was toward these digs that the widow Cox was headed at about eleven forty-five Thursday night when she spotted Mary Kelly coming out of The Britannia pub on the corner. Black Mary was no stranger to The Britannia. Many was the time she had rushed into this pub, after rolling some drunken sailor, to swap shawls with one of the other whores there. Thus disguised, she would take to the streets again, knowing that the police would be looking for her under a different description.

But this night Mary wore no shawl. Instead, she had on a dark red pelerine, and her hair, which she usually kept neatly pinned up, had tumbled down around her shoulders. She was, in fact, drunk, and she was not alone.

The man with Black Mary was short, stout and wore a round billycock hat, according to the widow Cox. About thirty-eight years of age, he had a blotchy face, a full, carroty mustache, and he was carrying a pail of beer in one hand. The widow followed the couple as they turned up Miller's Court, and said goodnight to them on Kelly's doorstep. Black Mary said goodnight; then, in a burst of foolish affability, announced, "Now I am going to have a song." The widow saw the couple enter No. 13, Kelly's room, then she heard the girl begin a sentimental Irish ballad, "Only a violet I plucked for my mother's grave." The voice might have been pleasing had its owner been sober, the widow reflected; as it was, it was thin, tearful and uncertain of the notes. The Cox woman remained in her room about a quarter of an hour, and when she came out she heard Kelly still singing, "Zillah, darling one, I plucked it and brought it to you," the husky voice quavered.

There was a light in Kelly's room, and she was still singing when the widow Cox returned at one o'clock, she claimed. By that time it had begun to rain, and so she remained by the fire a few minutes warming her hands before taking to the streets again. (The widow Cox seems to have been singularly restless this night, or rather, she seems to have had no luck in finding custom.) When she returned at three o'clock, the light was out in Kelly's room, and there was not a sound.

5

It rained intermittently during the night, with the result that roadworkers appeared early and began scattering fine gravel along the Victoria Embankment where the Lord Mayor's procession would pass, to prevent the horses hoofs from slipping. It would not do to have the chestnut mounts of the 10th Hussars, "The Princess of Wales' Own," sliding around on the wet pavement. November 9 was not only the date of the Lord Mayor's Show, it was the birthday of the Prince of Wales; and now, as if by way of reminder, guns began to boom in royal salute from the Tower of London and from the Horse Guards Parade. ("Dear Bertie's birthday," Queen Victoria noted in her diary. "May God bless him: He has a warm affectionate heart, and is a very dutiful and good son.")

From early morning the Greenyard, as the City stables were called, was the scene of tremendous bustle, as the Lord Mayor's coach had been brought there for harnessing. Built in 1757, the coach was a baroque affair, all gilt and ornateness, with painted panels attributed to Cipriani. The six shires that were to draw the coach ordinarily were employed by a local brewery, but on this occasion they were gaily caparisoned, and their drivers and "trouncers" had exchanged their brown uniforms and sugar-loaf hats for ceremonial scarlet and gold.

At ten o'clock that morning, while the Lord Mayor's coach was being put in readiness, John M'Carthy was in his chandler's shop in Dorset Street going over his books. Running a practiced finger down the ledger he noted that Mary Kelly was six weeks in arrears with her rent. Ordinarily, the rent for her room, which was 4*s.* 6*d.* per week, was payable in advance on a weekly basis, but M'Carthy, who liked Black Mary, had allowed himself to be put off by promises and blarney until now the sum due, he realized with a start, amounted to twenty-nine shillings.

"Bowyer," he called to his assistant, "go around to No. 13 Miller's Court and see what you can collect from the Kelly woman on the rent she owes us. She's been stalling us for weeks," he continued, throwing down his pen in disgust. "Tell her that from now on it's cash in advance, and that if she doesn't start paying off her arrears I'll have the bailiff on her. Remember," he cautioned his assistant, "don't come back empty-handed." Although he had only to duck around the corner to call on Mary Kelly, Thomas Bowyer reached for his hat, as though this piece of apparel somehow made his visit official. It was 10:45 A.M.

The Rt. Hon. James Whitehead was then in an antechamber of Mansion House robing for the ceremony which lay ahead. As he donned the scarlet gown, which was lined with white silk and edged with real sable, the Lord Mayor-elect had time to reflect upon the almost mystical nature of the ritual in which he was to figure. Even the insignia that he would handle was of uncertain provenance. His Lordship's crystal mace, which was spirally mounted with gold, was thought to date from Anglo-Saxon times, though no one knew for certain. Similarly, the frayed cloth-of-gold purse which was handed ceremonially to the incoming Lord Mayor may have been a gift from Elizabeth I. Still, no one knew, just as no one knew why aromatic herbs were scattered on the dais at Guildhall after a new Lord Mayor had been elected. It was enough that these things had once been invested with meaning for them to be lovingly preserved now.

The guns were still booming their birthday greeting to the heir apparent when Bowyer knocked at the door of No. 13 Miller's Court. Getting no reply, he knocked again, more insistently. "Lazy bitch," he muttered, "sleeping all day and whorin' all night." Next he tried the door only to find it locked. Being a rent collector Bowyer did not hesitate to apply his eye to the keyhole and he was surprised to find the key was missing. "Either she's bolted it from the inside, or she's done a flit," he thought aloud, and he rattled the door handle once more.

Around the corner and at right angles to the door were two windows which looked out upon dustbins and a water tap used by all the tenants of "M'Carthy's Rents." Bowyer remembered that the smaller of the windows had two broken panes, relic of a memorable row between Kelly and her paramour Joseph Barnett, and he discovered that the aperture thus formed was just large enough to pass a hand through. Dexterously he inserted his own hand through the crack, taking care to avoid the jagged edges of glass, and twitched the flimsy muslin curtain aside. What he saw as his eyes gradually adjusted to the murkiness within caused him to cry out in horror and to withdraw his hand so quickly that he almost cut it on the glass.

The wretched hovel which Mary Kelly called home was about twelve feet square and sparsely furnished. To the left of the window and directly opposite the door was a fireplace above which hung a cheap print titled, ironically enough, "The Fisherman's Widow." It was the room's sole attempt at decoration. In the far corner an open cupboard revealed a few bits of crockery, some empty ginger-beer bottles, and a crust of bread. From there the eye traveled downward to the bed, which was the chief article of furniture in the room. The bedclothes had been ripped off and lay tangled with bloodstained garments at the foot of the bed. Upon the blood-soaked mattress lay a raw mass of human flesh that had once been Mary Kelly. Between the bed and a nearby table Jack the Ripper had performed an operation, a cold blooded experiment in anatomy which for sheer horror would be difficult to surpass, as I can attest after having seen a police photograph of the results.

The poor woman lay on her back, entirely naked. Her throat had been cut from ear to ear, right down to the spinal column. Her ears and nose had been cut off, and the face otherwise slashed until its features were completely obliterated. The stomach and abdomen had been ripped open, the liver removed and placed on the right thigh. The lower portion of the body, including the uterus, had been cut out.

There were bloodstains even on the wall. Laid out on the table beside the bed was the final horror. There, like pieces in a nauseating jigsaw, were what first appeared to be little mounds of flesh, but which proved to be the victim's breasts. Symmetrically arranged alongside them were her heart and kidneys. It was like the work of some mad charcutier. There were even bits of flesh hanging from the picture-frame nails.

Bowyer did not stay long enough to take in all of these details, but ran to fetch his employer, who returned with him to Kelly's room and peered through the window. "The sight I saw was even more ghastly than I had prepared myself for," M'Carthy commented later. "All those lumps of flesh lying on the table — it was more the work of a devil than of a man."

6

Low women in pattens, high ladies in satins
And Cousins Suburban, in flame-colour'd turbans

. . . .

All, all to see the Lord May'r's Show!

Thus did Thomas Hood seek to capture the spirit of the Lord Mayor's Show. What this pageant was like in 1888 is even more graphically portrayed in the painting by William Logsdail which Sir James Whitehead commissioned, and which now hangs in the Guildhall Library.

Against the backdrop of the Royal Exchange reflected in the wet pavement three footmen, their calves encased in flesh-colored hose, advance, followed by the baroque magnificence of the Lord Mayor's coach. In the distance can be seen a detachment of the 19th Hussars, their dark blue tunics decorated with gold chain, their busbies surmounted by stiff white plumes. But it is not the pomp and splendor which hold the eye in this bit of Victoriana, but the crowd scenes, which appear to be faithfully depicted.

And what a curious, tattered, half-starved crowd it is — a motley of all that is most miserable and forlorn in the capital.

A mongrel dog has run into the street. A small boy stoops to retrieve from the mud a silk topper, knocked off by some ruffian, no doubt. And along the line of march Sir Charles Warren's blue-coated reinforcements are shown restraining the mob in its enthusiasm.

Enthusiasm is, perhaps, too strong a term, for not all of the ragged bystanders were friendly disposed. A hostile demonstration greeted the procession when it turned into Mincing Lane, and even *The Times* was forced to admit that "at certain points in the procession there was undoubtedly a good deal of jeering." This *The Times* attributed in equal parts to the Lord Mayor's political views (he was a Liberal) and to the absence from the show of the so-called "circus element." Although there were admittedly a great many roughs in the crowds, *The Times* commented on "the entire absence of any dangerous elements," thus giving the lie to Sir Charles Warren and his fears of a socialist insurrection.

While the Lord Mayor's procession wound through City streets on its way to the Law Courts in the Strand, another of those little comedies of errors which plagued the Ripper case was being enacted in Miller's Court, where Scotland Yard detectives, led by Inspector Frederick G. Abberline, had assembled in force. Dr. George B. Phillips, the divisional police surgeon, also arrived to make his examination *in situ* only to find that the murder investigation had hit an unexpected snag. As one of his final acts in office, Sir Charles Warren had issued orders that, in the event of another Ripper murder, neither the premises nor the body was to be disturbed until bloodhounds had been summoned and placed on the scent of the murderer.

The difficulty was that Warren had neglected to inform his subordinates where the bloodhounds were kept. Some officers thought they were with a veterinary surgeon at Thornton Heath, others, that they were kept at the Portland Road police station. Two precious hours were to be wasted in waiting for

Barnaby and Burgho to arrive — only to discover that these sagacious beasts had been returned to their owner, Edwin Brough of Scarborough, a fortnight earlier.

Meanwhile the police, unable to break into Kelly's room, milled around in the court, while its terrified inhabitants, forbidden to leave their dwellings, were held virtually prisoner. Superintendent Arnold finally arrived from the Yard to countermand the order, but it was one-thirty before the door to No. 13 splintered under M'Carthy's pickaxe, and police burst into Mary Kelly's room.

The Lord Mayor's procession by this time was approaching Fleet Street from St. Paul's. At one point where the procession was momentarily held up, the people at the windows and on the balconies improvised an edifying entertainment for His Lordship which consisted of tossing coppers, and sometimes silver, to the tatterdemalion crowd below. "The roadway, covered with a thin coating of greasy mud, was as slippery as ice," reported the *Daily Telegraph*, "and the fun was to see the street boys, and men for that matter, dart across to catch the descending copper or scramble for it in the indescribably filthy kennel. The noticeable feature of the game," the *Telegraph* added, "was its absolute fairness and uniform good nature."

But now, as the procession swung into Fleet Street from Ludgate Circus, where the crowds were densest, news of the Miller's Court murder burst with full fury upon the bystanders. Suddenly, seemingly from nowhere, newsboys appeared, the ink scarcely dry on the papers they waved, and began to shout: MURDER — WHITECHAPEL — 'ORRIBLE — ANOTHER MURDER — MUTILATIONS — JACK THE RIPPER — LATEST VICTIM. At this, pandemonium broke out, at least among a section of the audience. Spectators snatched the newspaper placards announcing the revolting murder and held them up to the police who were desperately striving to keep order. "Yah, look at this!" they jeered.

A band of medical students, some linked arm in arm, chose this moment to rush down Ludgate Hill knocking off the hats of passersby with their canes. Their leader, in a sheer excess of animal spirits, jumped onto the back of a police constable, knocking him to the ground, and then proceeded to bite the constable's thumb. All the "circus element," which the incoming Lord Mayor had tried hard to suppress as being beneath the dignity of the Corporation of London, came boiling to the top. For Sir James Whitehead the day lay in ruins. Scores of arrests were made. Six policemen were seen to haul one young man face downward away to the nearest station. But from here to the Law Courts in the Strand the Lord Mayor's procession was a rout, or, to put it more bluntly, Jack the Ripper had stolen the show.

"The murderer chose his time well," the *Star* commented editorially, and went on to expound a theory that the murderer was "one of those diseased creatures who, drunk with an insane love of notoriety, are determined to be the sensation of the hour . . . If that was his intention he succeeded beyond all expectation. He got his sensation. While the well-stuffed calves of the City footmen were being paraded for the laughter of London, his victim was lying cold in a foul, dimly lit court in Whitechapel."

7

The puppet figure in the gilded coach was on its way back to Guildhall, having fulfilled its ritual function, when a one-horse cart pulled up in Dorset Street opposite Miller's Court. The driver and his helper jumped down, pulled from the back of the cart a long, white coffin, dirty and scratched from constant use, and disappeared with it through the passageway. Although the police had cordoned off Dorset Street at both ends to keep out curiosity seekers, news that the body was about to be removed brought people running from the doss houses located in that street, so that when the carriers reappeared, their coffined burden obviously heavier, quite a crowd had collected. "The demeanor of the poor people was all that could be desired," reported *The Times.* "Ragged caps were doffed and slatternly-looking women shed tears as the shell . . . was placed in the van." The remains of Mary Kelly were then driven to Shoreditch mortuary.

That evening Sir James Whitehead was host to 850 guests at a banquet in Guildhall. The glittering assemblage, which included generals in full-dress uniform and diplomats with colorful sashes and decorations, filed into the banquet hall to the music of Handel's March from *Scipio,* the last to enter being the Lord Mayor himself, resplendent in a robe of black silk damask trimmed with gold lace and embroidery.

At the same hour three thousand of East London's poor gathered at the Great Assembly Hall, Mile End Road, for a meat tea provided through the Lord Mayor's generosity. In the absence of Handel's music, the progress of Whitechapel's neediest was not quite so orderly. "The mob seemed determined to besiege the hall," the *East London Advertiser* reported. "Seeing the state of affairs a reinforcement of police was sent for, but it was not till some 30 or 40 minutes after the time stated on the tickets for the supper to begin that the legitimate ticket-holders were able to obtain an entrance into the hall, this being effected by the extra police forming a cordon round the gates and only allowing those who showed tickets to pass."

At Guildhall two picturesque carvers, robed in white and mounted in pulpits, wielded their carving knives on the roast beef of old England. In addition, 700 quarts of turtle soup, 100 turkeys, 250 fowls and 200 dishes of venison were consumed on this occasion. "Pray charge your glasses," the Toast Master commanded, and the health of Her Majesty the Queen was proposed. In the lull which followed this toast, a representative of the *Pall Mall Gazette* overheard one alderman say to another, "Did it happen in our ward?" "Oh, no, not in our ward," the second alderman replied. "Ah, well, it's not so bad then," the other observed with an evident sense of relief. They were, of course, referring to the murder.

At the beanfeast in the Great Assembly Hall 3000 pork pies, 1500 pounds of cake, 825 half-quartern loaves and 6000 apples disappeared down the gullets of the East End hungry before one could say "God Save the Queen." It was, as "Grateful Pauper" wrote to the *City Press* the next day, "a beautiful tea and lumping weight."

Meanwhile, back at Guildhall Lord Salisbury, the Prime Minister, arose to make the principal address of the evening. His was the delicate task of saying nothing to offend the Lord Mayor, who was a Liberal, and hence on the "outs" with the government on such issues as Home Rule. Still, none need have feared, for Lord Salisbury's remarks were as full of orotund nonsense as those of M. du Norpoid, Proust's archetypal diplomat. Her Majesty's Government, he declared, attached no importance to "small wars and rumors of war"—these were "merely the surf which marked the edge of the advancing wave of civilization." Only an "uninformed opinion" egged on by chauvinism could bring on a war. (The following day *Fremdenblatt,* the mouthpiece of the Austrian Foreign Office, interpreted this as a dig at France "where there is unfortunately a party which looks upon war as a question of national honor.") Lord Salisbury ended by calling for a "Big Navy." "There is no part of the British people that wants war," he cried, and sat down to thunderous applause.

The beanfeast in Mile End Road ended with a magic lantern show and a concert by the Crusaders Temperance Brass Band, followed by three cheers for the new Lord Mayor and Lady Mayoress. A telegram was dispatched to the latter couple thanking them for their kindness in providing the meat tea.

Charity seemed to be in the air, for at Sandringham earlier in the day the Prince of Wales had celebrated his birthday by feting three hundred laborers on the estate with a slap-up meal in the carriage house of the Royal Mews. In the evening there were fireworks and the future Edward VII was host at a county ball.

8

While the polity applauded a bigger Navy, and royalty danced the Gay Gordons, what was left of Mary Jane Kelly, originally of County Limerick, Ireland, lay on a slab in the mortuary at Shoreditch. Working at top speed, it took two skilled surgeons and their assistants seven hours to reassemble the body so that it could be identified and be given a decent burial. The coroner's jury, at least, would be spared the ordeal of viewing the cadaver in its original mutilated condition.

The police denied that any of the body's organs were missing, but *The Times* flatly contradicted this. "We are enabled to state on good authority that notwithstanding all that has been said to the contrary, a portion of the bodily organs was missing. The police, and with them the divisional surgeon, have arrived at the conclusion that it is in the interest of justice not to disclose the details of the professional inquiry." The police surgeon however did admit that Kelly was in the early stages of pregnancy, and another newspaper account hints broadly that the missing portion was the fetus.

Meanwhile, the police subjected No. 13 Miller's Court to a minute scrutiny in search of clues. In the grate they found a large quantity of ashes as evidence that a fierce fire had been built up. So hot was it, in fact, that the rim, the handle and the spout of a teakettle had been burned away. In sifting the ashes they found remnants of clothing — the charred rim and wirework of a woman's felt hat and a burnt piece of velvet, all that remained of a velvet jacket which had belonged to Kelly, and which Kelly's friend Maria Harvey said was missing. Harvey stated that two men's cotton shirts which she had given to the decedent were likewise missing.

Inspector Abberline was of the opinion that the murderer had built up the fire, throwing on clothing and anything else he could lay hands on, in order that he could see to perform his horrific dissection. (The killer appears to have overlooked a candle which was stuck in a broken wineglass, and which was barely half consumed.) The great wonder is, of course, that the fire was not seen through the window by other tenants of Miller's Court who, as we shall see, were in and out the rickety tenement at all hours that night.

Had they chanced to peer through the window, they would have seen the Ripper at work. According to police estimates, it took him at least two hours to complete his dissection. When he had finished he barricaded the door by moving a heavy chest of drawers against it, and then escaped by climbing out the window.

CHAPTER XIV

A HURRIED INQUEST

CLOSE TO midnight on the night of the murder the widow Cox, it will be recalled, had encountered Mary Kelly, who was drunk and in the company of a man with a carroty-colored mustache. The widow had followed them up the narrow passageway known as Miller's Court, said goodnight to Kelly, and watched the couple go into No. 13 and shut the door, after which she heard Kelly singing "Sweet Violets" in her gin-husky voice. But Black Mary had not retired for the night, if another witness is to be believed. *Hours later she was seen on the streets of Spitalfields by someone she knew.*

George Hutchinson had once worked as a night watchman, which meant that, accustomed to sleeplessness, he often prowled the streets at odd hours of the night. In the early hours of Friday, November 9, it was not insomnia, but destitution that forced him to walk the streets, a condition known as "carrying the banner" in the East End. For George had been out of work for many weeks. Still, the powers of observation acquired as a watchman stood him in good stead as he turned the corner from Whitechapel Road and surveyed Commercial Street, now strangely silent at 2 A.M. He noted first of all a swarthy-looking man lounging on the corner beneath a gas lamp. But he hardly had time to take in this stranger when he spotted coming toward him from the direction of Dorset Street Mary Kelly. At once his face brightened.

The watchman and Kelly were old friends. When he had been working steadily he had often treated her to a seat in the fourpenny gods at the Cambridge Music Hall, or had bought her pink gins at The Britannia. Now, seeing her alone at this late hour, and in a "spreeish" mood, as he later described it, Hutchinson thought himself in luck. For Kelly had the reputation of being as open-handed with money as she was with her other favors. Already, as he watched her approach, Hutchinson could see himself with the price of a doss in his pocket, or, better still, curled up in Kelly's bed.

But gods other than those at the Cambridge now intervened to give his hopes a cruel twist. Before the watchman could open his mouth to pour out his woes, Kelly was on about her own troubles. The rent was due, she had had nothing to eat, could he lend her half a crown? She promised to repay it before the weekend was out. Wordlessly, like some seriocomic mime, he pulled out his empty pockets, spread his hands in a gesture of mock despair.

With the same comically sad air he watched Kelly move off, saw her slow her pace as she passed the swarthy man standing on the corner of Thrawl Street, saw the man put out a detaining hand. The man said something which caused them both to laugh, then the couple walked slowly back, the man's arm circling Kelly's waist. As they passed him, Hutchinson mechanically noted that the man wore taupe-colored spats.

What impulse prompted Hutchinson to follow this couple? Was it the faint stirrings of envy? After all, the ex-watchman had only lately fancied himself in Kelly's bed. Or was it simply from boredom? Spitalfields offered few enough distractions at this hour of morning. Again, he may have had the makings of a voyeur. Whatever his reason, Hutchinson now trailed the couple as they turned into Dorset Street. He saw them stand for a moment in front of Miller's Court, heard Kelly exclaim, "Oh, I've lost my handkerchief," whereupon the man whipped a red bandanna from his pocket, made a few playful passes with it, as though he were a toreador. Then they disappeared into the court together.

Hutchinson hesitated a few minutes, then tiptoed up the court to No. 13, but the light was already out in Kelly's room and he could hear no sound. Retracing his steps, he took up a waiting stance in front of Miller's Court. Waiting for what? "Blowed if I know," he would have answered if pressed to explain. As he stood there he heard the ponderous tread of a constable walking his beat in Commercial Street. Once he saw a man dart into a doss house farther down Dorset Street. After waiting three-quarters of an hour for the man in the dark spats to reappear, Hutchinson reluctantly gave up his vigil. The rest of the night he tramped the streets, his fists jammed deep into his pockets.

"My suspicions were instantly aroused," he later told the press, "at seeing so well-dressed a man in this part of London. I felt there was something queer about it." Queer, indeed, if the inventory of the man's clothing which Hutchinson gave is correct. "He was wearing a long, dark coat trimmed with astrakhan, a white collar with a black necktie, in which was fixed a horseshoe pin . . . He also wore a massive gold watch chain from which hung a seal with a red stone." As for the man's physical characteristics, he was about thirty-five years old, five feet six inches tall, of dark complexion, with dark eyes, bushy eyebrows, a mustache which curled up at the ends. He looked like a foreigner, in Hutchinson's opinion.

It is a pity that Hutchinson, who talked freely enough to the press, was never called as an inquest witness, for then he could have been cross-examined. What is one to make of the bizarre details he furnished to the press? His ability to discern in a dimly lit street that the man's tiepin was horseshoe-shaped, that his spats were taupe-colored, that a red stone hung from his watch chain — all of this smacks of the near miraculous.

Was it not the description of the villain who regularly popped up from the trapdoor at the Cambridge?

Yet Hutchinson stuck to his story, and this despite repeated efforts of the police to break it down. Chief Inspector Abberline grilled the watchman relentlessly. By a series of snap questions the inspector sought to cross him up on details. But Hutchinson's answers were always the same. "How could you see a red handkerchief so far away?" Abberline demanded. "He flourished the handkerchief in front of her," Hutchinson replied. "It caught the lamplight. He waved it about like a bullfighter and made her laugh."

If Hutchinson invented the stranger, then his performance was all the more remarkable, for he had everything to lose by making his statement voluntarily. After all, he had not slept anywhere the night of the murder; but he had, by his own admission, been at the scene of the crime at the hour when it was committed.

2

Characteristically, Queen Victoria was one of the first to react to the Kelly murder with a call for action. From Balmoral Castle in Scotland she sent a tart reminder to her Prime Minister, the Marquis of Salisbury: "This new most ghastly murder shows the absolute necessity for some very decided action. All these courts must be lit, and our detectives improved. They are not what they should be." Querulously she complained, "You promised when the first murder took place to consult with your colleagues about it."

Goaded by the Queen's telegram, Lord Salisbury summoned his Cabinet to No. 10, Downing Street Saturday morning, November 10. (How it must have pleased Jack the Ripper to learn that he was the subject of a Cabinet debate.) After some discussion, the Cabinet agreed to the unprecedented step of offering a free pardon to anyone who was not an actual party to the Kelly murder who would give information concerning the same. The police notice read:

> Whereas on November 8 or 9 in Miller's Court, Dorset Street, Spitalfields, Mary Jane Kelly was murdered by some person or persons unknown, the Secretary of State will advise the grant of Her Majesty's pardon to any accomplice not being a person who contrived or actually committed the murder who shall give such information and evidence as shall lead to the discovery and conviction of the person or persons who committed the murder.

That Jack the Ripper was a lone operator must have been fairly obvious from the start. This, for example, explained his almost miraculous ability to elude detection. But the police evidently felt that the Ripper was being shielded by a friend or relative who, knowing him to be insane and a killer, was still reluctant to give him up for fear of being incriminated as an accomplice. Lord Salisbury and his colleagues might better have combined their free pardon offer with a sizable reward, which would have appealed to the mercenary. As it was, their offer fell on barren soil.

3

The public sensation created by the previous Ripper murders was as nothing compared to that which followed the Miller's Court affair. In East London the lynch spirit was held in check only by the presence of large numbers of uniformed police. The fact that the Kelly murder occurred on the weekend of the Lord Mayor's Show when East Enders were in a holiday mood and spending freely on drink did not help matters. As the pub doors swung to and fro, one caught lurid snatches of conversation mingled with the sour smell of beer.

In Dorset Street itself a line of rough-looking characters stood with their backs to the wall opposite Miller's Court, smoking their short clay pipes and bandying obscene jests with passers-by. Now and then hoarse-voiced vendors threaded their way through the crowd brandishing crimson-covered pamphlets, which they identified as, "The Whitechapel Blood Book — only a penny!" To aggravate matters, the first anniversary of "Bloody Sunday," when Sir Charles Warren had used his blue-coats to club the unemployed, fell on this particular weekend, and thousands gathered in Hyde Park to hear William Morris and R. Cunninghame Graham, the Scottish laird, demand Warren's immediate resignation, unaware that it had already been accepted. As the weekend wore on, the tension mounted. It was as though East Enders were waiting for a signal to take the law into their own hands.

4

Ironically, the new Lord Mayor chose this particular Saturday, November 10, to preside for the first time at Mansion House in his capacity of Chief Magistrate of the City of London. Perhaps there was just a trace of sarcasm in his voice as, taking his seat, he remarked upon the "very orderly, well-conducted and good-humored character of the crowd" that had watched the Lord Mayor's procession.

This done, His Lordship got down to the business of the day, there being thirty-eight charges, mostly involving pickpockets who had been active during the passage of this same procession.[1] The most interesting of these cases was the theft of a

[1] The petty thefts committed during the Lord Mayor's Show in 1888 were nothing compared to what happened on Mafeking Day, May 17, 1900. When news of the relief of Mafeking became known in the City, thirty-six watches were said to have changed hands in ten minutes in front of Mansion House. Cheering Kitchener and Baden-Powell, the thieves knocked people's hats over their eyes and shook hands effusively while stripping their victims of all their possessions. The Lord Mayor from his balcony beamed benevolently on Her Majesty's subjects who showed such enthusiasm.

gold repeater watch, valued at £146, from an attaché of the Imperial Russian Embassy at Berlin who happened to be in London on Friday, November 9. This embassy official was making his way to the Deutsche Bank in Throgmorton Street between one and two o'clock on that day, he testified, when he encountered the Lord Mayor's procession and "suddenly found himself surrounded by roughs who began to push and hustle him." He next discovered that his overcoat was unbuttoned, and that his watch chain had been cut. Meanwhile, the watch itself was tossed from hand to hand until finally one of the confederates had the misfortune to be short-stopped by a cop. The Lord Mayor listened to this story with a certain amount of sympathy, then sentenced the three pickpockets involved, who had pleaded guilty, to six weeks' hard labor each.

5

The weekend did not pass without incidents of an uglier nature in the East End. On Sunday evening a half-blind old lady named Mrs. Humphries, who lived with her daughter in the George Yard buildings, groped her way into the courtyard to empty the slops, and as she entered the outhouse a young man, who had been courting her daughter, darted past her. Trembling with fear, Mrs. Humphries called out, "Who is it?" Unfortunately, the young man was afflicted with a stammer, and before he could even blurt out his name the old lady had raised a fearful hue and cry. As though they had been waiting for just this cue policemen and plainclothes detectives converged from all directions on the hapless suitor, and led him off to the Leman Street station.

Even greater was the excitement an hour later when a man whose face was made up to resemble a skull stood on the corner of Wentworth and Commercial Streets and shouted, "I am Jack the Ripper!" This man had blackened his face with burnt cork, and painted wide rings of white around his eyes so that he gave a truly eerie impression. He had but little time to create a sensation, however, for he was seized by two men, one of them a discharged soldier; and once more the mob appeared as if by magic from the wings with bloodcurdling cries of "Lynch him!" Sticks were raised, and the black-faced man might well have been battered had it not been for the arrival of those other figurants, the police. As it was, it took four constables and as many bystanders to subdue the man. He was taken to the Leman Street station, where he identified himself as a doctor at St. George's hospital, Hyde Park Corner, but refused to give his name.

According to crime writer Edwin T. Woodhall, "The Man with the White Eyes" met with a sticky end. "About three weeks later," Woodhall writes, "his body was recovered from the Thames by the River Police, near Hungerford Bridge. A paddle boat tied to the Waterloo Pier was shifted and caused the black swollen body to come to the surface, for it had been lodged under the wheel. The black burnt cork and white paint on the already decomposing features were hideously evident." Woodhall has confused two different stories, but he was not alone in believing that Jack the Ripper committed suicide immediately following the Mary Kelly murder by throwing himself in the Thames. This was a view shared by high police officials, as will presently be related.

6

The inquest into the death of Mary Jane Kelly, which opened at the Shoreditch Town Hall on November 12, differed from the inquests into the deaths of the other Ripper victims in several important respects. In the first place, the inquest was presided over by a different coroner. Gone was the genial, if foppish

Wynne R. Baxter, that self-appointed gadfly of the Metropolitan police, whose *ex parte* criticisms of these same law minions had stung them to fury. In his place the police had secured the much more pliant Dr. Roderick MacDonald, a Liberal Member of Parliament, who had served as District Medical Officer for Poplar before becoming Coroner for Northeast Middlesex.

Secondly, in contrast to the other Ripper inquests, which were dragged out over a period of weeks, the Kelly inquest was abruptly terminated at the end of the first day. Far from trying to elicit as much information as possible to help them in their inquiries, the police seemed determined to hush up the circumstances surrounding the Miller's Court murder. In this they were ably abetted by Dr. MacDonald, who himself had served as police surgeon for K-Division, and who thus was accustomed to working very closely with the authorities.

That a tug-of-war was going on behind the scenes became evident in the opening exchange between Dr. MacDonald and one of the jurors:

JUROR: I do not see why we should have the inquest thrown on our shoulders when the murder did not happen in our district, but in Whitechapel.

CORONER'S OFFICER (Mr. Hammond): It did not happen in Whitechapel.

CORONER (severely): Do you think that we do not know what we are doing here? The jury are summoned in the ordinary way, and they have no business to object. If they persist in their objection I shall know how to deal with them. Does any juror persist in objecting?

JUROR: We are summoned for the Shoreditch district. This affair happened in Spitalfields.

CORONER: It happened within my district.

ANOTHER JURYMAN: This is not my district. I come from Whitechapel, and Mr. Baxter is my coroner.

CORONER: I am not going to discuss the subject with the

jurymen at all. If any juryman says he distinctly objects, let him say so. (After a pause): I may tell the jurymen that jurisdiction lies where the body lies, not where it was found.

Later, Dr. MacDonald saw fit to refer again to the bitter behind-scenes jurisdictional wrangle, this time addressing himself to the reporters present whose newspapers had made a "great fuss" over the inquest switch. He had had no communication with Mr. Wynne Baxter, he said. "The body is in my jurisdiction, it was taken to my mortuary, and that is the end of the matter," he announced.

Having been duly sworn, the jurors were conducted by Inspector Abberline to view the body, which was lying in a coarse wooden shell in the mortuary adjoining Shoreditch Church. Only the decedent's face was visible, the mutilated body mercifully being concealed by a dirty gray cloth. "The face resembled one of those horrible wax anatomical specimens," noted the *Pall Mall Gazette*. "The eyes were the only vestiges of humanity. The rest was so scored and slashed that it was impossible to say where the flesh began and the cuts ended." The jury then inspected the room in Miller's Court, Dorset Street, where the murder had been committed, and returned to the town hall to hear testimony.

First witness to be called was Joseph Barnett, the Billingsgate fish porter with whom Kelly had lived up to the time of her death. He had last seen Kelly alive between 7:30 and 7:45 P.M. on Thursday, November 8, when he called upon her at No. 13 Miller's Court and found her with another prostitute, Maria Harvey.

Q (CORONER): Were you on good terms with the deceased?

A: Yes, on friendly terms, but when we parted I told her I had no work, and had nothing to give her, for which I was sorry.

Q: Did you have a drink together?

A: No, Mary was quite sober.

Q: Was she, generally speaking, of sober habits?

A: When she was with me I found her of sober habits, but she has been drunk in my presence several times.

Thomas Bowyer, the rent collector, told of the horrible discovery when he put his hand through the broken windowpane, twitched aside the curtain and saw "two pieces of flesh lying on the table." His testimony, which added nothing new to what he had told the press, was corroborated by John M'Carthy, Kelly's landlord.

Next came a parade of Dorset Street characters, women who, like Kelly, hustled a living in the streets. In the beginning they may have had Kelly's fresh looks, but by now most of them had grown gray in prostitution. Their shawls wrapped tightly around them, they answered the coroner's questions rather truculently, or with a slightly comic air. Pride of place went to Mary Ann Cox, the widow who had seen Kelly at 11:45 P.M. with the man with the carroty mustache, and who now told of her own various comings and goings on the night of the murder. When the widow returned to her room for the last time at about 3 A.M. the light in Kelly's room was out, she told the inquest jury.

Q (CORONER): Did you go to sleep?

A: No, I was upset. I didn't even bother to undress, not being sleepy. I just laid down on the bed.

Q: Did you hear any noises or any cries?

A: I heard a man who lives in the court leave for work at Spitalfields market.

Q: Did you hear anything else?

A: I heard a man go down the court at six-fifteen. That would be too late for the market.

Q: From what house did he come?

A: I don't know.

Q: Did you hear the door bang after him?

A: No.

Q: Then he must have walked up the court and back again?

A: Yes.

Q: It might have been a policeman?

A: It might have been.

The next witness was Elizabeth Prater, a prostitute who occupied the room directly above Mary Kelly's. She was out hustling all Thursday night, she told the jury, and she did not direct her footsteps toward Miller's Court until 1 A.M., and even then she stood on the street corner for about twenty minutes hoping to pick up a customer. Had there been a light in No. 13 she would have noticed it as she climbed the stairs to her own room, she testified. She saw none, however. Had Kelly or anyone else moved about in the room below Prater would have heard them, the walls being of very flimsy structure; but she heard no one. Prater barricaded her door with two tables, then climbed into bed and slept soundly for two hours. "A kitten disturbed me at about three-thirty or three forty-five," she explained to the jury. "As I turned over to go back to sleep I heard a faint cry of 'Oh, murder.'" It seemed to come from the court.

Q: Do you often hear cries of 'Murder'?

A: It is not unusual in the street. I took no notice of it.

Q: Did you hear it a second time?

A: No.

Q: Did you hear beds or tables being pulled about?

A: None whatsoever. I went back to sleep and awoke at five A.M.

Q: What did you do then?

A: I went downstairs and saw some men harnessing horses. At a quarter to six I was in The Ten Bells.

Q: Did you see any strangers in The Ten Bells?

A: No.

Q: What did you do then?

A: I went back to bed and slept until eleven A.M.

Q: You heard no singing downstairs?

A: None whatsoever. I would have heard the singing distinctly, but it was quiet at one-thirty.

Sarah Lewis, a laundress living at No. 24 Great Pearl Street, next took the stand and told of going to Miller's Court at 2:30 A.M. Friday to visit a friend, Mrs. Keyler, who occupied the house opposite Mary Kelly's. As she turned into the court, she noticed a man standing opposite the entrance and looking down the court as though he were waiting for someone. He was stout, not very tall, and he wore a black "wide-awake" hat. (Unfortunately, we possess no description of George Hutchinson, but the man Mrs. Lewis saw may well have been Hutchinson, who, according to his claim, maintained a vigil outside Miller's Court until 3 A.M.) The laundress said that she dozed in a chair at Mrs. Keyler's until 3:30 A.M. when she heard the clock of Christ Church, Spitalfields, strike the half hour.

Q: What woke you up?

A: I could not sleep. I sat awake until nearly four, when I heard a female's voice shouting "Murder" loudly. It seemed like the voice of a young woman. It sounded at our door. There was only the one scream.

Q: Were you afraid? Did you wake anybody up?

A: No. I took no notice as I heard only the one scream.

Q: You stayed at Mrs. Keyler's house until what time?

A: Until 5:30 P.M. Friday. The police would not let us out of the court.

The testimony of the next witness was at such variance to the known facts that the coroner cautioned her to be very careful concerning her evidence. She was Caroline Maxwell, wife of the lodging-house keeper at No. 14 Dorset Street, which was directly opposite to Miller's Court, and she now stated under oath that she saw Mary Kelly standing at the entrance to Miller's Court at *8 o'clock Friday morning.* She was quite positive that it was the deceased, even though she had only spoken to

Kelly once or twice before, and she was equally certain as to the time because her husband had just finished work.

Q (CORONER): Did you speak to her?

A: Yes. It was unusual to see her up at that hour. I spoke across the street, "What, Mary, brings you up so early?" She said, "Oh, Carrie, I do feel so bad."

Q: And yet you say you had only spoken to her twice previously? You knew her name, and she knew yours?

A: Oh, yes, by being about in the lodging house.

Q: What did she say?

A: She said, "I've had a glass of beer, and I've brought it up again." I imagine she had been in The Britannia beer shop on the corner. I left her saying that I could pity her feelings.

Q: Then what did you do?

A: I went to Bishopsgate Street to get my husband's breakfast.

Q: Did you see Kelly again?

A: Yes. When I returned I saw her outside The Britannia public house talking to a man.

Q: This would be about what time?

A: It was about a quarter to nine.

Q: What description can you give of the man?

A: I could not give you any, as they were at some distance.

INSP. ABBERLINE (interrupting): The distance is about sixteen yards.

A: I am sure it was the deceased. I am willing to swear it.

Q: You are sworn now. Was he a tall man?

A: No, he was a little taller than me and stout.

INSP. ABBERLINE: On consideration, I should say the distance as twenty-five yards.

Q: What clothes had the man?

A: Dark clothes. He seemed to have a plaid coat on. I could not say what sort of hat he had.

Q: What sort of dress had the deceased?

A: A dark skirt, a velvet body, a maroon shawl, and no hat.

Q: Have you ever seen her the worse for drink?

A: I have seen her in drink, but she was not a notorious character.

Maria Harvey, of No. 3 New Court, Dorset Street, who was with Kelly all Thursday afternoon, was next called as a witness.

Q: Were you in the house when Joe Barnett called?

A: Yes. I left shortly after Joe arrived. I said, "Well Mary Jane, I shall not see you this evening."

Q: Did you leave any articles with Kelly?

A: Yes, I left with her two men's dirty shirts, a little boy's shirt, a black overcoat, a black crepe bonnet with black satin strings, a pawn ticket for a gray shawl on which two shillings had been lent, and a little girl's white petticoat.

Q: Have you seen any of these articles since?

A: Yes, I saw the black overcoat in a room in the court on Friday afternoon.

The coroner then called upon Dr. George Bagster Phillips, the police divisional surgeon, to give a preliminary report of his post-mortem findings. This Dr. Phillips did without going into any detail concerning the wounds inflicted. Immediate cause of death the surgeon gave as severance of the right carotid artery. The jury asked no questions at this stage, it being understood that more detailed evidence of the medical examination would be given at a future hearing.

One can therefore imagine the surprise among the spectators present at the inquest when shortly afterward Coroner MacDonald abruptly terminated the proceedings and recorded the jury's verdict of "willful murder against some person or persons unknown." The coroner had not thought fit to ask Dr. Phillips if any portions of the body were missing. Nor had he sought to establish the nature of the weapon with which Mary Kelly was murdered.

British Common Law since Edward I has required that "all

the injuries of the body, also all the wounds, ought to be viewed; and the length, breadth, and deepness, with what weapon, and in what part of the body the wound or hurt is . . . all which things must be enrolled in the roll of the coroner." Dr. MacDonald knew this. After all, as a police surgeon, he had been called upon often enough to testify at inquests. Yet he chose deliberately to suppress this evidence.

"There is other evidence which I do not propose to call," he announced rather grandly at the close of the inquest, "for if we at once make public every fact brought forward in connection with this terrible murder the ends of justice might be retarded." What did he mean by this extraordinary statement? Was he being guided by Scotland Yard, which had been so anxious to get the inquest out of Coroner Wynne Baxter's hands? What were the police trying to hide?

7

From the evidence of the inquest witnesses, and assuming this evidence to be correct, it is possible to draw up a rough timetable of movements in and about Miller's Court on the night of the murder:

11:45 P.M. — Kelly and a shabbily dressed man are seen coming out of The Britannia pub by the widow Cox, who follows the couple up Miller's Court, sees them enter No. 13. After remaining in her room for fifteen minutes, the widow goes out again.

1:00 A.M. — The widow Cox returns to Miller's Court, hears Kelly singing as she passes the window of No. 13.

1:20 A.M. — Elizabeth Prater, who lives above Kelly, returns to her room, but sees no light in No. 13, nor does she hear any noise.

2:00 A.M. — George Hutchinson sees Kelly in Commercial Street with a well-dressed man, follows them to Miller's Court.

2:30 A.M. — Sarah Lewis goes calling in Miller's Court, sees a man standing on the sidewalk opposite the court. (*Note:* This may have been Hutchinson.)

3:00 A.M. — Hutchinson abandons watch on Miller's Court.

3:30–4:00 A.M. — A cry of "Murder!" is heard by both Elizabeth Prater and Sarah Lewis, but neither of them pays any attention to it.

6:15 A.M. — The widow Cox hears someone leave Miller's Court.

8:00–8:45 A.M. — Mrs. Maxwell sees Kelly first standing at the entrance to Miller's Court, then later talking to a man in front of The Britannia pub, according to her claim.

10:45 A.M. — Rent Collector Thomas Bowyer discovers the murder.

The first thing that strikes the observer is the extraordinary amount of nocturnal activity centering on "M'Carthy's Rents," which turns out to be nothing more than a brothel with at least three prostitutes besides Mary Kelly occupying its crib houses. It might truthfully be said that if Miller's Court slept at all, it slept with one eye open. Sarah Lewis thinks nothing of paying a social call there at 2:30 A.M. and falls asleep while sitting upright in her friend's chair. And what is one to make of the widow Cox, who pops in and out of her room at least three times between midnight and three o'clock, when she finally stretches out on the bed without bothering to remove her clothes? The reason she gives for this latter eccentricity is that she was feeling upset, but upset about what?

And then there is Elizabeth Prater, another whore, who occupies the room above Kelly. Prater is so destitute that she does a street-corner stand at 1:20 A.M. hoping to catch some unwary customer, according to her testimony. Yet when she does go back to her room she barricades the door with two tables. Barricades the door against whom?

But the wonders do not stop there. Both Elizabeth Prater and Sarah Lewis told the coroner's jury that they heard a cry of "Murder!" at about 3:30 A.M. Prater said it was in a faint voice, while Lewis said that it was a loud scream. But neither of them paid the slightest attention to the cry. Cries of "Murder!" were common in these parts, they told the inquest — they were nothing to become alarmed about. The cry would seem to fix the time of the killing at between 3:30 and 4 A.M. If it took the killer two hours to complete his grisly dissection, as the police estimated that it did, it would mean that he left Miller's Court at about 6 A.M., when the widow Cox said that she heard a man depart.

There is nothing irreconcilable in the shabbily dressed man with whom Kelly was seen by the widow Cox shortly after midnight, and the flashily dressed character whom Hutchinson saw in her company two hours later. The fact that he was shabby in appearance suggests that the first man may have tried to sponge on Kelly's hospitality, hoping to enjoy free lunch with his beer, so to speak. (Incidentally, it is difficult enough to picture Jack the Ripper with a carroty mustache and wearing a billy-cock hat but when the widow Cox assures us that he was carrying a pail of beer in one hand, she is really stretching credulity.)

The probability is that having got rid of her small-beer lover, Kelly took to the street again, where she was seen by Hutchinson at 2 A.M. This was not unusual, as we have already seen from the comings and goings in Miller's Court. And after all, the rent collector was due on the morrow. Kelly knew that she would have to pay something on account or be thrown out of her miserable digs. Poor Black Mary, she might have spared herself the trouble, for death was about to present an even more pressing Account Due.

8

Mary Kelly was given an impressive funeral, paid for by Henry Wilton, who had been clerk of St. Leonard's Church, Shoreditch, for fifty years. Promptly at noon on Sunday, November 18, the bell of St. Leonard's began to toll, apparently as a signal for every housewife in the neighborhood to abandon preparations for the Sunday dinner and to come running, for the crowd which gathered in front of the church was composed mostly of women. In no time the thoroughfare was completely blocked, and the police, who seem to have anticipated just such a crowd, had their hands full keeping order.

The coffin was borne on the shoulders of four men. It was of polished elm with metal mounts, and on the coffin plate was engraved the French variant of the decedent's name "Marie Jeanette Kelly, died 9th November, 1888, aged 25." Boys at a Leytonstone school contributed the floral cross made of heart's ease which rested on top the coffin alongside two crowns of artificial flowers from The Ten Bells and The Britannia pubs respectively (the *East London Advertiser* noted that the wreaths bore cards inscribed by "friends using certain public houses in common with the murdered woman").

The sight of the coffin affected the crowd greatly, according to the *Advertiser*. "Round the open car in which it was placed men and women struggled desperately to get to touch the coffin. Women with faces streaming with tears cried out, 'God forgive her' and every man's head was bared in token of sympathy."

The hearse was followed to St. Patrick's Catholic cemetery at Leytonstone by two mourners' coaches, one containing Joseph Barnett, the Billingsgate fish porter, looking dignified in unaccustomed blue serge. In the other coach were the widow Cox, Maria Harvey and three other women, all of whom had been fortifying themselves for the journey at a public house close to the churchgate. At a few minutes before 2 P.M. the cortege reached St. Patrick's where it was met by Father Colomban, who kept the burial service brief. In agreeing to pay for the funeral Mr. Wilton let it be known that if the public wished to share in the expense their contributions would be welcome. Any surplus would be used to erect a tombstone, he added. No tombstone was ever erected.

9

The Kelly murder gave rise to apocryphal stories, a number of which were gathered by Daniel Farson, popular TV compère, and televised in November, 1959.[3] One of these legends concerns the funeral itself, and was told by a Cockney type. "My mother," he said, "was at the cemetery that afternoon visiting another grave. When all the mourners had left, she and her friend noticed one man who had stayed behind. After some time, believing himself to be alone, he parted the boards above the grave and spat down on it."

Another of Mr. Farson's guests was a Mrs. Little, who claimed that her mother had moved into No. 13 Miller's Court after the murder. "There was a picture of the Crucifixion on the wall," she related, "and behind it was a bloody imprint of a hand. No matter how many times it was painted over it always showed through. Many smartly dressed gentlemen used to visit the house to see it."

[3] "Farson's Guide to the British," an Associated-Rediffusion two-part program televised on November 5 and 12, 1959.

CHAPTER XV

JILL THE RIPPER AND OTHERS

The abrupt conclusion of the Kelly inquest left the Ripper mystery dangling in midair. After some unseemly scuffling behind the scenes, the final curtain had been rung down hastily at the end of the second act, leaving the spectator to grope his way from the darkened theater, his mind awhirl with unanswered questions. Why had Coroner MacDonald been in such a hurry to end the proceedings? Was he afraid that his jurisdiction would be successfully challenged if he prolonged them longer? Or was he taking orders from Scotland Yard? Why had he suppressed the autopsy report? To this day no one knows for certain what organs, if any, were missing from Mary Kelly's body. Such information might have been useful in establishing whether or not a pattern of murder existed.

Why was George Hutchinson, the night watchman, not called as a witness? Hutchinson's story, if it had stood up to questioning, might likewise have thrown light on the case, for it placed Mary Kelly on the streets hours after she had been seen by the widow Cox. Hutchinson also gave a detailed description of the man with whom she was seen. And what about Caroline Maxwell, who swore that she saw Kelly as late as 8 A.M. on the morning she was discovered murdered? Why was no effort made to clear up the discrepancies in her story? Or would this have involved "other evidence which I do not propose to call," in the words of Coroner MacDonald?

In the intervening years amateur detectives have sought to write a third act to a mystery which seemingly defies solution, and their answers have been as varied as the men who have supplied them.[1]

Most assiduous of the early amateurs was Edward K. Larkins, an employee of Her Majesty's Customs, who, over a period of three years, made himself a thorough nuisance at the Home Office and at Scotland Yard. Larkins claimed that the murders were the work of not one, but two killers, whom he identified as Portuguese seamen working abroad the cattleboats *City of Oporto* and *City of Cork.* The two men, however, were not accomplices, according to this Customs official.

"The first murder, I assume, was committed by one man out of revenge; those which followed were committed by another man in a spirit of devilry," Larkins wrote in a memorandum dated March 8, 1889. He then named his suspects. "The cattlemen who were in this country on board the vessels when these murders took place were Manuel Crux Xavier and José Laurence."

Larkins worked out an elaborate chart showing that the *City of Oporto,* with Xavier aboard, had been tied up in the London docks on August 31, when Mary Ann Nicholls was found murdered, while Laurence had been in London aboard the *City of Cork* on the dates of the other four murders. On the strength of this evidence Larkins urged the British Consul at Oporto to have the two culprits arrested and extradited to England at once. When the Consul declined to do so, Larkins sent off a scorching letter. "Immediately the excitement is over I shall . . . invite the opinion of the public as to whether you are a fit person to be in charge of British interests abroad," the Customs official warned. As late as 1891 Larkins was still bombarding the Home Secretary and the Metropolitan Police Commissioner with memoranda concerning the Ripper case.

[1] See Appendix B.

Another who placed the Ripper at sea, but this time in the role of a deep-sea fisherman, was Dr. D. G. Halsted, who began his medical career in 1884 as an intern at the London Hospital in Whitechapel Road, and who thus had a ringside seat for the Ripper murders, so to speak. Dr. Halsted, who spent some time as a medical missionary to the fishing fleet off Dogger Bank, writes:

> I believe that after the last murder in November the Ripper joined the North Sea fishing fleet, where he was well out of the reach of the Law, and his presence would pass almost unnoticed among the scum of humanity who were to be found on those ships . . . Such suspicions were certainly confirmed when one heard about the bodies sometimes picked up by the trawlers in their nets, some the victims of shipwreck or accident, but others fairly obviously the result of foul play aboard ship.[2]

Dr. Halsted adds an interesting note concerning Jack the Ripper's supposed medical knowledge. "The great surgical skill which he used to apply to his female victims," he writes, "could easily have been picked up by a man accustomed to boning and filleting fish."

2

The Victorians shied violently away from the possibility that the Whitechapel killer could be a woman. The idea of a denatured Lady Macbeth of the Stews operating in their midst was repugnant to all their conceptions of the gentler sex. Indeed, it was not until 1938 that the Jill the Ripper theory was seriously put forward, its exponent being William Stewart, commercial artist turned detective. According to Stewart, the killer was a midwife, possibly connected with an abortion racket.[3]

[2] D. G. Halsted, *Doctor in the Nineties*. London: 1959.
[3] William Stewart, *Jack the Ripper: A New Theory*. London: 1939.

Only a midwife, he argues, would be free to roam the streets of Whitechapel at night without exciting suspicion, even though there might be bloodstains on her clothing. Only a midwife would have the elementary knowledge of anatomy which the Ripper displayed. Lastly, "She would have known each of her victims and had their confidence — an absolutely necessary factor when every strange person was suspect by the women who were killed."

Even if discovered bending over the body of a freshly murdered victim, Jill would have had the perfect alibi. "All she had to say was that she was passing when she came upon the body and at first thought the dead woman required her professional attention. She had started to make an examination when to her horror she found the woman had been murdered." It is only when he comes to the question of motive that Stewart seems to be on uncertain ground.

As an abortionist, Jill the Ripper may well have been denounced to the police by one of the women she had helped, Stewart argues. "A highly-strung, imaginative woman, thrust into prison for such practices, would consider herself a martyr," he says. "Brooding over what she would consider to be an act of treachery, she would eventually convince herself that she had every justification for the murder of such women as those who had denounced her."

The author uses the Mary Kelly murder to clinch his argument. Kelly, it will be recalled, was three months pregnant at the time of her death. What would be more natural than that Kelly, to whom a child would spell disaster, should seek the services of an abortionist to terminate her pregnancy? What more natural than that such an abortionist should be admitted to Kelly's room without an alarm being raised, and that the latter should undress for an examination?

In his quest for straws with which to build bricks Stewart seems to have overlooked a strong hint thrown out by Joseph

Barnett, her paramour, that Kelly was a lesbian, or at any rate that she had lesbian tendencies, a trait not uncommon to prostitutes. If this were true, it would open up a whole new line of investigation.

Barnett told police that he and Black Mary had been living together happily until one Maria Harvey, whom he identified as "this woman of immoral character," intervened in their lives. The market porter did not mind the demands Harvey made upon Kelly's time, but when she proceeded to share their conjugal bed he "objected strongly," he said. Finally, after Harvey had been there two or three nights, he quarreled with Kelly and left her, moving to 24 New Street, Bishopsgate. This was on October 30, or little more than a week before Black Mary was murdered. "Kelly would never have gone wrong again, and I would never have left her, had it not been for the bad women stopping with her," Barnett declared.

Here is a lead which would have been more rewarding for Stewart to follow than his midwife theory. It at least offers a powerful motive for murder: that of jealousy on the part of some vengeful female.

The fact that Caroline Maxwell thought she saw Black Mary standing in front of Miller's Court hours after she had been murdered raises the possibility that the killer, if not a woman, may have made his escape in woman's clothing, at least upon this one occasion. A twenty-nine-year-old doctor named Arthur Conan Doyle, who had published his first Sherlock Holmes story only the previous year, was among those who in 1888 thought that the Ripper disguised himself as a woman to escape detection. Of his father's theory Adrian Conan Doyle writes from Switzerland:

> More than thirty years having passed, it is difficult to recall his views in detail on the Ripper case. However, I do remem-

ber that he considered it likely that the man had a rough knowledge of surgery and probably clothed himself as a woman to avoid undue attention by the police and to approach his victims without arousing suspicion on their part.

So much for the amateurs' efforts to unravel the great Ripper mystery. Let us now take a look at the professionals.

3

"I cannot recall that my grandfather, General Sir Charles Warren, ever stated in writing, his personal views on the identity of Jack the Ripper," writes Watkin W. Williams in reply to my query.[4] Nor did Warren ever express such views in conversation with his grandson. "It was a subject about which he very seldom spoke," asserts Mr. Williams, who is a master at Eton College. "My impression is that he believed the murderer to be a sex maniac who committed suicide after the Miller's Court murder — possibly the young doctor whose body was found in the Thames on December 31st, 1888."

But if Sir Charles Warren was reticent about expressing an opinion in the Ripper case, other police officers were not. Unlike the amateurs whose nominations for the Ripper have varied from midwives to deep-sea fishermen, the professionals showed a remarkable unanimity as to who Jack the Ripper actually was. If one includes Sir Charles Warren on the strength of his grand-

[4] When General Warren resigned as Police Commissioner, he was succeeded by James Monro. But the public had by no means heard the last of Warren. With the outbreak of the Boer War in 1899, he was recalled from the inactive list, made second in command to General Sir Redvers Buller, of the Natal Field Force. When young Lieutenant Winston Churchill broke the news of the Spion Kop disaster to General Warren at the latter's field headquarters, he records that Warren "took it all very calmly . . . He was a charming old gentleman," Churchill adds. "I was genuinely sorry for him. I was also sorry for the Army." General Warren retired in 1905 to devote himself to the Boy Scout movement. He went to his Valhalla in 1927, at the age of eighty-seven.

son's testimony, six out of seven of the police experts who have concerned themselves with the case at one time or another believed the Ripper to be a doctor of medicine. The six who shared this view were Warren, Chief Inspector Abberline, Major Henry Smith, Sir Melville Macnaghten, Sir Basil Thomson and Detective Sergeant Leeson.

This finding looks quite impressive until one examines it closely. Of the sextet only Warren and Abberline held senior posts at Scotland Yard at the time of the Whitechapel murders, and Abberline was convinced that the Ripper and George Chapman, the poisoner, were one and the same person. Major (later Lieutenant Colonel Sir) Henry Smith, an Assistant Police Commissioner for the City of London, was concerned directly with only one murder, that of Catherine Eddowes, and held no fixed views concerning the Ripper's identity, as far as I have been able to make out.

Of the remaining police officers Sir Melville Macnaghten did not join Scotland Yard until six months after the murders, and then only in the capacity of assistant chief constable; while Sir Basil Thomson did not join the Yard as CID head until 1913. Therefore, neither of these men could have had firsthand knowledge of the murders. As for Leeson, he was only a rookie constable pounding a beat in Whitechapel during the period that the Ripper operated, and it is unlikely that his superiors would have taken him into their confidence. This leaves unaccounted for the views of Sir Robert Anderson, Assistant Police Commissioner and head of the CID in 1888.

"Having regard to the interest attaching to the case," Sir Robert Anderson writes in his memoirs, "I am almost tempted to disclose the identity of the murderer . . . But no public benefit would result from such a course, and the traditions of my old department would suffer." Sir Robert does tell us that the Ripper was a "low-class Polish Jew."

It is a remarkable fact that people of that class in the East-end will not give one of their number to Gentile justice . . . I will merely add that the only person who ever had a good view of the murderer unhesitatingly identified the suspect the instant he was confronted with him; but he refused to give evidence against him. In saying that he was a Polish Jew I am merely stating a definitely ascertained fact.

We have encountered this titillation technique once before when Sir Robert refused to divulge the name of the Fleet Street journalist whom he accused of forging the letters signed "Jack the Ripper." Again, the traditions of his old department would have suffered. But in this instance it seems highly irresponsible, for John Pizer, a Polish Jew, had been arrested as a Ripper suspect at the time of the Leather Apron hysteria. Either Anderson is trying to cast doubt on the innocence of Pizer, or else he is merely indulging in anti-Semiticism. (Note the insinuation that the only reason the Ripper went free is that a co-religionist refused to testify against him.) There is a third possibility, and that is that Anderson is talking through his hat, for Sir Robert, it will be recalled, left for a month's holiday in Switzerland on the day the Ripper claimed his second victim, Annie Chapman. He did not return to London until the third and fourth murders had been committed. Sir Robert therefore can hardly claim to have been diligent about the Ripper investigation.

Criminals executed for other murders have been favorite nominees to fill the Ripper's shoes. Thus, Dr. Thomas Neill Cream, the notorious poisoner who murdered four prostitutes, was said to have cried on the scaffold, "I am Jack the —" just as the trapdoor was sprung. Billington, the executioner, is said to have sworn that he heard Cream utter these words. The only flaw to this story is that Cream was serving a sentence in an American prison at the time of the Whitechapel murders.

On the twenty-first day of May — Frederick Deeming passed away;

. . . .

Ta-ra-da-boom-di-ay! This is the happy day,
An East-end holiday, The Ripper's gone away.

This ditty was inspired by the execution on May 21, 1893, in Melbourne, Australia, of Frederick Deeming, thief, confidence trickster, bank robber and bigamist. In 1891 Deeming murdered his wife and four children, cemented their bodies under the scullery floor of their house in Rainhill, Liverpool, and then emigrated to Australia. His Liverpool crimes were not discovered until after he had disposed of a second wife in similar fashion in Melbourne. He was executed before a large crowd by two hangmen, one disguised by a black beard and the other by a white one, and for many years the belief persisted in some circles that he was Jack the Ripper.[5] Indeed, while awaiting execution he was said to have confessed to being the Ripper. L. C. Douthwaite, in his book *Mass Murder*, nails this lie to the mast:

> Whether he confessed or not — and in view of an egotism that, however infamously attained, was avid for limelight, it is by no means unlikely that he did — the assertion was false. Proof of this is absolute. At the time of the Jack the Ripper murders, Deeming was in prison.

4

Chief Inspector Abberline was certain that Jack the Ripper was in reality George Chapman, alias Severin Klosowski, a Polish barber-surgeon, who was hanged in 1903 after poisoning

[5] Apparently a plaster case made from Deeming's death mask was for a long time pointed out by guides at Scotland Yard's "Black Museum" as being the features of Jack the Ripper. I am indebted for this information to F. C. Hails, coroner of Stoke-on-Trent, who says that his particular guide told him confidentially, "We think that he's the man."

his three wives. So convinced was he of this identity that when Chapman was arrested Abberline smacked his hands together and exclaimed, "The police have got Jack the Ripper at last!" Nor was the police inspector alone in believing Chapman to be the Ripper. "Chapman, like the Ripper, was ambidextrous," writes Superintendent Arthur F. Neil of Scotland Yard. "The only description ever given by an eye-witness of the Ripper tallied exactly with Chapman, even to the height, deep-sunk eyes, sallow complexion and thick black moustache." Because these two police officials never wavered in their belief concerning Chapman's qualifications as the Ripper it might be well to look into his history more closely.

As Superintendent Neil noted, Chapman had a thick black mustache which gave his face a brutish appearance. "I have never seen such a villain," remarked Edward Carson, the famous criminal lawyer who led for the Crown at Chapman's trial. "He looked like some evil, wild beast," Carson continued. "I almost expected him to leap over the dock and attack me."

Chapman (real name Klosowski) was born in Poland in December, 1865, which would make him twenty-three years old at the time of the Ripper murders. In Poland he learned the trade of feldsher, a sort of barber's assistant trained to do minor doctoring. When he emigrated to London's Whitechapel in June, 1887, he found work as a barber-surgeon, removing warts and performing simple operations. He later married a Polish girl in London and took her to New Jersey, U.S.A., where he deserted her.

Returning to England, Chapman settled in Hastings. Here in October, 1895, he contracted the first of a series of bigamous marriages. It was with a Mrs. Spink, who was short, blond and plump, and a distinct asset to her husband's barbering business for not only did Mrs. Spink lather the customers — she beguiled them with music on the piano while Chapman shaved them. On April 3, 1897, Chapman bought an ounce of tartar emetic, which contains deadly antimony, a registered poison. Shortly afterwards Mrs. Spink began to waste away, her death on Christmas Day, 1897, being recorded as due to phthisis.

Next we find Chapman as mine host at The Prince of Wales tavern in Finsbury, London, and "married" to one Bessie Taylor, a barmaid. Bessie died on February 13, 1901, aged thirty-six, her death being attributed to "exhaustion from vomiting and diarrhea." She was succeeded six months later, both in the capacity of barmaid and wife, by Maud Marsh, who in turn died of vomiting, diarrhea and abdominal pains. This time, however, Chapman had been careless. Impatient to finish her off, he had administered strychnine to Maud.

The Polish barber was arrested for the murder of Maud Marsh on October 25, 1902. The bodies of Mrs. Spink and Bessie Taylor were exhumed and both showed traces of antimony. In sentencing Chapman to death the judge omitted the customary abjuration, "May the Lord have mercy on your soul."

Hargrave L. Adam, who edited *The Trial of George Chapman,* came to the conclusion that Chapman and the Ripper were one and the same person on the following evidence.

(1) The first Whitechapel murder occurred shortly after Chapman's arrival from Warsaw, and all during the autumn of 1888 he was never very far from the scenes of the various Ripper crimes. (2) The description (presumably Hutchinson's) of a man seen with Mary Kelly just before she was murdered was "a most faithful description of Chapman," according to Adam. (3) The use of "Americanisms" in the Ripper letters tallied with the fact that Chapman had spent two years in the United States and frequently posed as an American. (4) Finally, Adam points out that Chapman possessed the requisite surgical skill to be the Ripper. Before coming to England he had worked as a hospital assistant in Praga, as a "barber's sur-

geon" with the Russian Army, and the Polish government had issued a junior surgeon's certificate to him in 1886.[6]

Some of Adam's arguments are easily disposed of. For example, Chapman may have tried to pass himself off as a Yankee, but he would not have been very adept at the use of American slang in 1888 for the simple reason that he did not visit the United States until 1890. Both Adam and Superintendent Arthur F. Neil make much of the fact that Chapman resembled the man whom Hutchinson saw with Mary Kelly on the night she was murdered. But then Chapman's thickset, brutish looks tallied with almost all the descriptions of Ripper suspects furnished to the police, with this exception: most of these descriptions were of middle-aged men. Chapman as already noted was only twenty-three years old at the time of the Whitechapel murders.

The question of the Ripper's surgical skill will be dealt with later, but it should be pointed out here that the women whom Chapman murdered differed greatly from the Ripper's down-and-outers. The Ripper scoured the sewers of the East End for his victims, but Mrs. Spink and her sisters *in extremis* came from respectable, working-class homes. The very fact that Chapman found it necessary to go through a parody of marriage with his intended victims argues for their moral sobriety.

The most crushing argument against Chapman's being Jack the Ripper is, of course, the fact that he was a poisoner, choosing to dispatch his victims by this cruel, but refined method. Psychiatrists and criminologists who down the years have studied the mentality of poisoners find that they have little in common with sadists of the Ripper type. Adam anticipates this objection and tries to get around it by saying, "If Chapman was actually Jack the Ripper, poisoning, *as a much safer means of killing,* might easily have suggested itself to him. Having

[6] H. L. Adam, *The Trial of George Chapman.* London: 1930.

changed his method, it became, of course, imperative that he should seek an entirely different class of victims." (My italics.)

To make this bland assertion is to ignore the whole point of the murders and to misread the Ripper's character completely. The Ripper was not interested in "a much safer means of killing." He chose the most dangerous and the most public means of murder possible, his crimes being characterized by increasing audacity. Far from seeking safety, he deliberately called attention to himself.

5

The latest theory concerning Jack the Ripper, that he was a Russian named Alexander Pedachenko, is really a variant of Chapman, the demon poisoner. However, the Pedachenko theory is ably argued by Donald McCormick, a Fleet Street journalist, who cites as one of his authorities Rasputin the mad Russian monk.[7] Briefly, McCormick believes that Pedachenko was sent to London as a Czarist secret agent to spy on the anarchists, and that he committed the Whitechapel murders in order to discredit the anarchists and to get them deported from Britain.

Pedachenko, as described by McCormick, had much in common with Chapman. Both men were feldshers, or barber-surgeons qualified to do minor doctoring; and both were employed in this capacity in London's poorer districts, removing warts and treating skin diseases, as well as cutting hair. McCormick, however, is not content to let the matter rest there; he insists upon giving the arm of coincidence another twist. Pedachenko, according to the journalist, assisted at a clinic *attended by four of the Ripper's victims — Tabram, Chapman, Nicholls and Kelly* — St. Saviour's Infirmary in Walworth. (Why these four should journey all the way to Walworth on

[7] Donald McCormick, *The Identity of Jack the Ripper.* London: 1959.

the south bank of the Thames, McCormick does not say, but he cites Dr. Dutton as his authority for this information.) After the Whitechapel murders, Pedachenko allegedly was smuggled out of London and back to Russia, where he died in a lunatic asylum in 1908.

According to the *Ochrana Gazette,* a confidential bulletin circulating among the Czarist secret police, Pedachenko was wanted for the murder of a woman in the Montmartre district of Paris in 1886, and he may have fled to London in order to escape arrest. He disguised himself as a woman on occasions, the *Gazette* asserts, and then goes on to describe him as having, "heavy, black eyebrows and a moustache which he usually wore curled and waxed at the ends"! (McCormick gets around this contradiction neatly by recalling the burnt-out teakettle which was found in the fireplace ashes in Mary Kelly's room. What was the kettle used for? "Not to make tea," McCormick assures us, "but perhaps to boil water for Pedachenko to shave off his moustache." This done, the Russian disguised himself in Kelly's clothing and made his escape.)

There remains the question of motive, always the bugbear when it concerns Jack the Ripper. McCormick quotes from the so-called "secret papers" of Rasputin to the effect that the Czarist police loosed their greatest criminal lunatic on London "in order to exhibit to the world certain defects of the English police system" — i.e., to show up Sir Charles Warren and his minions for the bumbling, ineffective force that they were. But McCormick suggests as a more plausible explanation of the murders that they were part of a Czarist plot to discredit the Russian anarchists who were living in London. This would explain why, for example, Elizabeth Stride's body was found outside the International Workmen's Educational Club in Berner Street, a rendezvous for Russian and Polish socialists. Sir Basil Thomson lent his weight to this theory. "Certainly part of the policy of the Czarist Secret Service," he declared in a letter, "was to discredit anarchist organizations by means of trumped up charges of terrorism and robbery. The Peter the Painter affair proved that." (Sir Basil was referring to the Sidney Street Siege.)

McCormick states that Dr. Dutton was "quite emphatic" that the Ripper was Pedachenko, and that the doctor's summaries of the evidence were "level-headed, cautious assessments of fact . . . He did not put forward any wild theories." To the contrary, the good doctor time after time put forth statements without supporting evidence. For example, his statement that four of the Ripper's victims attended a clinic in Walworth where Pedachenko was an assistant "right up to the time of their deaths" — what proof did he have for this wild assertion? This is only one of the self-serving statements quoted by McCormick as emanating from Dr. Dutton, who seems to have run with both the hares and the hounds during the course of his inquiries concerning the Ripper case. In the absence of better proof, Dr. Dutton's statement that Pedachenko and the Ripper were one and the same person must be treated with great reserve.

The professionals — the police experts and others — are no more helpful in establishing the Ripper's identity than the amateurs. If anything, they are more confused. They seem to be mesmerized by the Ripper's supposed medical knowledge and unconsciously, perhaps, to have accepted the cliché of "the man with the little black bag." In fact, the little black bag seems to have become the King Charles's head of everyone who has ever gone near the Ripper case.[8]

[8] In his book *The Fatal Caress* (New York: 1947), Richard H. Barker advances the notion that Jack the Ripper was a middle-aged professor from one of the London colleges with a passion for playing practical jokes, and that he carried in his little black bag nothing more lethal than manuscripts and lecture notes. "Such a theory," Barker writes, "helps to explain the one fault that can reasonably be attributed to Jack — his incorrigible long-windedness, his inability to stop, when it was perfectly clear that his public had had enough."

Similarly the experts cannot bring themselves to believe that Jack the Ripper might have been an Englishman. No, he was dark, swarthy, foreign-looking, the very opposite of the conventional blue-eyed Englishman with his fresh complexion. The Ripper was, in fact, a Portuguese, a Russian or a Pole — one can take one's pick. After the welter of speculation we have just surveyed, it comes as no surprise to read in *Reynold's News* of fairly recent date: "Nothing in the years that have passed has come to light to alter the Yard's theory, which marked the closing of their file on the most callous murderer in police history: 'He was a Polish sailor.' "

CHAPTER XVI

SHAW WRITES A LETTER

"Now that the Ripper has been so successful in calling attention for the moment to the social question . . ." Thus does George Bernard Shaw begin a letter to the *Star* in which he discusses the Whitechapel murders. To Shaw, then aged thirty-two, the identity of Jack the Ripper was quite simple; he was a social reformer of "independent genius." The young playwright, who had already established a reputation for himself as a moralist and a wit, used the Ripper as a means of scoring points against the propertied classes; and yet his thesis has more logic to recommend it than most of the lucubrations of the so-called experts we have just examined. In his letter to the *Star*, headed "Blood Money to Whitechapel," he begins by contrasting conditions before and after the coming of the Ripper.

> Less than a year ago [Shaw writes], the West-end press was literally clamoring for the blood of the people — hounding Sir Charles Warren to thrash and muzzle the scum who dared to complain that they were starving . . . behaving, in short, as the propertied class always does behave when the workers throw it into a frenzy of terror by venturing to show their teeth.

Since the beginning of the Whitechapel murders, the press, however, had undergone a remarkable change of heart. Editors now wrote with feeling about the "Dark Annies" in their midst, and the air was loud with *mea culpas.*

> Whilst we conventional Social Democrats were wasting our time on education, agitation and organization, some independent genius has taken the matter in hand, and by simply murdering and disembowelling four women, converted the proprietary press to an inept sort of communism. The moral is a pretty one, and the Insurrectionists, the Dynamitards, the Invincibles and the extreme left of the Anarchist party will not be slow to draw it . . . Every gaol blown up, every window broken, every shop looted, every corpse found disembowelled means another ten pound not for "ransom."

Shaw then refers to the unemployment riots of 1886, when stones were heaved through the windows of the Carlton Club in Pall Mall with such effect that panic-stricken officialdom hastily raised the Mansion House Fund for the Relief of Distress from £3000 to £78,000. "It remains to be seen how much these murders may prove worth to the East End in *panem et circenses.*" The young music critic, as he was then, cannot resist taking a sans-culottish jibe at the aristocracy.

> If the habits of Duchesses only admitted of their being decoyed into Whitechapel backyards [he declares], a single experiment in slaughterhouse anatomy on an aristocratic victim might fetch in a round half million and save the necessity of sacrificing four women of the people.

The possibility that Jack the Ripper may have been a zealous, if misguided social reformer had occurred independently to the *Star* only to be rejected out of hand. "Finally," the *Star* suggests editorially, "there is the off-chance — too horrible to contemplate — that we have a social experimentation abroad determined to make the classes see and feel how the masses live." Too horrible to contemplate — to the Victorian mind the idea of murder being used as an instrument of social reform was just as unthinkable as was the notion of a killer who was also a practical joker, and who signed himself "Saucy Jack." They preferred to regard the Whitechapel murders as being motiveless. "Sexual murders are the most difficult of all for police to bring home to the perpetrators," writes Sir Melville Macnaghten, "for motives there are none; only a lust for blood, and in many cases a hatred of woman as woman."

Still others had turned over in their minds the idea that the Ripper murders might have had a social or political content without realizing the full implications of this possibility. *The Lancet,* the medical journal, even speaks of the murders as having "served a good purpose," that purpose being to "awaken the public conscience." Reverend Samuel Barnett, of Toynbee Hall, held that "the murders were, it may almost be said, bound to come . . . The Whitechapel horrors," he added, "will not be in vain if at last the public conscience awakes to consider the life which these horrors reveal." His wife, Henrietta Barnett, whom we have already met as the organizer of the Whitechapel women's petition, went further.

Commenting on how powerfully the murders had served as a stimulus for housing reform, Mrs. Barnett wrote, "Verily, it was the crucifixion of these poor lost souls which saved the district." Even *Commonweal,* the organ of William Morris's socialism, was forced to concede that "in our age of contradictions and absurdities, a fiend-murderer may become a more effective reformer than all the honest propagandists in the world."

"The murders were . . . bound to come." If they were bound to come, were they not, by the same token, bound to occur in East London?

2

Jack the Ripper was almost Aristotelian when it came to observing the dramatic unities. In the matter of locale, for example, what better setting for serial murder than London's East End, always supposing that one killed in order to call attention to social injustice? And not the whole of the East End either but a tiny segment of it near Spitalfields market and bounded by Whitechapel Road, "the evil quarter mile," as Mr. Barnett called it. Was this choice fortuitious? *The Lancet* gives the answer in remarking editorially, "It is worthy of note that the crimes have been committed in *precisely the same district where, as sanitary reformers, we have often demanded the intervention of the authorities.*" (My italics.)

The victims, themselves, with one exception, were strikingly alike, which is the second unity that the Ripper observed. They were prostitutes who were past their prime, and who were now reduced to the depths of degradation. They were the bundles of rags whom Jack London found sleeping in the shadow of Christ Church, Spitalfields, and who he was assured would sell their souls for tuppence. The exception, of course, was Mary Kelly, who was still young and had her looks.

There was even a certain unity of time imposed upon the pattern of murder, a unity which has nothing to do, incidentally, with the lunar theory advanced by L. Forbes Winslow, the alienist.[1] The Ripper was a weekend killer. All five murders were committed on either the first or last weekend of the month in the interval between Friday night and Monday morning. Was this not in order to achieve maximum notoriety? East London was thronged with people on the weekend, some attracted by the open-air market in Petticoat Lane, others showing off their finery in Whitechapel Road. What better means of creating horror and consternation than to confront this multitude with bloodstains not yet dry on the pavement?

The acid test of the Ripper's intention came with the Kelly

[1] Winslow, however, was right in asserting that all five murders occurred either when the new moon rose, or when the moon had entered its last quarter, according to *Whitaker's Almanack* for 1888. The heavenly configuration on September 7, the eve of the Annie Chapman murder, was of a particularly ominous character, both Mercury and Venus being in conjunction with the moon, according to the *Almanack*.

murder, for which he shrewdly chose a public holiday, the Lord Mayor's Show. Long before this festive occasion arrived, a Fleet Street reporter predicted that if the Ripper intended further crimes, he would choose the morning of November 9. "A marked day, a day of great excitement, would just suit him if his motive was to show himself the boss criminal of the century," the reporter is quoted by the *Spectator* as saying.

And what of the public manner in which these crimes were committed? The victims, with the exception of Mary Kelly, had their throats cut in the open air. Their bodies were mutilated, then left on the public highway for all the world to see. Absolutely no attempt was made at concealment. On the contrary, here was murder that deliberately called attention to itself. The pattern could not have been more distinctive had Jack the Ripper pinned his calling card to the petticoats of each of his victims.

3

"The strangler is obviously not a monster with horns coming out of his head." Thus did Detective Lieutenant John J. Donovan, of the Boston police, comment on the Boston Strangler in May, 1963, after the strangler's eighth victim had been found with a nylon stocking twisted around her neck.[2] "He is almost certainly a very respectable young man, well-spoken, and probably wearing a well-cut Ivy League suit." With the exception of the Ivy League suit, this description could fit equally well Jack the Ripper. While everything indicates that the Ripper suffered from a split personality, that he was a real-life Jekyll and Hyde case, he undoubtedly was quiet-spoken, with nothing in his looks or manner to attract attention, let alone to raise alarm.

English law has a rather apt phrase to describe such an

[2] The *Daily Express*, May 16, 1963.

average man. He is known in legal parlance as "the Man on the Clapham Omnibus." In his averageness Jack the Ripper was the very apotheosis of this omnibus straphanger.

Probably the only reliable description of the Ripper was that furnished by Joseph Lawende, the commercial traveler, who saw Catherine Eddowes standing close to a man in Mitre Square just ten minutes before she was found murdered. "It was bright moonlight, almost as light as day, and he saw them distinctly," remarks Major Henry Smith, the deputy City police commissioner, adding, "This was, without doubt, the murderer and his victim." Here is Lawende's description of the man: about thirty years of age, five-feet nine inches in height, *shabby appearance, fair complexion and having a small fair mustache,* dressed in something like navy serge and wearing a cloth cap with a peak. (My italics.) Note the "shabby appearance" — we are a long way here from the music-hall villain wearing the astrakhan-trimmed coat and the spats, the horseshoe-shaped tiepin, the massive gold watch chain with the red stone set in its seal. And the "fair complexion, fair mustache" puts us in another world from those other villains — the dark, swarthy, barber-surgeons of Russian or Polish descent.

"The killer has a silver tongue," Detective Lieutenant Donovan remarked of the Boston Strangler. "In each case he had struck up an acquaintanceship with his victim and had won her confidence." The same might be said with equal conviction of Jack the Ripper. Here was someone who knew how to approach prostitutes without arousing their suspicion, who could talk their language, catch them off guard. And it should be remembered that the whores who worked Whitechapel were in a state bordering on hysteria all during that Autumn of Terror when the unknown killer was decimating their ranks. There were suggestions in the press that pistols should be issued to the harlotry of Whitechapel, and at least one of these drabs carried a police whistle and used it, as has been noted, when she was accosted by a drunken licensed victualer.

Whether or not the Ripper lived in the East End, and I am strongly inclined to think that he did not, he certainly knew its geography. He knew the shortcuts between streets, which alleys were blind, which streets led to dead ends. He knew, for example, that there was a public sink up an alley from Dorset Street, and he washed his hands there after murdering Catherine Eddowes, the police arriving before all the blood-stained water had drained away. He also knew which lodging houses had interconnecting doors, and how to run the maze of their courts without being detected. He had studied the terrain as a general might study a situation map.

For his life depended upon his knowledge of the area. On the night of the double murder, for example, when the police were hot on his heels, one false turning, one misstep would have landed him in the arms of the law. He knew the habits of the local police patrols intimately. He had evidently timed their rounds, trained himself to recognize their measured tread, noted their wooden lack of perception. If Jack the Ripper was not actually of the East End, and all indications are that he was not, he was certainly omnipresent there. He hovered over this slum-ridden, crime-infested area like some evil genius.

4

In the weeks that followed the Mary Kelly murder an extraordinary state of affairs revealed itself at Scotland Yard. Far from redoubling its efforts to apprehend the killer, the Yard actually appeared to relax its vigilance. The senior inspectors assigned to the Ripper case were withdrawn. So were the constables who had been sent into the East End as reinforcements. The Commercial Street station, which had been field headquarters for cigar-chewing detectives in bowler hats, once more reverted to normal.

Stone cross marking the grave of Montague John Druitt in Wimborne Cemetery, Wimborne, Dorset.

James W. Bousfield, of Stepney, East London, holding one of the watch chains which Martha Tabram hawked for a living. Martha, who had lodged with the Bousfields at one time, was found murdered on August 7, 1888. It is doubtful, however, that she was one of the Ripper's victims.

Mrs. Annie Tapper, now in her eighties, who claims she sold a bunch of grapes to Jack the Ripper on the night of the double murder, September 30, 1888. He was "dressed for a wedding," she maintains.

“Ripper’s Corner” in Mitre Square, where the body of Catherine Eddowes was found. Even before the bloodstains had been washed away, a mother drew her infant from beneath her shawl and held it above the heads of the bystanders. “Does it want to see the blood?” she crooned. “And so it shall, bless its heart.” Today, “Ripper’s Corner” is shown to visitors as one of the outstanding sights of East London.

The spot in Buck's Row (now Durward Street), Whitechapel, where Mary Ann Nicholls, the Ripper's first victim, was found with her throat slit.

The Working Lads' Institute in Whitechapel Road where several of the Ripper murder inquests were held. In 1888 East London, with a population larger than that of Philadephia, had not a single morgue, and inquests were usually held in the back parlors of saloon bars.

Below: The Interior as it is today, almost unchanged from the Ripper's day. Around this table sat the coroner's juries. The same biblical text stared down at them from the walls.

Westfield, the house where Montague John Druitt was born in Wimborne, Dorset.

One of the "model" dwellings which replaced the doss houses in Flower and Dean Street, Spitalfields. Slum clearance of this sort was given impetus by Jack the Ripper, but, as can be seen from this photograph, the Victorians replaced one type of slum by another.

Commissioner while his men sought these "sagacious beasts." Hours later it was found that they had long since been returned to their kennels in Scarborough.

By getting lost in the fog and generally making a nuisance of themselves, the bloodhounds Barnaby and Burgho provided a much-needed comic relief to what was pure tragedy. After Mary Kelly was found murdered, the investigation was delayed on orders from the Metropolitan Police

Above: Bemonocled Sir Charles Warren rides his hobby horse into battle. His efforts to militarize the police were no match for the cunning of the Whitechapel killer.

Punch satirizes the police for their failure to apprehend the killer. The cop on the beat took the rap for the bumbling ineptitude of his superiors. *Reproduced by permission of* Punch.

Opposite: The Ripper not only hastened the resignation of Warren as police chief, but nearly unseated Home Secretary Henry Matthews, who was accused of "philandering with pothouse Tories while God's poor are being slaughtered wholesale in London." Even Lord Salisbury, the Prime Minister, did not escape criticism.

Scene of the Miller's Court murder as depicted by an artist in one of the "penny dreadfuls." The silk-hatted villain seen entering No. 13 with Mary Kelly carries the inevitable black bag, in this case a Gladstone. Hand luggage of this type soon went out of vogue once the Ripper had begun his operations.

The Oxford and Cambridge undergraduates at Toynbee Hall continued to patrol East End streets after dark all that winter — until February, 1889, to be exact, by which time the patrollers were "unable to bear the long hours and exposure," according to the *Toynbee Record.* But their example was ignored by the police. In fact, the police were so confident that the last had been heard of the Whitechapel killer that they disbanded their special patrols. What made Scotland Yard so sure that it would not be bothered by Jack the Ripper again? Why did it believe that he had disappeared from the face of the earth?

Albert Backert, of the Whitechapel Vigilance Committee, provides us with the answer. Backert failed to share the general optimism at Scotland Yard. In fact, he was so sure that the Ripper would strike again that he held his Whitechapel Vigilance Committee in reserve, ready to activate it at a moment's notice. Seeing that Scotland Yard did not intend to pursue the killer further, Backert sought an interview with the police early in March, 1889, at which he complained bitterly about police complacency. The result of that interview he noted down:

> I was asked if I would agree to be sworn to secrecy, on the understanding that I was given certain information [Backert recalled]. Foolishly, I agreed. It was then suggested to me that the Vigilance Committee and its patrols might be disbanded *as the police were quite certain that the Ripper was dead.* I protested that, as I had been sworn to secrecy, I really ought to be given more information than this. "It isn't necessary for you to know any more," I was told. "The man in question is dead. *He was fished out of the Thames two months ago* and it would only cause pain to relatives if we said any more than that."
>
> I again protested that I had been sworn to secrecy for nothing, that I was really no wiser than before. "If there are no

> more murders, I shall respect this confidence, but if there are any more I shall consider I am absolved from my pledge of secrecy." The police then got very tough. They told me a pledge was a solemn matter, that *anyone who put out stories that the Ripper was still alive might be proceeded against for causing a public mischief.* However, they agreed that if there were any other murders which the police were satisfied could be Ripper murders, that was another matter. [My italics.][3]

Backert was convinced that the police were either pulling his leg, or trying to get rid of him and his vigilante committee, which they had regarded as a nuisance from the start. "I never believed the yarn," he confesed, "though I kept my pledge until after the [Alice] McKenzie murder in 1891."

Backert was wrong on one count. The theory that Jack the Ripper committed suicide shortly after the Kelly murder by drowning himself in the Thames was no leg pull. It was the firm conviction of two police chiefs. Three, if one includes Sir Charles Warren.

The suicide theme is taken up by a number of crime writers who were in the confidence of Scotland Yard. Thus, after declaring that police "strongly suspected" a certain doctor of being the Ripper, Major Arthur Griffiths states that "he disappeared immediately after the last murder . . . On the last day of that year, seven weeks later, his body was found floating in the Thames and was said to have been in the water a month." Basil Thomson, who became Assistant Police Commissioner in charge of CID in 1913, pinpoints the doctor's nationality. "The belief of the CID officers at the time," he writes, "was that they [the murders] were the work of an insane Russian doctor and that this man escaped arrest by committing suicide at the end of 1888."

Sir John Moylan, OBE, police historian and onetime assistant

[3] Backert's statement is quoted by Donald McCormick, who got it, apparently, from Dr. Thomas Dutton's papers.

under-secretary at the Home Office, refrains from speculating as to the Ripper's nationality, but merely notes, "The murderer it is now certain escaped justice by committing suicide at the end of 1888." We have already encountered the suicide earlier in the case of Edwin T. Woodhall, a crime writer who was once a member of the CID. Woodhall, it will be recalled, told how the body of a Ripper suspect who blacked his face with burnt cork was found in the Thames when a paddle boat tied to Waterloo Pier was shifted. "The black burnt cork and white paint on the already decomposing features were hideously evident," Woodhall claimed.

None of these men, be it noted, was actually engaged on the Ripper murder investigation of 1888. Why then were they so positive that the Ripper had drowned himself after the Miller's Court murder? Why this unanimity of opinion? What were the "circumstances which left little doubt in the official mind"? It is time now to get to the bottom of this mystery.

CHAPTER XVII

THE RIPPER AS A SUICIDE

THE MAN responsible for spreading the story that Jack the Ripper drowned himself after the Kelly murder was Sir Melville Macnaghten, who served as Assistant Police Commissioner in charge of the CID from 1903 until 1913. In his memoirs Macnaghten speaks of the two great disappointments of his life, the one being that he never played cricket for Eton against Harrow. "The second," he writes, "was that I became a detective officer six months after Jack the Ripper committed suicide, and never had a go at that fascinating individual."

Macnaghten's father was at one time chairman of the East India Company, and Sir Melville's education, as already indicated, was Eton; therefore his choice of the Metropolitan Police as a career was as surprising as the fact that he joined the force in the humble role of assistant chief constable. His police career, however, was a distinguished one, and although he never had a go at the Ripper he handled many other important cases, including some celebrated homicides. He was knighted for his services in 1907, retired in 1913 because of ill health.

Hargrave L. Adam describes Sir Melville as being "deliberate, self-contained, secretive, courteous, with a keen eye and cautious tongue," and he then refers to his head as being "crammed full with official secrets." One of these official secrets, according to Adam, was the identity of Jack the Ripper.

Adam quotes Macnaghten as saying that he had "documentary proof" of the Ripper's identity, but that he had burnt the papers — "an unprecedented thing, surely for a police official to do," comments Adam.[1] Donald McCormick repeats this story about the destruction of documents. "Sir Melville Macnaghten's views," McCormick writes, "are specially interesting if only because on one occasion he stated that he had 'documentary proof of the identity of the criminal, but that he burnt the papers' . . . This is an amazing admission from a senior police officer," he added.

Macnaghten's daughter, the Dowager Lady Aberconway, thinks that if her father did make such a statement, he did so in order to silence his cronies at the Garrick Club, who were always pestering him with queries concerning Jack the Ripper. She denies, however, that her father actually destroyed any documentary proof concerning the Ripper's identity. In a letter to the *New Statesman* of November 7, 1959, Lady Aberconway declares: "I possess my father's private notes on Jack the Ripper in which he names three individuals 'against whom police held very reasonable suspicion' and states which of these three, in his judgment, was the actual killer."

It is these notes which have furnished the basis of all subsequent assertions that Jack the Ripper committed suicide. Major Arthur Griffiths, for example, copied the notes almost verbatim, merely omitting the names of the three individuals whom the police strongly suspected. More recently the notes were used in a television reconstruction of the Ripper crimes which Daniel Farson presented to a British audience. This time Macnaghten's chief suspect was described in some detail but not named, although the initials "M. J. D." were given and his death certificate was shown on the television screen with the name blocked out.

Macnaghten's notes on Jack the Ripper were written in 1894,

[1] H. L. Adam, *op. cit.*

or six years after the Whitechapel murders. They were written in response to a series of articles which had appeared in *The Sun* in February, 1894, and which had tried to pin the Ripper's crimes on a harmless fetishist named Thomas Cutbush.[2] Macnaghten is evidently concerned to scotch rumors which seek to keep the Ripper legend alive by attributing to him various unsolved murders of a violent character, and he certainly succeeds in giving the lie to the *Sun*'s wild assertions concerning Cutbush. He then goes on to assert that "the Whitechapel murderer had five victims and five only," which he enumerates as Mary Ann Nicholls, Annie Chapman, Elizabeth Stride, Catherine Eddowes and Mary Kelly. As to why the Ripper ceased to operate after November 9, 1888, Macnaghten writes:

> A much more rational and workable theory, to my way of thinking, is that the Ripper's brain gave way altogether after his awful glut in Miller's-court, and that he then committed suicide, or, as a less likely alternative, was found to be hopelessly insane by his relatives, that they, suspecting the worst, had him confined in a lunatic asylum . . .
>
> I enumerate the cases of three men against whom the police held very reasonable suspicion. Personally, and after much careful and deliberate consideration, I am inclined to exonerate the last two, *but I have always held strong opinions regarding No. 1, and the more I think the matter over, the stronger do these opinions become.* The truth, however, will never be known, and did, indeed, at one time lie at the bottom of the Thames, if my conjectures be correct.
>
> *No. 1.* Mr. M. J. Druitt, *a doctor of about 41 years of age and of fairly good family, who disappeared at the time of the Miller's-court murder, and whose body was found floating in the Thames on 3rd December, i.e. seven weeks after the said murder. The body was said to have been in the water for a month, or more — on it was found a season ticket between Blackheath and London. From private information I have*

[2] See Appendix B.

little doubt but that his own family suspected this man of being the Whitechapel murderer; and it was alleged that he was sexually insane.

No. 2. KOSMINSKI, a Polish Jew, who lived in the very heart of the district where the murders were committed. He had become insane owing to many years indulgence in solitary vices. He had a great hatred of women with strong homicidal tendencies. He was (and I believe is) detained in a lunatic asylum about March, 1889. This man in appearance strongly resembled the individual seen by the City P.C. near Mitre-square.

No. 3. MICHAEL OSTROG, a mad Russian doctor and a convict and unquestionably a homicidal maniac. This man was said to have been habitually cruel to women, and for a long time was known to have carried about with him surgical knives and other instruments; his antecedents were of the very worst and his whereabouts at the time of the Whitechapel murders could never be satisfactorily accounted for. He is still alive. [My italics.]

In his memoirs published in 1914, Macnaghten again speculates about the identity of Jack the Ripper, obviously referring to the notes he had made twenty years earlier. But this time there is no mention of the Polish Jew or of the Russian doctor, nor does Sir Melville give the name of the individual upon whom his suspicion had finally fastened. Nor is he inclined to believe any longer that this individual had ever been committed to an asylum by his relatives. Of this chief suspect he volunteers the following additional information:

The man of course was a sexual maniac . . . I do not think that there was anything of religious mania about the real Simon Pure, nor do I believe that he had ever been detained in an asylum, nor lived in lodgings. I incline to the belief that the individual who held up London in terror resided with his own people; that he absented himself from home at certain times, and that he committed suicide on or about the 10th November, 1888.

Sir Melville Macnaghten certainly had strong views concerning this individual, whom he had identified earlier as "M. J. Druitt, a doctor of about 41 years of age," views which he communicated to Major Arthur Griffiths, a onetime Inspector of Her Majesty's Prisons, among others. Journalist George R. Sims, another of Macnaghten's cronies, also apparently heard the story, for in his memoirs he says that the Ripper was a doctor, and confirms that "his body was found in the Thames after it had been in the river for nearly a month . . ." He goes on, "There were circumstances which left little doubt in the official mind as to the Ripper's identity." In an earlier work he paints the picture of the Ripper as a homicidal maniac leading the ordinary life of a free citizen:

> He rode in tramcars and omnibuses [Sims asserts]. He traveled to Whitechapel by the underground railway, often late at night. Probably on several occasions he had but one fellow-passenger in the compartment with him, and that may have been a woman . . . Some of us must have passed him in the street, sat with him perhaps at a cafe or a restaurant. He was a man of birth and education, and had sufficient means to keep himself without work. For a whole year at least he was a free man, exercising all the privileges of freedom. And yet he was a homicidal maniac of the most diabolical kind.[3]

2

"I never kept a diary, nor even possessed a notebook," Sir Melville boasts in his memoirs. It is perhaps unfortunate that the CID chief did not keep a notebook, for, relying upon his memory concerning events which had occurred many years earlier, he has allowed a number of errors to creep into his discussions of the Ripper case, both in the notes he made in 1894 and in his memoirs published in 1914. For example, in

[3] George R. Sims, *The Mysteries of Modern London.* London: 1906.

the memoirs he prefaces his remarks about Jack the Ripper by saying, "Although . . . the Whitechapel murderer, in all probability, put an end to himself soon after the Dorset Street affair in November, 1888, *certain facts pointing to this conclusion were not in possession of the police till some years after I became a detective officer.*" (My italics.) Here, of course, Macnaghten's memory is clearly at fault, as attested by Albert Backert's statement. It will be recalled that Backert, as a member of the Whitechapel Vigilance Committee, was called in by Scotland Yard as early as March, 1889, and told to call off the street patrols because "the police were quite certain that the Ripper was dead," his body having been "fished out of the Thames two months ago." (Backert's interview at Scotland Yard would have taken place before Sir Melville Macnaghten had even joined the Yard.)

Again, in his 1894 notes, Sir Melville describes the Polish suspect Kosminski as "strongly resembling the individual seen by the City P.C. near Mitre Square" the night Catherine Eddowes was found murdered. I can find no reference to a City police constable having seen a man near Mitre Square either immediately before or immediately after the murder. To the contrary, P.C. Edward Watkins, who walked this particular beat, testified at the inquest that he had encountered no one near the square. Apparently Macnaghten has confused the City constable with Joseph Lawende, the commercial traveler, who definitely saw a man and woman talking together in Mitre Square fifteen minutes before the murder was discovered.

Macnaghten makes the greatest error of all in describing his No. 1 suspect as "a doctor of about 41 years of age." Montague John Druitt was only thirty-one years old when he committed suicide, and he was not a doctor. He was a barrister who had been called to the Bar at the Inner Temple in April, 1885. His father, William Druitt, however, was a surgeon. So were his grandfather, his uncle and his cousin. Montague John Druitt, barrister at law, came from a long line of Fellows of the Royal College of Surgeons.

3

Leonard Matters, in his book on Jack the Ripper, scoffs at the assertion that the Ripper's body was found floating in the Thames. "There is no warrant whatever for this assertion," he writes, "and all the theories based on it, all the confident assurances that the police had found 'their man' are worthless." Donald McCormick is inclined to agree. "The simple test for the theory," says McCormick, "is to find out what doctor was found drowned in the Thames on the last day of December 1888. And as soon as this test is applied the theory is destroyed. For in none of the leading London morning or evening papers of the day is there any report of such an incident at any time between 9 November, 1888, and the end of January 1889. Nor do the obituary columns of the newspapers, nor those of the *Medical Directory* for 1889 and 1890 provide any clues." It is a pity that McCormick did not cast his net a bit wider, for had he done so his patience might have been rewarded. For example, had he searched *The County of Middlesex Independent* for Wednesday, January 2, 1889, he would have come across the following item, which occupied ten lines at the bottom of page 3:

> FOUND IN THE RIVER — The body of a well-dressed man was discovered on Monday in the river off Thornycroft's torpedo works, by a waterman named Winslow. The police were communicated with and the deceased was conveyed to the mortuary. The body, which is that of a man about 40 years of age, has been in the water about a month. From certain papers found on the body friends at Bournemouth have been telegraphed to. An inquest will be held today [Wednesday].

Elsewhere the paper, which was published in Brentford, noted that there was a "dense fog" on Monday, December 31, the day the body was found. Then, on January 5, 1889, the *Independent* identified the water-soaked corpse and gave a short account of the inquest:

SUICIDE IN THE THAMES — Dr. Diplock held an inquiry at the "Lamb Tap," Chiswick, on Wednesday of the body of a gentleman named Montague John Druit [sic], 31 years of age, which was found by a waterman floating in the Thames off Thorneycroft's, on Monday. *The pockets of the deceased were found to contain stones.* The jury returned a verdict of "Suicide during temporary insanity." [My italics.]

For further details concerning Montague John Druitt one must turn to *The Southern Guardian* of January 5, 1889, where the following item appears:

SAD DEATH OF A LOCAL BARRISTER: An inquiry was on Wednesday held by Dr. Diplock, at Chiswick, respecting the death of Montague John Druitt, 31 years of age, who was found drowned in the Thames. The deceased was identified by his brother, a solicitor residing at Bournemouth, who stated that the deceased was a barrister-at-law, but had recently been an assistant at a school in Blackheath. The deceased had left a letter, addressed to Mr. Valentine, of the school, in which he alluded to suicide. Evidence having been given as to discovering deceased in the Thames — upon his body were found a cheque for £50 and £16 in gold — the Jury returned a verdict of "Suicide whilst of unsound mind."

The deceased gentleman was well known and much respected in this neighbourhood. He was a barrister of bright talent, he had a promising future before him, and his untimely end is deeply deplored. The funeral took place in Wimborne cemetery on Thursday afternoon, and the body was followed to the grave by the deceased's relatives and a few friends . . .

4

Montague John Druitt was born on August 15, 1857, in Wimborne, Dorset (present pop. 4487), which is in the heart of what is known as the Hardy country. Westward lies the vast, bracken-covered "Egdon Heath" of Thomas Hardy's novels, while closer at hand are villages whose names are but thinly disguised in his works. Hardy, himself, lived in Wimborne Minster, or "Warborne" as it became in his writings, in the early 1880's, and he would thus have been a familiar figure to Montague John, then in his early manhood. Wimborne's name is Saxon and derives from the bourne or brook called the Wim which flows through the town, and which is now known perversely enough as the Allen. But it is the Minister half of the town's corporate name which inspires the most pride, referring to the handsome church beneath which Ethelred, the Saxon King, is said to be buried. To the local mind the very presence of the Minster, with its astronomical clock, its chained library of rare books, its central tower dating from the twelfth century, confers "cathedral status" upon this market town.

In this "cathedral city in miniature," as the official guidebook describes it, Dr. William Druitt, the father of Montague John, was a man of some standing. Not only was he Wimborne's leading surgeon and physician, but he was a Justice of the Peace, a member of the Anglican Church Governing Body and a governor of the 389-year-old Grammar School, which had been founded by Lady Margaret, the Countess of Richmond and mother of King Henry VII. "A strong Churchman and a Conservative," is the way the *Wimborne Guardian* describes Dr. Druitt. "He had strong sentiments respecting administration of some portions of the Poor Law," the newspaper adds, without specifying what these strong sentiments were. Himself the son of a surgeon, Dr. Robert Druitt, William of Wimborne became a member of the London Society of Apothecaries in 1842, a Fellow of the Royal College of Surgeons in 1849. In June, 1854, at the age of thirty-four, he married a Dorset girl who was ten years his junior.

It was a fashionable wedding, celebrated in St. James's, Westminster, and the match considerably enhanced Dr. Druitt's fortunes, his wife Ann bringing with her rich farmland located in the Dorset village of Child Okeford. Henceforth, Dr. Druitt added to his other distinctions that of being a gentleman farmer. The couple had seven children, Montague John being the second son.

The Druitt family's prominence may be measured by the fact that Westfield, where Montague John was born, was easily the biggest and most imposing house in the town. Some say that this long, low English country house of gray stone was used by Dr. Druitt as a private mental hospital for aristocratic patients, but I have been unable to verify these rumors. At any rate, it stood in magnificent grounds, screened from prying eyes by tall trees, and with wide, sweeping drives leading up to its entrance. In addition to the stables where the horses and carriages were kept, there were two cottages on the estate for the servants.

It was in this upper middle class environment that Montague John grew up. That he was a bright boy there can be no doubt, for at the age of thirteen, in competitive exams, he won a scholarship to Winchester College, located in the nearby county of Hampshire. He was to spend the next six years, perhaps the most crucial years of his life from the standpoint of character formation, at this famous public school.

Winchester College, whose motto is "Manners Makyth Man," was founded in 1382 by William of Wykeham, Bishop of Winchester and twice Lord Chancellor, who proposed to instruct seventy "pore and needy Scholars" and a few fee-paying Commoners in "grammaticals." Today, although the number of Scholars is still restricted to seventy, they are outnumbered seven to one by the so-called Commoners, who pay £498 a year for the privilege of attending this ancient institution. Traditionally, Winchester's headmasters have been Bishops, but the school has nurtured radical thought. In modern times it has produced Sir Stafford Cripps, Chancellor of the Exchequer in the postwar Labor Government. The late Hugh Gaitskell, leader of the Labor Party Opposition, was also a Wykehamist, as the Winchester boys are called. So are several present Labor Members of Parliament. With an unusually high ratio of teachers per pupil, Winchester College offers perhaps the finest education in England today.

Surrounded by high walls of flint and stone, Winchester has all the appearance of an armed fortress. Even the original fourteenth century windows are slitlike, precautions which become understandable when one recalls that the college was founded shortly after the Peasants' Revolt and when the bloody conflict of Town and Gown in Oxford in 1355 was still a vivid memory. The effect, however, is a gloomy one.

As one of seventy Scholars, Druitt led a privileged life at Winchester. He lived in a chamber with ancient oak-paneled walls and high-backed, wooden study cubicles that were darkened with age. He wore a black gown to distinguish himself from the Commoners, who wore jackets and straw boaters. He dined in a lofty hall surrounded by the portraits of Bishops, and ate from a wooden trencher similar to those used in medieval times.

From his school record Montague John emerges as a completely extrovert type. He was active in sports, debating, and, one suspects, school politics. He even won a literary prize, though the subject of his essay is not now known. It was only when he turned to acting that Druitt fell short of the mark. His first and last appearance with the Shakespeare Society was as Sir Toby Belch in *Twelfth Night,* and concerning this performance *The Wykehamist,* the school paper, comments: "But of the inadequacy of Druitt as Sir Toby, what are we to say? It can be better imagined than described."

Montague John more than made up on the playing fields for what he lacked in stage presence. He was a first-rate cricketer, playing for the school's First Eleven ("Lords," it is called) during the summer of 1876, usually as opening bowler. He was an excellent racquets player and distinguished himself at Fives, an ancient form of handball. In 1874 with a partner he won the Senior Double Fives and the following year he was School Fives champion.

But Druitt's first love was debate, which undoubtedly had a strong bearing on his choice of the law as a career. Almost from the start he was active in the Debating Society, becoming its treasurer in his senior year. In his choice of debate topics Montague John betrays a strong political bias. For example, he was an admirer of Gladstone, although he did not think much of the Liberal Party as such. As for European politics, he was Jacobin in his sympathies, and in a debate in November, 1873, defended the French Republic, which was then threatened by monarchist plotters. In another debate he attacked Bismarck's influence in Europe as "morally and socially a curse to the world." In a final appearance before the Debating Society he upheld the present generation against its predecessors, who were responsible for such evils as slavery and the subjugation of women. "The old theory of government was 'man is made for States,'" he pointed out. "Is it not a vast improvement that States should be made for man, as they are now?"

Not all of Druitt's forensic tilts were in this serious vein. In a debate on the motion, "That the present bondage to fashion is a social evil," he took the side of fashion, advancing the typical Victorian argument that the styles of the 1870's were a "graceful combination of beauty and utility." He also championed Wordsworth against his detractors, finding it a great merit on the part of the poet that he was "a bulwark of Protestantism." [4]

[4] One suspects that the Wordsworth debate was inspired, in part, by malice, for the poet's nephew had at one time been Assistant Headmaster at Winchester, and, as such, had been heartily disliked for introducing "the steam-heated atmosphere of a pious clique," as one Winchester historian describes it. Charles

In his final year at Winchester Druitt was elected Prefect of Chapel, which was one of the top school honors. He was also among the nineteen seniors who were successful in the Oxford and Cambridge Exams in the autumn of 1875, and the following year he was awarded a Winchester Scholarship to New College, Oxford. Thus, Montague John, at the age of nineteen and on the threshold of University, was one of the most promising of Winchester's Class of 1876, good alike at sports and studies. The school could pride itself on having molded him into a "muscular Christian," although his political leanings were decidedly radical.

That Druitt did not fulfill this promise at Oxford is a matter of some mystification. Was he one of those volcanoes that erupt at an early stage, then quickly subside to a sputtering crater? Or, finding the competition at Oxford too tough, did he surrender to mediocrity without a struggle? Certainly, his university record was anything but brilliant. He began well enough by taking a Second Class Honors in Classical Moderations in 1878, but by the end of the Easter term in 1880 he had slid back to a Third Class Honors in Classics. He was, however, elected steward of the Junior Common Room, which attests to his popularity with the other New College undergraduates. That same year, 1880, he left Oxford with his B.A. (Druitt later knew a moment of post-graduate glory when, as a newly qualified barrister, he returned to Winchester with an "Old Wykehamist" team and thrashed the First Eleven at cricket, Druitt scoring 38 runs in the first innings and 23 in the second.)

5

In 1882, as, indeed, today, the expense involved in becoming a barrister was prohibitive to all save the well-to-do. The would-

---

Wordsworth, the nephew, had his favorites among the boys who were known as "Holy Joes," and who were bullied by the other Wykehamists.

be barrister would first have to apply to one of the four Inns of Court, which are the only institutions through which a person may be admitted to the Bar. This first hurdle entailed the payment of a sizable admission fee (at present £84. 5*s.*). The neophyte would then have to give an undertaking to his Inn not to engage in a trade until he had passed the Bar finals. Tradition required that he eat seventy-two dinners in Hall during the next three years, and the wine bill itself could prove a costly item. At Gray's Inn, for example, the senior of the mess by custom toasted every gentleman present during dinner, mentioning each by name. The examinations which the student took from time to time each carried large stamp fees, and when eventually he was called to the Bar there was a Call Fee (at present fixed at £60).

With this in mind, it is not surprising to find Montague John in 1882 borrowing, with his father's consent, against a £500 legacy which his father had set aside in his will for just this purpose. His finances thus assured, young Druitt applied for admittance to the Inner Temple, and was accepted on May 17, 1882. There then began for him another round of student life. He learned to submit to the ordeal of the dinner in Hall where, surrounded by the portraits of former Benchers, in facial expression not unlike the glum Bishops whose portraits he had memorized at Winchester, he drank his claret, listened to the witty oratory. For the next three years he boned up on his Blackstone, sat for his exams. Then, on April 29, 1885, came Call Night, when Druitt, dressed in the traditional black gown, was "called" before the Benchers of the Inn. Through the magic of a handshake he became a full-fledged barrister.

Any jubilation Montague John may have felt at having won his independence was cut short by the death of his father in September, 1885. Dr. William Druitt, who died of a heart attack, left an estate valued at £16,579 and a peculiar will. Under the terms of the latter the use of all rents and other income from the estate, together with "my horses, carriages . . . and all my wine, coal, corn and other articles of consumption," went to the doctor's widow, Ann Druitt. The will provided legacies of £6000 each for the three daughters on condition that they did not marry before the age of twenty-one. The farm at Child Okeford, Dorset, went to the eldest son, William. This left very little of the father's worldly goods to be divided among the three remaining sons. It may be that having provided them with university educations (all four sons attended Oxford), the doctor felt himself quits with his male issue, and that his chief concern, therefore, was to leave suitable dowries for his daughters, the youngest, Ethel, being only fourteen when he died. Whatever his reasoning, the doctor's will seemed bound to create discontent.

Meanwhile, Montague John went ahead and rented chambers in the Inner Temple at No. 9 King's Bench Walk, a tree-shaded avenue which had echoed the roistering of drunken Knights Templar until they were expelled from these precincts in the fourteenth century. In the 1880's, however, bachelor digs in the Inner Temple were quite sedate, and cheap — for £60 a year one could rent two or three rooms, usually with a few rats thrown in. Druitt had his name painted in spidery black letters on the wooden panel outside his door. He joined the Western Circuit and Winchester Sessions. He settled down to wait for business. But, apparently, the clients never came.

"The tragedies of the Inns — the life stories of men who have come enthusiastic to the profession of the law, and have utterly failed — would fill as many pages as are contained in a complete set of Law Reports," writes George R. Sims, a journalist who was contemporary with Druitt. Sims adds that of the eight thousand barristers who had been called to the Bar only one in eight was making a living. This was in the days before Legal Aid, which gave the poor some standing in the courts. Only the well-to-do could afford to become involved in legal actions in those days.

Montague John was not to be found among the one-eighth who made the legal profession pay, for in 1888 he was a teaching assistant at a private school in Blackheath run by a Mr. George Valentine at No. 9 Eliot Place. Had he acted with impetuosity in throwing up his law career? It is hard to say. Perhaps he intended to resume it at a later date, for he still retained his chambers at No. 9 King's Bench Walk.

6

Blackheath lies high above the river Thames just south of Greenwich. To the historian the name recalls the Wat Tyler rebellion of 1381. It was here, too, that the citizens of London paid homage to Henry V upon his return from the Battle of Agincourt in 1415. To the sportsman Blackheath suggests golf, for it was here that golf was first introduced to England by James I, who brought the game with him from Scotland. (It was still played on the heath as late as 1918.) But in Victorian times Blackheath was noted for its "cramming shops," those fee-paying prep schools which served as recruiting centers for Eton, Harrow and the other great public schools, and foremost among these "cramming shops" was the establishment run by Mr. George Valentine at No. 9 Eliot Place, which overlooks the heath.

Curiously enough, No. 9 was the only one in the row of fine Georgian houses in Eliot Place to be demolished; it was pulled down in 1910 and replaced by a "semi-detached" which stands out from its neighbors like a rotten tooth. As early as 1811 there had been a school at No. 9, which Benjamin Disraeli had attended as a boarder. In those days the school, although Anglican, had a reputation for being liberal in religious matters, and young Disraeli was allowed to receive instruction in Hebrew from a rabbi on Saturdays.[5] The school was also somewhat snob-ridden. Thus, in 1865, it was selected from among the other Blackheath schools to send half a dozen boys once a week to play with Prince Arthur, the future Duke of Connaught, who was then in residence with a tutor at Ranger's House, Greenwich Park.[6]

Indications are that when Montague John Druitt joined the teaching staff some twenty years later, the school at No. 9 had degenerated into a glorified version of the Dotheboys Hall pictured by Dickens in *Nicholas Nickleby*. According to the census figures, forty-two boarders were crammed into the school's confined quarters, which were also made to accommodate three resident masters and seven servants, including a cook, a kitchen maid and three housemaids. To Druitt, accustomed to the spacious quadrangles of Winchester, with its equally roomy chambers, the overcrowding at Mr. Valentine's school must have seemed intolerable.

But in the autumn of 1888 Druitt would not have had much time to reflect upon the sad reversal of his fortunes. When the school broke up for the Christmas holidays on December 1, he was to gaze upon No. 9 Eliot Place for the last time.

7

Montague John Druitt was last seen alive on Monday, December 3, 1888. That day dawned rainy and dismal, London catch-

[5] A contemporary contributes this interesting picture of the future Prime Minister as a schoolboy: "He was always full of fun; and at Midsummer when he went home for the holidays in the basket of the Blackheath coach, fired away at the passers-by with his pea-shooter."

[6] In at least one former pupil the school at No. 9 seems to have instilled nothing but gloom. Writing in the *Home Counties Magazine* in 1905, N. F. Abell tells of the first day he spent there as a boarder. "More than forty years ago I was left at a school in Eliot-place, Blackheath," he writes. "I never cross Blackheath on a late autumn afternoon without recalling the impression made upon me by the chilliness and dreariness, the gloom of the dark-lined heath, the leafless dripping trees, the sombre brick wall . . . and the line of gaunt, unlovely houses which formed Eliot Place. (Mr. Abell, of course, is reflecting the Victorian distaste for Georgian architecture.)

ing the tail end of the southwesterly gales which lashed the coast. As the day advanced the news proved to be nearly as dull as the weather. In the House of Commons Gladstone, then nearing his eightieth birthday, accused the police of using brutality against Irish nationalists, and Gladstone, in turn, was accused of pettifogging. James Monro arrived at Scotland Yard that Monday to take up his duties as Metropolitan Police Commissioner. The Dowager Lady Kinnaird, who had hoped to employ Bible colporteurs to turn darkest Whitechapel into a bower of the Lord, died quietly in her sleep. Nine paupers were bound over for trial for inciting a riot at the Islington Workhouse. As the day wore on the flooding of the Thames gave rise to some alarm, the river having overflowed onto the towpaths near Windsor.

At some time during this dreary, blustery day Druitt went for a walk along this swollen river, and, at some point, in a mood of desperation, he threw himself into its rapid current, having first carefully weighted his body with stones. His body was not recovered from the Thames until nearly a month later.

Druitt's suicide seems to have been the signal for disaster to overwhelm his family. Certainly his mother, Ann Druitt, never recovered from the shock. Shortly afterward she was removed to a private mental hospital in Chiswick, not far from where her son's body had been fished from the Thames. Mrs. Druitt died there, aged fifty-nine, on December 15, 1890, two years and twelve days after Montague John had taken his life. "Melancholia" is the cause of death recorded on her death certificate, after which the attending physician has noted: "Brain disease, 21 months; Acute pneumonia, 8 days; Exhaustion." If the physician is right, Mrs. Druitt's decline dates almost exactly from that rainy December day in 1888 when her son disappeared. Six months after the mother's death Westfield, Montague John's birthplace, was put up for sale.

CHAPTER XVIII

A SENSE OF SIN

MONTAGUE JOHN DRUITT'S suicide leaves a trail of question marks behind it. What, for example, were the contents of the letter which he addressed to Mr. Valentine of the Blackheath school? Did it contain a confession of murder? What about the money that was found on his body, the check for £50 and the £16 in gold? This was an unusual amount for a schoolmaster to carry on his person. Had he drawn the money from the bank with the intention of fleeing? If so, why did he change his mind, throw himself into the Thames? "The probability is," Macnaghten writes, "that after the awful glut of Miller's Court his brain gave way altogether and he committed suicide . . ."

Finally, upon what did the police base their "strong suspicion" that Druitt was Jack the Ripper? This suspicion amounted to conviction if the statement of Albert Backert is taken into account. Having been sworn to secrecy by Scotland Yard in March, 1889, Backert, it will be recalled, was told "the police were quite certain that the Ripper was dead . . . He was fished out of the Thames two months ago." The police even threatened to prosecute Backert if he persisted in putting it about that the Ripper was still alive. What was the basis of this certainty? The bizarre manner of Druitt's suicide? The evidence would have to be more compelling than that. A signed murder confession in the hands of Mr. Valentine? But this, in itself, would prove nothing. Dozens of cranks, some harmless, some otherwise, had come forward to confess the Ripper's crimes during the course of the investigation.

The key to the mystery probably lies in Macnaghten's statement: "From private information I have little doubt but that his own family suspected this man of being the Whitechapel murderer." At some time between December 3, when he was last seen alive, and December 31, when his body was taken from the Thames, Montague John Druitt's family must have reported his disappearance to the police. In reporting him missing, did one of the Druitts seize the occasion to confide to the police the family's private fears concerning Montague John? In all likelihood this is what happened, in view of Macnaghten's statement. It is even possible that prior to December 3, the family had decided to commit Druitt to an insane asylum and had enlisted police aid to this end. This would explain such evidence of precipitant flight as the large sum of money found on his body.

In building up its hypothetical case against Druitt as Jack the Ripper, Scotland Yard would have to hurdle some formidable obstacles. There was, for example, Druitt's presence in Whitechapel to be accounted for. What was a man of his education and refined family background doing in the stews of East London? This would be the first question to occur to the Victorian mind. The Victorians sanctioned visits to the East End providing they were connected with moral uplift. In fact, slumming of this sort was all the rage in the 1880's. *Punch* even ran a cartoon showing a group of obviously gentlefolk, clad in aseptic-looking mackintoshes, about to set out for "a dear little slum in the Minories." But consorting with "those vile creatures," that was another matter. The Victorian ethos did not admit of such *nostalgie de la boue*.

And yet some of Druitt's contemporaries who were also men of refinement indulged such peculiar tastes. Walter Sickert, the Edwardian painter, had a decided predilection for low life, frequenting cheap music halls and other places of ill-repute. As has already been noted, Sickert dined out on the story that he had once lived in Jack the Ripper's digs. Swinburne was another example. Haunted by memories of the flogging block at Eton, the poet frequented a brothel in St. John's Wood whose speciality was flagellation, *le vice anglais.* ("My life has been enlivened of late by a fair friend who keeps a maison de supplice," he confided in a letter to a friend. "There is occasional balm in Gilead," he added). And yet Swinburne's sexual aberration was the "anguished sensitivity which was of the very essence of his being," if his latest biographer is to be believed.

Then there was William Ewart Gladstone, four times Britain's Prime Minister. Gladstone's efforts to redeem fallen women were the despair of his family and his friends. Acting from the purest of motives, the Liberal statesman used to roam the streets of Soho at night picking up prostitutes and taking them home to his wife. On one occasion a youth who saw Gladstone with a tart tried to blackmail him. On another, a group of Gladstone's political enemies planned to have him shadowed by private detectives. The gossip became so clamorous that in 1886 it finally reached Queen Victoria's ears. The Queen used it as yet another weapon against her Prime Minister.

But one does not have to postulate vice as an explanation for Druitt's presence in the East End. There was Toynbee Hall, the universities settlement founded by Reverend Samuel Barnett in 1884. As an undergraduate, Druitt could not have escaped hearing of the plans to build Toynbee Hall, for Mr. Barnett was a frequent visitor to Oxford in the mid-seventies. In those days Oxford was in a ferment of social reform, students and dons alike reacting against the soulless doctrines of laissez-faire economics. After listening to Mr. Barnett describe the horrors of Spitalfields, where the mass lived "without knowledge, without hope, and often without help," many of Druitt's classmates volunteered to spend their vacations doing social work in the East End.

2

Answering "the call from the East," these undergraduates now flocked to Whitechapel. With more enthusiasm than practical sense, they helped to administer the "top boots and blankets" funds which the Barnetts founded. They assisted at flower shows, concerts, *conversaziones,* which were designed to bridge the gulf between classes and masses by bringing culture to the latter. When Toynbee Hall opened its doors as a residential settlement in 1885, a majority of its settlers were Oxonians, some of them Druitt's college mates. For example, Cyril Jackson, the future chairman of the London County Council, who was then active at Toynbee Hall, was from New College. It would be natural, therefore, that Druitt should turn to Toynbee Hall not only as a means of recreation, but as an opportunity to do good. With his love of polemic, it would be natural that he should take part in the weekly "Smoking Conferences," or "Tobacco Parliaments," as they were called, where social questions were heatedly debated by clerks in cloth caps and earnest settlement workers wearing "old school ties." Here Druitt would have been exposed to Fabian Socialism, for Bernard Shaw and the Webbs were frequent visitors to Toynbee Hall.[1]

"The sense of sin has been the starting point of progress," Reverend Samuel Barnett remarked on more than one occasion. Certainly, the environs of Toynbee Hall were not lacking in

[1] Another visitor was Vladimir Ilyich Lenin. When John Morley, onetime Secretary of state for India, lectured at Toynbee Hall in 1902 he was closely questioned by a foreigner with bulbous brow and pointed beard who gave his name as Jacob Richter, the German alias Lenin used during his London exile. Lenin so impressed the Toynbee Hallers that Dean Robinson asked him around to tea the following Sunday.

sinful examples. This tiny replica of Oxford, which was faithful in detail from its front quadrangle to its crenellated clock tower, was located in the very heart of Spitalfields. Its back door opened onto the George Yard buildings (now Gunthorpe Street) where a school for juvenile thieves had once flourished. According to Mayhew, the female Fagin who ran this padding-ken used to admonish her young charges as they set out for "work" in the morning, "Now, my little dears, do the best you can, and may God bless you."

And not only thieving — on the first floor landing of these same George Yard buildings the body of Martha Tabram was found with blood issuing from thirty-nine stab wounds. Within a five minutes' walk of Toynbee Hall, Annie Chapman and Mary Kelly were murdered. It is not surprising, therefore, that the Toynbee residents were eager to form themselves into a vigilance committee to hunt Jack the Ripper. One suspects that they acted less from disinterested motives than from a desire to divert suspicion from themselves. Indeed, a Toynbee resident remarked to me jestingly that not even the saintly Mr. Barnett had escaped local suspicion as being the Whitechapel killer.

3

"Suicide whilst of unsound mind," was the verdict returned at the coroner's inquest into Montague John Druitt's death. For how long had his mind been unsound? There is no way of knowing, although Macnaghten indicates that his family had long "suspected the worst."

Might not someone of Druitt's education and refinement whose mind was delicately balanced at best, have been pushed to the edge of insanity by the sights around him in London's East End? The nightly spectacle of women selling their bodies for tuppence or a stale crust of bread had sickened Jack London on his brief visit to Spitalfields. What might not it have done to a Montague John Druitt, whose mind had become unhinged? Such a man, overwhelmed by a sense of hopelessness and futility, might he not have conceived it as his mission to call attention to these evils, even to the extent of committing murder? Stranger deeds have been recorded in history as springing from just such motives.

Reverend Samuel Barnett spoke of "a passion for righteousness" in describing the social worker's mission in the East End, declaring that the downtrodden could be saved only by "the mercy which can be angry as well as pitiful." These are curious words. As filtered through a warped intelligence they could be interpreted literally as a call to action, even to murder in the last, desperate extreme. Was this the case with the Whitechapel killer?

4

"Time has been wasted in looking for Jack the Ripper among the rags of Whitechapel," Alfred E. Knowles, a retired Pinkerton detective living in London, told a *Daily Telegraph* reporter. "The assassin must have means at his command whereby he can change his abode, personal appearance and dress at will." The detective then took Scotland Yard severely to task for not maintaining a watch on the railway stations located near the City and the East End, particularly late at night on weekends. "By that means every passenger . . . would have been scrutinized."

That the police had wasted their time in looking for the Ripper in East End doss houses should have been evident from the start. Even burglars shunned these rookeries according to Montagu Williams, the police court magistrate. For a burglar "to have anything like a fixed abode, where his goings and comings would be scrutinized, would indeed be fatal to his enterprise," Williams declares, "for he carries about with him in his tools conclusive proof of his guilt." How much more conclusive as proof of a murderer's guilt would have been his bloodstained clothing. How much greater therefore would have been the murderer's need to shun the common lodging house. To book a bed in one of these would mean that the killer risked being turned over to the police straightaway by his fellow dossers, providing that they did not lynch him first.

Dr. Thomas Dutton, too, was positive that the Ripper did not live in the East End. "But it seemed certain that he must live near to the East-end," Dr. Dutton adds, "and the area south of the river — Lambeth, Walworth and Camberwell — seemed a likely neighborhood." No doubt the fact that Montague John Druitt taught school south of the river weighed with the police in building up their hypothetical case for Druitt's being Jack the Ripper. It would help to explain, for example, the Ripper's seemingly miraculous ability to elude the police, for Blackheath had almost direct railway connection with East London via the Cannon Street station, which is located in the City. Thus for someone living in Blackheath it would have been possible to slip in and out of Whitechapel unnoticed. (The police kept no watch on the station.) Moreover, supposing Druitt to be the Ripper, it would have been possible for him to flee the scene of his crimes without running the gamut of Middlesex Street, Bishopsgate or any of the other populous thoroughfares that lead to North London or to the West End. He would merely have had to gain Cannon Street station via back streets and alleys, or so the police must have reckoned.

Tempting as it is, I am inclined to reject this explanation as not being consonant with the facts in the case. For one thing, the London–Blackheath season ticket found on Druitt's body indicates that he did not live in Blackheath, but commuted to and from his work. For another, there were no all-night trains connecting London and Blackheath. According to the timetables in *Bradshaw's Guide* for 1888, the last train for Blackheath left Cannon Street on the Southeastern Railway line at 11:40 P.M., although a later train stopping at Blackheath left London Bridge just south of the Thames at twelve twenty-five. Obviously neither of these trains would have been of any use to the killer in making his escape, as all five of the Ripper murders occurred between the hours of 12:35 and 4 A.M. The earliest morning train leaving Cannon Street station for Blackheath was at 5:10 A.M., but if the killer had waited for this train he would have trebled his chances of being caught.

Druitt would have had no need to return to Blackheath. A much safer refuge was close at hand, one to which he could quickly repair if the police were on his heels. For Montague John still retained his chambers at No. 9 King's Bench Walk in the Inner Temple, and this cloistered legal enclave was within easy walking distance of the East End and of the scene of the Ripper crimes. Moreover, the Inner Temple could be approached by two routes, both equally deserted at night. Coming from the City, it could be reached via Fleet Street, where only the occasional printer would be stirring after midnight; or it could be approached via the Embankment along the Thames. There were three gates leading to the Inner Temple, including the one in Tudor Street, just off Bouverie Street. A word to a sleepy night porter in his lodge would have gained Druitt instant admittance at any one of these gates without being questioned, or even being seen.

Jack the Ripper's need for privacy was absolute. As *The Times* pointed out, "More probably he is a man lodging in a comparatively decent house in the district, to which he would be able to retire quickly, and in which, once it was reached, he would be able at his leisure to remove from his person all traces of his hideous crime." Is the Inner Temple the answer to the conundrum posed by the vanishing Ripper? Does this explain his miraculous escapes?

5

Finally, there remains the question of Jack the Ripper's surgical skill. Sir Melville Macnaghten, writing from memory six years after the event, made the fundamental error of describing Druitt as a doctor. But would the fact that he was a barrister and not a doctor of medicine tend to eliminate Druitt as a suspect? The truth is that the experts were hopelessly in disagreement as to the amount of medical knowledge the Ripper possessed. Dr. Rees Ralph Llewellyn, testifying at the Polly Nicholls inquest, held that the mutilations were "deftly and fairly skillfully performed." Dr. George B. Phillips, at the Chapman inquest, said, "The mode in which the uterus was extracted showed some anatomical knowledge," a judgment with which *The Lancet* agreed. "Obviously," the medical journal observed, "the work was that of an expert — of one, at least, who had such knowledge of anatomical or pathological examinations as to be enabled to secure the pelvic organs with one sweep of the knife."

Dr. Frederick G. Brown, who carried out the postmortem examination of Catherine Eddowes, concluded that the killer showed "a good deal of knowledge as to the positions of organs in the abdominal cavity and the way of removing them." But he was flatly contradicted by two surgeons, Dr. George W. Sequeira and Dr. William S. Saunders, who had assisted him at the autopsy, and who followed him to the witness stand. Both of these medicos testified that, in their opinion, the Ripper had shown no particular anatomical skill. Dr. Thomas Dutton felt that the Ripper's knowledge of surgery was no greater than that which a feldsher, or barber-surgeon, would have possessed. "I am quite prepared to admit that by English standards the technique of the Ripper was not in the same class as that of a highly proficient English surgeon," Dr. Dutton is quoted by Donald McCormick as saying. "Speed was the substitute for skill," he added. "And, without doubt, the Ripper was a fast operator, much faster than the average British surgeon could possibly have been." It seems commonplace to remark that both speed and skill could have come with practice, in which the Ripper was not lacking.

Finally, there is the opinion of Dr. D. G. Halsted, quoted earlier, that the Ripper's surgical skill was no greater than that which could have been acquired by a deep-sea fisherman in boning and filleting fish. To conclude, I can only point to the medical background of the Druitt family, which I have traced earlier. Montague John's father, his grandfather, his uncle and his cousin were all surgeons. It is more than possible, indeed it is probable that Druitt as an interested spectator, sat in the amphitheater of the operating room and watched his father practice his art. He would thus have gained some knowledge of surgery even though that knowledge was rudimentary.

6

"The truth, however, will never be known, and did, indeed at one time lie at the bottom of the Thames, if my conjectures be correct," writes Sir Melville Macnaghten in his notes on Jack the Ripper. Sir Melville would appear to be unduly pessimistic in his conclusions. In all likelihood the truth is locked up in a steel filing cabinet at Scotland Yard; or perhaps it lies buried in some musty attic among letters that have long since been forgotten, photographs that have faded, the lock of hair that is mouldy with age. If it could be found, the suicide note which Montague John Druitt addressed to Mr. Valentine, for example, might throw some light on the mystery. But rather than to force the attic or the Thames to yield their secrets, it might be more profitable to consider what produces a Jack the Ripper, what causes him to go on his murderous rampage. For despite the advances in forensic science, little more is known today about the psychology of the criminal or the ecology of crime than was known at the time of the Whitechapel murders.

By a weird coincidence, in looking up Montague John Druitt's obituary in *The Southern Guardian* for January 5, 1889, I found on an adjacent page an article headed "Murder and Science," which was very much to the point. I quote it in part:

> Suppose we catch the Whitechapel murderer, can we not, before handing him over to the executioner or the authorities at Broadmoor, make a really decent effort to discover his antecedents, and his parentage, to trace back every step of his career, every hereditary instinct, every acquired taste, every moral slip, every mental idiosyncrasy? Surely the time has come for such an effort as this. We are face to face with some mysterious and awful product of modern civilization . . .

This article was written seventy-five years ago or long before the present university chairs of criminology had been endowed.

7

A strange mixup in identity almost denied me access to the birth records of the Druitt family in Wimborne, Dorset. I was mistaken for a member of the Church of Latter-Day Saints, or the Mormons, as they are better known. For many years Mormons from America have been microfilming birth records in various English vestries as part of their program for retroactively baptizing their dead ancestors. But this genealogical research has aroused considerable animosity on the part of the Established Church. Thus, when I applied to see the parish registers at the Minster, the atmosphere was distinctly hostile in the oak-paneled vestry hung with its red cassocks. It was only after I had assured the verger that I was not one of the Latter-Day Saints that the latter became cooperative.

In the end the verger not only gave me access to the parish registers, but took me on a conducted tour of the ancient

Minster, pointing out various memorials to the Druitt family as we went along. The stained glass window in the South Transept, for example, is a memorial to Dr. William Druitt, Montague John's father, donated by his surviving children in 1892. It is a fine example of Clayton and Bell stained glass of its period, I was told. One of the daughters had also given silver plate to the Minster, but this was locked up the day I visited.

My business at the Minster completed, I asked a roadmender the way to Wimborne Cemetery, then took the road leading to Blandford which he indicated. The road passes by Westfield, the former Druitt family seat, which has seen some transformations since Montague John's day. From the outside, the house itself looks much the same as when Montague John played there as a boy. But the trees have been felled, the sweeping approaches to the house are gone. The estate was sold in 1891 to Sir William Watts, K.C.B., of Bournemouth, and later fell into the hands of the Rt. Hon. Gertrude Floyer, Dowager Countess of Moray, who died there in 1928. After her death the interior of the house was chopped up into a number of small service flats, and these are now flanked by a modern structure, a hideous collection of mortar and bricks known as "Moray Court."

Whoever laid out Wimborne Cemetery was evidently bent upon sparing the Lord hard work, for its arrangements represents a preliminary sorting against Judgment Day. On the left side of a central gravel walk members of the Established Church sleep peacefully in their graves; on the right side are buried the Non-Conformists. At the top of a rise are two graystone chapels, identical in all respects save their articles of faith. The caretaker, a young man in Wellington boots and with cheeks rubbed raw by the November cold, looked at me quizzically when I asked to be shown the Druitt family plot. "Druitt? That's a name I know," he said in the nasal accent that is peculiar to Dorset. He then led me along the gravel path to the Anglican chapel on the left. There in hallowed ground alongside the chapel I found what I was looking for.

Montague John Druitt's grave is marked by a crude stone cross spotted with lichen. The inscription at its base has been eroded by time, but one can still make it out: "In Memory of Mon. Jno. Druitt, December 4, 1888. Aged 31." Behind it, his parents, William and Ann Druitt are interred in a common grave. Alongside Montague John lies his elder brother, William, who died a bachelor in February, 1909, at the age of fifty-two. "They died young in those days," the caretaker beside me remarked, having noted the brothers' ages from their tombstones. "Neither of these two blokes seems to have had his fair share of life." I agreed that this was the case.

CHAPTER XIX

EPITAPH FOR THE RIPPER

THE HEADLINE of the *Daily Express* for February 8, 1960, bristled with action verbs of the sort that headline writers take pride in:

WHERE JACK THE RIPPER STRUCK
TWO MEN FALL AS GUNS BLAZE

The story underneath began: "In squalid, deserted Duval street — where Jack the Ripper murdered Mary Jane Kelly in 1888 — three men stepped out of a car yesterday and went into the Pen Club. A few minutes later they backed out. A Soho club manager, shot in the head, staggered after them. Then he crumpled in a heap — to die in the gutter. A second man, once a promising middleweight boxer, shot in the stomach, fell over the body. The gangsters' car drove off." That was all, or nearly all — gunplay and murder involving rival gangsters and of a sort that is not too uncommon in a metropolis the size of London. And yet it set up an echo. Duval Street was formerly Dorset Street, which changed its name following the notoriety visited upon it by the slaying of Mary Jane Kelly. Murder striking twice in the same spot is perhaps not too uncommon either. But that is not the point.

The important thing is that Jack the Ripper has never died as far as the average Londoner is concerned. Mothers frighten their children with his name. Headline writers keep it alive.

Even Elizabeth Taylor, the Hollywood film actress, evoked the Ripper's memory in a recent television documentary on London. Unfortunately, the Ripper is remembered for the wrong reasons.

2

It has been my contention that the series of murders with which the Ripper's name is bracketed followed a certain pattern, that they had a peculiar rhythm of their own, and that it was only the obtuseness of his Victorian contemporaries which made them insensible to this pattern and this rhythm. Above all, my contention has been that the internal evidence in the case points to the use of murder as a means of social protest. The proof of this contention, of course, would be if the murders had actually resulted in reform, if the Ripper had left some lasting monument. Did he, in fact, leave East London a changed place?

The authors of Volume XXVII of the *Survey of London,* which deals with Spitalfields, have no hesitation in crediting him with certain reforms. "When the Whitechapel murders of Jack the Ripper startled London in the latter half of 1888, the condition of these common lodging-houses was forcibly brought to the attention of the public," the *Survey* declares. Again: "The Whitechapel murders undoubtedly gave a further impetus towards the rebuilding of the Flower and Dean-street area." As far back as 1875 the Metropolitan Board of Works had condemned as unfit for habitation houses in this area which accommodated four thousand persons, but nothing was done about it. Nothing was done about it until thirteen years later when Jack the Ripper decided to lend a hand.

The Ripper spurred to action Reverend Samuel Barnett of Toynbee Hall, who, in turn, enlisted the aid of Philanthropy. As early as October, 1888, while the Ripper was still exploring Whitechapel with his knife, Mr. Barnett wrote to his brother about a "big housing scheme." "At present we must keep quiet," the Reverend declared, "but I think we may try to rebuild the whole bad quarter." The clergyman added that £200,000 capital would be needed to float the limited liability company of which his wife, Henrietta Barnett, would become a director. "If she can turn a den of thieves into a Temple of God she may die happy," he concluded.

A year later the Reverend was still fighting the good battle with the rent rackers on the one hand, and the Four Percenters on the other. But victory was in sight. The area which the clergyman was determined to clean up contained no fewer than 146 registered lodging houses with more than 6000 beds. In Flower and Dean Street alone there were 1500 beds, most of them occupied by thieves and prostitutes of the "Dark Annie" sort who flitted from doss to doss. "This reform is vast," Mr. Barnett wrote to his brother in October, 1889, "and when it is done we shall be able to sing *Nunc Dimittis.*"

The reform, indeed, was vast. But, thanks to the impetus given by the Ripper, the decade 1888–97 saw a proliferation of building societies, whose aims were as charitable as their names were long — "The Metropolitan Association for Improving the Dwellings of the Industrious Classes," for example. Mr. Barnett's limited company bought up sites in Thrawl Street and Wentworth Street, tore down the lodging houses and erected "model dwellings." By 1892 nearly the whole of the north side of Flower and Dean Street had been cleared and "models" put up by the Four Per Cent Industrial Dwellings Company.

In demolishing the old doss houses, the wreckers "laid bare the secret dens of a century of infamy," in the words of one contemporary writer. They let air and light into basements where men and women had lived like wolves in their lairs. Walls infested with vermin, large blocks of creeping things, came crashing down in clouds of choking dust. Bedding, likewise verminous, was burned. In some of the doss houses conditions were so bad that the demolition gangs demanded extra pay and a generous ration of beer before they would enter them.

Unfortunately, the "model dwellings" which replaced the doss houses were designed to contain poverty, rather than to alleviate it, and, like many other Victorian good works, they were doomed from the start. For one thing, they lacked the warmth and camaraderie of the common lodging houses, noisome as these latter were. In a doss-house kitchen one could at least expect to find sympathy, a sentiment which was as pervasive as the smell of bloaters, whereas in the new tenements toadying for favors seems to have been the rule. A group of bachelor mechanics, interviewed by the magazine *The Builder,* gave this explanation why they preferred a doss house to the "model" flats which had been erected for their benefit in Spicer Street, Spitalfields: "They liked their tea better, they said, if they took it beside someone who would supply the place in conversation of a mother or sister."

3

By some stroke of irony, the six-story Victorian tenements in Spitalfields which Jack the Ripper inspired survived the Blitz. These barracklike "model dwellings," which were the pride of Reverend Samuel Barnett, escaped unscathed, although the incendiaries fell in neighboring streets. Some say that they were spared because Christ Church, Spitalfields, was used as a landmark by the Luftwaffe, that the Heinkels guided on the church spire in dropping their bombs on the city farther west. Whatever the reason, these tenement buildings remain as a grim reminder of Spitalfields' past, and as a monument to the Ripper. Not that he lacks monuments. The corner in Mitre Square where Catherine Eddowes was disemboweled is known to this day as "Ripper's Corner," and is a tourist showplace. (Nearly every East Ender I talked to in connection with this book offered, incidentally, to take me to the various murder sites. They are well known and frequently visited by the local inhabitants.)

It is in wandering around the area at night, when the garment factories are empty and the loading bays at Spitalfields market have shut down, that one feels the presence of Jack the Ripper. At night Commercial Street is now so silent and deserted that in passing Christ Church one fancies that one can hear the death-watch beetles gnawing away at the fabric of this, Nicholas Hawksmoor's most noble spire. But the old landmarks are still there. On the corner is The Ten Bells pub where Mary Kelly used to stop by for a quick gin. Standing outside as a customer pushes through the saloon bar door, one listens for the ghostly laughter of Mary Kelly and her sisters in trade. But no, The Ten Bells at night is now quite sedate. Its customers are respectable working-class types who linger long over a pint of beer. An air of stagnation hangs over the whole district. Somehow one feels that Spitalfields is cursed, that this is unhallowed ground. The war certainly put a finish to it, but perhaps the area never really recovered from the awful affair of Miller's Court. Even the bricks seem to give off an odor of poverty and vice.

Two blocks away is No. 29 Hanbury Street, where Annie Chapman was found with her head nearly severed from her body. To the right of the door lettering informs one that "N. Brill, Hairdresser-Perfumer" once occupied the premises, but all that is left of Mr. Brill today is a row of dirty milk bottles in the front window. From the front door a passage leads to the backyard, which is exactly as it was when "Dark Annie" met her fate there. Nothing, one feels, has been changed. The words which the *Daily Telegraph* used in commenting upon this terrible event have the same ring of truth about them today that they had seventy-five years ago, and, in closing, I can do no better than quote them:

Dark Annie's spirit still walks Whitechapel, unavenged by Justice . . . And yet even this forlorn, despised citizeness of London cannot be said to have suffered in vain. On the contrary, she has effected more by her death than many long speeches in Parliament and countless columns of letters to the newspapers could have brought about. She has forced innumerable people who never gave a serious thought before to the subject to realize how it is and where it is that our vast floating population — the waifs and strays of our thoroughfares — live and sleep at night and what sort of accommodation our rich and enlightened capital provides for them, after so many Acts of Parliament passed to improve the dwellings of the poor, and so many millions spent by our Board of Works, our vestries . . . "Dark Annie" will effect in one way what fifty Secretaries of State could never accomplish . . .

Some mention was made at the inquest upon Annie Chapman of a wild proposal to photograph her glazed eyes, and so try if the dying retina would present any image of the cruel monster who killed her and mutilated her. Better have listened with ear of imagination at her poor swollen lips, for, without much fancy, a Home Secretary or Chairman of the Metropolitan Board of Works might have heard them murmuring: "We, your murdered sisters, are what the dreadful homes where we live have made us. Behind your fine squares and handsome streets you continue to leave our wild-beast lairs unchanged and uncleansed. The slums kill us, body and soul, with filth and shame and spread fever and death among your gentry also, while they are spawning beds for crime and social discontent. When it is possible for the poor of London to live and sleep in decency you will not pick up from backyards so many corpses like mine."

APPENDIXES
BIBLIOGRAPHY
INDEX

APPENDIX A

As a mythmaker Jack the Ripper has shown himself to be without rival among criminals, from the standpoint of both the number and the potency of the myths he has evoked. The aura of mystery surrounding the Whitechapel murders has intrigued men of all nations, and has given rise to novels, plays, films, and even operas, dating from 1888 to the present day. In his introduction to *The Harlot Killer, The Story of Jack the Ripper in Fact and Fiction,* Anthony Boucher lists some of these fictional products that owe their inspiration to the Ripper, including an amusing Sherlock Holmes pastiche titled *Jack El Destripador.* (Inasmuch as Sherlock Holmes and Jack the Ripper made their public debuts at about the same time, pastiches of this sort have long been a favorite with Baker Street Irregulars.)

The Germans, in particular, took Jack the Ripper to their bosom in the 1920's, the anarchistic nature of his crimes fitting their black mood which sought an outlet in expressionist art. Thus the Ripper figures in the most interesting episode of *Waxworks,* a film directed by Paul Leni in 1924. In the film a starving young poet is engaged by a showman to turn out publicity about such waxworks figures as Haroun-al-Raschid, Ivan the Terrible. In the Ripper episode the poet dreams that he and the showman's daughter are being pursued through a weird, expressionist landscape by "Spring-Heeled Jack." Siegfried

Kracauer describes this episode as "among the greatest achievements of film art."

In Frank Wedekind's double drama, *Erdgeist* and *Die Büchse der Pandora,* the Ripper theme again finds its own special climate in a combination of sex, sadism and despair. This drama concerns Lulu, a whore who destroys men only to be destroyed in turn in a London garret by Jack the Ripper (a role which Wedekind himself played in the original stage production). The Wedekind drama, of course, inspired Alban Berg's unfinished opera, *Lulu,* which was first performed in Zurich in 1937; and there have been three film versions, the latest being an Austrian film which was released in 1962.

By far the most interesting film version of *Lulu* was that directed by G. W. Pabst in 1928, and starring Louise Brooks. Pabst turned the climax of the film into a veritable Walpurgisnacht with Lulu entertaining in her dingy London attic an African crown prince, a mute, a professor of philosophy, and finally, of course, Jack the Ripper who murders both her and her lesbian friend, the Countess Geschwitz.

Brecht's *Dreigroschenoper* owes as much for its inspiration to Jack the Ripper as it does to Gay's *The Beggar's Opera.* Mackie the Knife, Brecht tells us, is a capitalist appropriator of other men's crimes ("He takes the greatest care that all the boldest or, at least, the most fear-inspiring deeds of his subordinates are ascribed to himself"), but he shares one weakness with the real-life Ripper: he is a publicity hound. MacHeath "loved to read in the papers that his deeds were not committed for any material profit, but rather for sport, or for the satisfaction of a creative desire, or even because of an inexplicable demoniacal urge." The real-life Ripper followed the newspapers closely, laughed when the police claimed that they had picked up his scent. "The joke about Leather Apron gave me real fits," he wrote; adding, "They say I am a doctor now. Ha! Ha!"

The British shy away from expressionism in their handling of the Ripper theme in favor of naturalism. Thus, *Jack the Ripper,* a British film released in 1959, is a fairly straightforward reconstruction of the crimes. In this film a mad doctor, looking for the destroyer of his son, asks his intended victims, "Are you Mary Clarke?" as a prelude to carving them up with a scalpel. Among other means of exploiting the film, it was suggested that exhibitors "arrange for a man to parade the streets dressed in cloak and top hat complete with bag; have the title painted on the bag in white paint . . . This stunt," the filmmakers claimed, "will cause a lot of interest . . ."

The favorite Ripper myth, however, is that embodied in Mrs. Belloc Lowndes's novel, *The Lodger,* which saw life originally as a short story. This is the myth of a fiendish killer harbored in the bosom of an ordinary family whose members are unaware of his true identity. Five separate film versions of *The Lodger* have been made, the last being released in 1953. Most original is the silent film version made by Alfred Hitchcock in 1926 and starring Ivor Novello. This time the lodger is not the murderer, though he does everything to excite suspicion. Novello, looking pale and Christlike, is chased by a frenzied mob and nearly lynched before the real Avenger is brought to justice. This is the first British feature-length film made by Hitchcock, who was then only twenty-six, and it shows promise of the master to come in such scenes as the opening closeup of the Avenger's latest victim screaming, which dissolves into a crowd scene showing terror on the women's faces.

The other celluloid versions have followed Mrs. Lowndes's story line pretty closely, making Jack the Lodger out to be a religious maniac ("When the evil is cut out of a beautiful thing . . . then only the beauty remains"), but strengthening his motivation to murder. Thus, in the 1943 version of 20th Century–Fox, Laird Cregar has sworn to avenge a brilliant younger brother who has been ruined by an actress resembling Merle

Oberon. (This film contains a howler, incidentally, in that fingerprints are used to trap the killer; M. Bertillon's methods had not been adopted by Scotland Yard in 1888.) The 1953 remake of this film, titled *The Man in the Attic,* and starring Jack Palance, shows a decided advance in psychological insight. This time it is mother who is at the bottom of the woodpile, for Mother, it seems, wore tights ("And within him love and hatred are furiously ensnarled because of his actress mother's callous treatment of his father and himself," according to the press handout).

British composer Phyllis Tate turned *The Lodger* into an opera, which had its first performance at London's Royal Academy of Music on July 14, 1960, and which was televised in 1964. Miss Tate carefully observes the rules of Greek tragedy in that none of the murders occurs onstage, but she manages to convey the lodger's religious and sexual mania vividly enough by setting to music the words of Revelation 17 beginning, "I saw a woman sit upon a scarlet colored beast, full of names of blasphemy, having seven heads and ten horns." Gradually the landlady comes to realize that the quiet gentlemanly lodger who has saved her and her husband from destitution is an atrocious killer. The conflict in the landlady's mind — shall she hand over a mentally sick man to the law? — constitutes the core of the opera, together with what the composer calls "the sinister element." Miss Tate adds such innovations as a chorus of Cockney revelers who grow drunker, more savage and lewd as each murder is committed offstage.

The Ripper has traveled across the channel to appear as *Jack l'Eventreur* in a drama of the same name by André de Lorde at the Grand Guignol in Paris. It remained for film director Marcel Carne to satirize the Ripper crimes for all time in a wild film farce titled *Drôle de Drame,* made in 1937. In this film, which spoofs the methods of Scotland Yard in particular, Jean Louis Barrault plays the part of a Limehouse killer who specializes by slaughtering only butchers. The reason? He is a vegetarian who has sworn to avenge his animal friends.

APPENDIX B

IN FEBRUARY, 1894, the *Sun* put forward the sensational claim that it had solved the Whitechapel murder mystery. "We know the Christian name and surname of Jack the Ripper," the newspaper crowed. "We know his present habitation; our representatives have seen him, and we have in our possession a mass of declarations, documents and other proofs of his identity."

According to the *Sun*, its suspect had committed nine murders, including that of Frances Cole in 1891; in addition, he had assaulted six other women with intent to commit murder, stabbing them from behind. "He was at liberty and close to Whitechapel during all that period when the murders were committed," the report added, "and these murders immediately came to an end . . . from the moment he was safely under lock and key." As its clincher, the *Sun* boasted, "We have even a facsimile of the knife with which the murders were committed, purchased at the same place."

There was just one omission. The newspaper coyly refused to name its suspect, thereby offering its readers a potted version of *Hamlet* without the Prince of Danes. "At this moment our readers must be satisfied with less information than is at our disposal," it apologized. "Jack the Ripper has relatives; they are some of them in positions which would make them a target for natural curiosity . . . and we must abstain therefore from giving his name in the interest of the unfortunate, innocent and respectable connections."

Although it declined to name him, the *Sun*'s suspect for Jack the Ripper was, in fact, Thomas Cutbush, aged thirty, a relatively harmless fetishist who went around ripping women's dresses from behind with a knife. At the moment the articles appeared, Cutbush was being detained at Broadmoor, the asylum for the criminally insane, and the events which the articles referred to had occurred three years earlier — i.e., in 1891. The *Sun* was correct in stating that their suspect had "respectable connections" who would be embarrassed if his identity was disclosed: his uncle was a senior civil servant at the Colonial Office.

Cutbush's upbringing, however, had been entrusted to his mother and to a maiden aunt, both of whom were highly excitable. In 1888 he was living with these two female relatives in Kennington, on the south side of the Thames, and not within ten minutes' walking distance of Whitechapel, as the *Sun* had claimed.

As a young man Cutbush fancied that he had contracted a venereal disease. He became obsessed with the subject. He spent his days poring over medical textbooks, and went around dabbing his face with various ointments which he carried in his pockets. His nights, the *Sun* would have us believe, he spent prowling the streets, the prey of the sinister Hyde half of his nature. The *Sun*'s reporter rather outdid himself in picturing the aunt and mother keeping their nightly vigils. "While he has been out through the watches of the night on his fiendish work," the report reads, "one of them has sat up, waiting anxiously for his return . . . in imagination picturing this tiger who marched from crime to crime as some innocent, harmless and helpless child needing protection from the violence of others."

"Tiger" Cutbush was caught in the act on March 7, 1891, when Miss Isabel Anderson, eighteen, while walking with a female companion in Kennington Road, felt a tug at her dress from behind and heard a sound like that of cloth being ripped. She wheeled around in time to see a man with a knife in his right hand, but the man ran off before she could get a look at his features. Another man gave chase and caught Cutbush. Afterward Miss Anderson found that the lower part of her dress had been cut as if by a sharp instrument. In Cutbush's over-coat pocket police found a sheath knife whose blade was six inches long with a very sharp, curved point. This knife was traced to a shop in Houndsditch whose owner remembered having sold it to Cutbush. As to the *Sun*'s claim that it was the Whitechapel murder weapon, the knife had been sold to Cut-bush in February, 1891, or two years and three months after the last of the Ripper murders was committed.

In Cutbush's room police found a couple of paper dolls of women in indecent postures, pathetic collages composed of bodies cut from some old fashion plates to which legs had been added and made to represent naked thighs and pink stockings. According to the *Sun*, these were "rough drawings of the bodies of women and of their mutilations after the fashion of the Whitechapel murders."

The *Sun* was not content to chronicle the adventures of their supposed Jack the Ripper, but insisted upon visiting him in Broadmoor three years after he had been incarcerated there. The reporter, who lied his way into this institution, described Cutbush as being thin and walking with a slight stoop "as if his chest troubled him." His face was narrow, his forehead high and receding, but his eyes were what arrested the re-porter's attention. They were "large and dark," he wrote, "with the expression of the hunted animal in them." Poor Cutbush, the *Sun* determined to make him out a tiger to the very end.

BIBLIOGRAPHY

THE following works were published in London.

ADAM, H. L. *The Trial of George Chapman.* 1930.

———. *The Police Encyclopaedia.* 1920.

ANDERSON, SIR ROBERT. *The Lighter Side of My Official Life.* 1910.

BESANT, SIR WALTER. *East London.* 1901.

BOOTH, CHARLES. *Life and Labour of the People in London.* 1889–1902.

DILNOT, GEORGE. *The Story of Scotland Yard.* 1929.

GRIFFITHS, ARTHUR. *Mysteries of Police and Crime.* 1901.

HALSTED, D. G. *Doctor in the Nineties.* 1959.

LEESON, EX-DET. SERGEANT B. *Lost London.* 1934.

LONDON, JACK. *The People of the Abyss.* 1902.

MACNAGHTEN, SIR MELVILLE. *Days of My Years.* 1915.

MATTERS, LEONARD P. *The Mystery of Jack the Ripper.* 1948.

MAYHEW, HENRY. *London Labour and the London Poor.* 1851.

MCCORMICK, DONALD. *The Identity of Jack the Ripper.* 1959.

MOYLAN, SIR JOHN. *Scotland Yard and the Metropolitan Police.* 1929.

NEIL, SUPT. A. F. *Forty Years of Manhunting.* 1932.

O'DONNELL, ELLIOTT. *Great Thames Mysteries.* 1930.

PIMLOTT, J. A. R. *Toynbee Hall.* 1935.

PROTHERO, MARGARET. *The History of the C.I.D. at Scotland Yard.* 1931.

SIMS, GEORGE R. *Living London.* 1902.

———. *The Mysteries of Modern London.* 1906.

SINCLAIR, ROBERT. *East London.* 1950.

SITWELL, SIR OSBERT. *Noble Essences.* 1950.

SMITH, SIR HENRY. *From Constable to Commissioner.* 1910.

STEWART, WILLIAM. *Jack the Ripper, A New Theory.* 1939.

Survey of London, Vol. XXVII. "Spitalfields and Mile End New Town." 1957.

THOMSON, SIR BASIL. *The Story of Scotland Yard.* 1935.

WEBB, BEATRICE. *My Apprenticeship.* 1926.

WILLIAMS, WATKIN W. *The Life of Sir Charles Warren.* 1941.

WINSLOW, L. FORBES. *Recollections of Forty Years.* 1910.

WOODHALL, EDWIN T. *Jack the Ripper, or When London Walked in Terror.* 1937.

Newspapers and Periodicals Consulted: *The Times, The Daily Telegraph, The Daily News, The Star, The Daily Express, The Pall Mall Gazette, Reynolds News, The Financial News, The City Press, The East London Advertiser, The East London Observer, The Jewish Chronicle, Justice, Commonweal, Punch, The Lancet, The Illustrated London News, The Penny Illustrated Paper, Moonshine, The Toynbee Record, The Home Counties Magazine, Murray's Magazine.*

INDEX

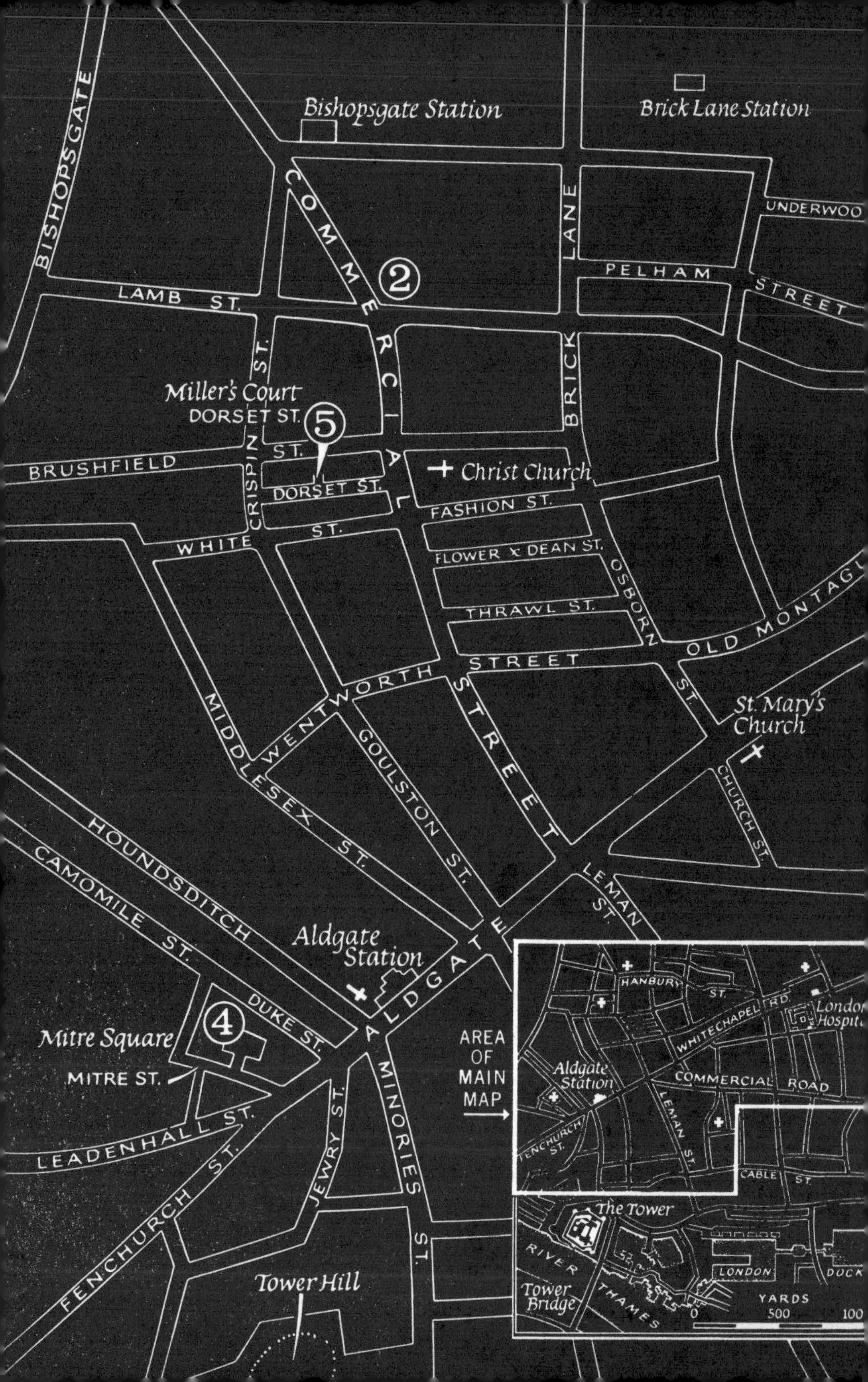
Bishopsgate Station
Brick Lane Station
BISHOPSGATE
COMMERCIAL STREET
2
BRICK LANE
UNDERWOO
PELHAM STREET
LAMB ST.
CRISPIN ST.
Miller's Court
DORSET ST.
5
BRUSHFIELD ST.
DORSET ST.
Christ Church
WHITE ST.
FASHION ST.
FLOWER & DEAN ST.
THRAWL ST.
OSBORN ST.
OLD MONTAGU
WENTWORTH STREET
St. Mary's Church
MIDDLESEX ST.
GOULSTON ST.
CHURCH ST.
HOUNDSDITCH
CAMOMILE ST.
LEMAN ST.
Aldgate Station
ALDGATE
DUKE ST.
4
Mitre Square
MITRE ST.
LEADENHALL ST.
JEWRY ST.
MINORIES ST.
FENCHURCH ST.
Tower Hill
AREA OF MAIN MAP
HANBURY ST.
WHITECHAPEL RD.
London Hospital
Aldgate Station
COMMERCIAL ROAD
LEMAN ST.
FENCHURCH ST.
CABLE ST.
The Tower
RIVER THAMES
Tower Bridge
LONDON
DOCK
YARDS
0
500
100